ALSO BY RICHARD N. HAASS

The Opportunity:
America's Moment to Alter History's Course

The Reluctant Sheriff:
The United States After the Cold War

The Bureaucratic Entrepreneur:
How to Be Effective in Any Unruly Organization
(initially published as *The Power to Persuade:*
How to Be Effective in Any Unruly Organization)

Intervention:
The Use of American Military Force in the Post–Cold War World

Conflicts Unending:
The United States and Regional Disputes

Beyond the INF Treaty:
Arms, Arms Control, and the Atlantic Alliance

Congressional Power:
Implications for American Security Policy

EDITED VOLUMES

Honey and Vinegar:
Incentives, Sanctions, and Foreign Policy
(co-edited with Meghan O'Sullivan)

Transatlantic Tensions:
The United States, Europe, and Problem Countries

Economic Sanctions and American Diplomacy

Superpower Arms Control: Setting the Record Straight
(co-edited with Albert Carnesale)

WAR OF NECESSITY
WAR OF CHOICE

A MEMOIR OF TWO IRAQ WARS

Richard N. Haass

SIMON & SCHUSTER   New York • London • Toronto • Sydney

SIMON & SCHUSTER
1230 Avenue of the Americas
New York, NY 10020

First Simon & Schuster hardcover edition May 2009

SIMON & SCHUSTER and colophon are registered trademarks
of Simon & Schuster, Inc.

For information about special discounts for bulk purchases,
please contact Simon & Schuster Special Sales at
1-800-456-6798 or business@simonandschuster.com.

The Simon & Schuster Speakers Bureau can bring authors to your live event.
For more information or to book an event contact the Simon & Schuster
Speakers Bureau at 866-248-3049 or visit our website at
www.simonspeakers.com.

Designed by Dana Sloan

Manufactured in the United States of America

10 9 8 7 6 5 4 3 2 1

Library of Congress Cataloging-in-Publication Data

Haass, Richard
    War of necessity : war of choice / by Richard N. Haass.
       p. cm.
       1. Iraq War, 2003—Causes. 2. Iraq War, 2003—Political aspects.
    3. Bush, George W. (George Walker), 1946—Political and social views.
    4. Persian Gulf War, 1991—Causes. 5. Persian Gulf War, 1991—Political
    aspects. 6. Bush, George, 1926—Political and social views. 7. United
    States—Politics and government—1989– 8. United States—Foreign
    relations—Middle East. 9. Middle East—Foreign relations—United
    States. 10. United States—Military policy. I. Title.
       DS79.764.U6H337   2009
       956.7044'3—dc22   2009004495

ISBN-13: 978-1-4165-4902-4
ISBN-10:   1-4165-4902-1

*To the Men and Women of the U.S. Armed Forces
who served in the two Iraq conflicts and to
Frederick C. Smith, who for thirty years has been all
that anyone could ask for in a friend*

CONTENTS

WAR OF NECESSITY
WAR OF CHOICE

1. A TALE OF TWO WARS

FOR TWO WEEKS, the U.S. intelligence community had monitored the gradual buildup of Iraq's armed forces along its southern border with Kuwait. The prevailing view within the administration of George H. W. Bush was that Iraqi military activity constituted a crude attempt to bludgeon Kuwait—oil rich, loaded with cash, and widely resented for the arrogance often displayed by its leaders—into lowering its oil output and dropping its objection to a higher price for the precious commodity. It was a view that I shared, much to the consternation of Charlie Allen, the crusty, veteran national intelligence officer for warning, who was convinced before anyone else that the Iraqis were not bluffing.

By August 1, 1990, however, it had become clear to all of us working on the issue that what we were seeing unfold was a good deal more than simply another act in the long-running theater of Arab diplomacy. Iraq had amassed too many troops and was doing too many of the things it would have to do if it were actually going to attack Kuwait rather than just threaten it. The Central Intelligence Agency issued an alert that predicted an attack was imminent. A special meeting of the "deputies" (the subcabinet group of senior officials representing the principal departments and agencies most involved in foreign and defense policy) was convened in one of the seventh-floor conference rooms at the State Department to discuss what was known and what the United States might do about it. It being August, many of the most senior people were away, escaping Washington's notorious heat and humidity. Secretary of State James Baker was off meeting in Siberia with his Soviet counterpart and was scheduled to go to Mongolia; Larry Eagleburger, his deputy, was taking the day off. Bob Kimmitt, normally the number three person at State but that day the acting secretary, chaired the session, as Bob Gates, the deputy national security advisor and the normal chair of the deputies, was on vacation. Besides others from various bureaus at State, there were representatives of several of the intelligence agencies and from both the civilian and military sides of the Defense Department. As the senior director for the Near East and South Asia on the staff of the National Security Council (NSC) and special assistant to the president, I was the principal person in attendance from the White House.

The meeting dragged on for most of the day as intelligence reports, ever more alarming, dribbled in. Saddam Hussein was up to something, although what that "something" was no one in the room knew. By late afternoon, a consensus had formed that we ought to make one last effort at dissuading the Iraqis from doing anything military. Given that Iraq was essentially a one-man show and that our ambassador was out of the country, this meant getting President Bush to contact Saddam. I was called upon to persuade the president to do so.

Normally I walked the half mile or so between the State Department and the White House, as time for exercise was hard to find given the long hours inevitably required by jobs such as mine. But with Iraq poised to attack Kuwait, the day was hardly one for a leisurely stroll. I got into the first cab I could find and rushed over to the West Wing office of my boss, Brent Scowcroft, formally the assistant to the president for national security affairs, commonly known as the national security advisor. I quickly laid it all out for him. He agreed that while it was a long shot—it was the middle of the night in Baghdad and it would be next to impossible to reach Saddam, much less affect his thinking—it made sense at least to present the option to the president.

By then, it was early evening in Washington. Brent picked up the phone, got the president on the line, and asked if the two of us could come to see him. Bush instantly agreed. We walked over to the sick bay on the ground floor of the residence, where the president was lying facedown on a doctor's examination table, having heat applied by the White House nurse to several joints sore from hitting a bucket of golf balls. I summarized the situation as best we knew it. An Iraqi attack of unknown scope and purpose seemed imminent, and the interagency group concluded we had nothing to lose by trying to reach Saddam and get him to call it off. The president shared our wonder that Saddam would actually do such a brazen thing as well as our skepticism that we could accomplish anything at this hour. But he agreed to try. The three of us then began to discuss just how to reach Saddam—whether it was best to go through our embassy in Baghdad (headed up at the time by Deputy Chief of Mission Joe Wilson, who years later would find himself a political target of the second Bush presidency when he questioned that administration's claim that Iraq was seeking to buy the raw material for a nuclear bomb) or through their embassy in Washington—when the phone rang. It was Bob Kimmitt on the line. He gave us the news that our embassy in Kuwait was reporting that firing had been heard in the streets. Iraq had invaded, although little else was clear. Our plan to phone Saddam had just become OBE—overtaken by events. Promising to stay in close touch with the president as we learned more, Brent and I returned to his office to discuss what steps needed taking right away. We then walked down to the Situation Room in the basement and convened a senior-level interagency meeting over the secure, closed-circuit television system that had been installed not too long before. The Gulf crisis, what would become the first major test of the post–Cold War world, was under way.

Nearly twelve years later, in early July 2002, I again found myself going from the State Department to the same West Wing office, now inhabited by President George W. Bush's national security advisor, Condoleezza Rice. It was one of my regular meetings with Condi, whom I had gotten to know well when we both worked on the NSC staff for Brent Scowcroft and with whom I'd stayed in close touch.

I was seeing Condi in my capacity as director of the State Department's Policy Planning Staff, a position I had accepted with Colin Powell, whom I had also gotten to know well when we worked with each other in the previous Bush administration. Most of my job involved being an all-purpose advisor and counselor to the secretary of state as well as the person who oversaw his in-house think tank. I also drew special assignments in my other role as a roving ambassador for the United States, something that made me the U.S. envoy to the Northern Ireland peace talks and, after the terrorist attacks of September 11, 2001, the U.S. coordinator for the future of Afghanistan. My meetings with Condi were not part of any formal interagency process but rather something informal, reflecting more than anything else our personal relationship.

As usual, I prepared on a yellow pad a list of the half-dozen or so issues I wanted to discuss during what normally was a thirty- to forty-five-minute meeting. At the top of my list was Iraq. For several weeks, those on my staff who dealt with Iraq and other Middle East issues had been reporting back that they sensed a shift, namely, that those at their level working at the Pentagon, the NSC, and the vice president's office who favored going to war with Iraq were sending signals that things were going their way. I did not share this enthusiasm for going to war, believing that we had other viable options and fearing that going to war would be much tougher than the advocates predicted. My related concern was that it would take an enormous toll on the rest of American foreign policy at the precise moment in history that the United States enjoyed a rare opportunity to exert extraordinary influence.

I began my meeting with Condi by noting that the administration seemed to be building momentum toward going to war with Iraq and that I harbored serious doubts about the wisdom of doing so. I reminded her that I knew something about this issue given my role in the previous Bush administration and my background in and with the Middle East. So I asked her directly, "Are you really sure you want to make Iraq the centerpiece of the administration's foreign policy?"

I was about to follow up with other questions when Condi cut me off. "You can save your breath, Richard. The president has already made up his mind on Iraq." The way she said it made clear that he had decided to go to war.

I was taken aback by the blunt substance and tone of her answer. Policy had gone much further than I had realized—and feared. I did not argue at that moment, for several reasons. As in previous conversations when I had voiced my views on Iraq, Condi's response made it clear that any more conversation at that point would be a waste of time. It is always important to pick your moments to make an unwelcome case, and this did not appear to be a promising one. I figured as well that there would be additional opportunities to argue my stance, if not with Condi, then with others in a position to make a difference.

Also accounting for my uncharacteristic reticence was the fact that my own opposition to going to war with Iraq was muted. At a recent dinner with two close friends, I had said I was 60/40 against initiating a war. My opposition was not stronger because of my assumption (derived from the available intelligence) that Iraq pos-

sessed both biological and chemical weapons. I also believed that if
we went to war we would go about it in a way reminiscent of how
we had gone about the previous Iraq war, that is, only with considerable international and domestic backing and only with enough forces
and sensible plans. Had I known then what I know now, namely,
that there were no weapons of mass destruction and that the intervention would be carried out with a marked absence of good judgment and competence, I would have been unalterably opposed. Still,
even then, I leaned against proceeding, fearing it would be much
more difficult than predicted given both the ambitious aims that
would inform any new war and the nature of Iraq.

Condi and I went through the rest of my list in a desultory fashion. I rushed back to the State Department, calling Colin Powell's
secretary, Marjorie Jackson, and asking to see him as soon as he was
free. Told to come right over, I quickly went down the hallway into
the reception area, through his large outer office that he rarely used
except for formal meetings, and then into the small study in the back
where he sat at his desk. Sitting on the small couch there, I told Powell what had happened in my meeting with Condi. He was typically
relaxed, skeptical that things had gone so far, thinking either Condi
was exaggerating or I had misread "my girlfriend," as he teasingly
tended to refer to her in my presence.

He was wrong. By the time Colin Powell had his dinner meeting
in the White House residence with the president and Condi a month
later, the issue on the table was not whether to go to war against Iraq
but how. Should the United States go beforehand to the U.N. Security Council? What about Congress? In the end, these proved to be
important but second-tier issues. The fundamental decision to go to
war against Saddam's Iraq had effectively been made by a president
and an administration with virtually no systematic, rigorous,
in-house debate. Less than a year later, the second Iraq war in just

over a decade had begun. It was a war that would prove to be one of the most contentious, unpopular, and costly in American history.

At first blush, the two wars appear similar. Both involved a president Bush and the United States in conflicts with Iraq and Saddam Hussein. There, however, the resemblance ends:

- The first was a limited, in many ways traditional war, one that sought to reverse Iraq's external aggression and restore the status quo ante; the second was an ambitious, even radical, initiative designed to oust and replace Iraq's leadership and, in so doing, create the foundations for a very different Middle East.

- The first war was essentially reactive and consistent with the universally accepted doctrine of self-defense; the second was a case of preventive war that enjoyed far less legal underpinning and political support.

- The first Iraq war was a truly multilateral affair, with dozens of countries ranging from Russia and Japan to Egypt and Syria forming an unprecedented international coalition and contributing in ways both varied (diplomatic, military, economic) and significant; the second war was for all intents and purposes unilateral, with the United States supported meaningfully by Great Britain and few others.

- The first Iraq war came about after more than a dozen U.N. Security Council resolutions failed to dislodge Saddam from Kuwait. The second war was launched with the backing of one new Security Council resolution and after the United States concluded it could not gain support for a second.

- For the first Iraq war, the United States went to the United Nations to gain backing that the administration believed would make it less difficult to build domestic and above all congressional support for using armed force; for the second war, the

United States went to Congress first and then sought U.N. authorization.

- The first war made use of more than 500,000 U.S. troops and was premised on the Powell Doctrine's bias toward employing overwhelming military force; the second war was designed by Secretary of Defense Donald Rumsfeld to minimize the number of U.S. armed forces (approximately 150,000) committed to the effort.

- The first Iraq war began with a prolonged phase in which airpower alone was used by the United States; the second war involved U.S. ground forces early on.

- The first war took place against the backdrop of a "false negative," in which most intelligence analysts and policy makers believed (incorrectly, as it turned out) that Saddam would not invade Kuwait; the second war took place against the backdrop of a "false positive," in which most intelligence analysts and policy makers believed (again incorrectly) that Saddam was hiding weapons of mass destruction. Indeed, in the run-up to the first war, the United States and the international community placed relatively little emphasis on weapons of mass destruction, although it later became clear that the world had badly underestimated the scale of Iraq's programs; in the run-up to the second Iraq war, considerable emphasis was placed on weapons of mass destruction, although it later became clear that U.S. officials badly overestimated Iraqi capabilities.

- Those who opposed the first Iraq war underestimated the costs of allowing the status quo to stand and overestimated the costs of going to war to evict Iraq from Kuwait; those who favored the second Iraq war underestimated the costs of going to war and overestimated the costs of allowing the status quo to stand.

- The first Iraq war proved to be controversial at home at the outset but ended up being wildly popular; the second Iraq war was initiated with broad congressional and public backing but over time became widely unpopular.

- The first Iraq war cost considerably less than $100 billion and, because of the contributions of coalition states, cost the U.S. government next to nothing. The second war has cost the United States as much as $1 trillion and possibly (depending on the accounting) considerably more. The tab is still rising and there is no chance of getting anyone to share more than a modest piece of it if that.
- The first war claimed a few hundred American lives; the latter more than four thousand.

What else can be said about these wars? Wars can be defined any number of ways: civil wars, wars of national liberation, world wars, cold wars, counterinsurgencies, a global war on terrorism, wars of attrition, defensive wars, nuclear wars, limited wars, just wars, and preventive wars all come to mind. What these and other such descriptions tend to reflect is scale, purpose, duration, the means employed, the nature of the conflict, and/or the nature of the undertaking.

There is, however, another way to think about war. Wars can either be viewed as essentially unavoidable, that is, as acts of necessity, or just the opposite, reflecting conscious choice when other reasonable policies are available but are deemed to be less attractive.

History offers us numerous examples of each. Any list of modern wars of necessity from the American perspective would include World War II and the Korean War. Wars of choice undertaken by the United States would include Vietnam, Bosnia, Kosovo, and, a century before, the Spanish-American War.

The distinction is by no means confined to the United States. Menachem Begin, the former prime minister of Israel, differentiated between what he called "wars of choice" and "wars of no alternative." Speaking in 1982 during Israel's war in Lebanon (Operation Peace for Galilee), he stated his view that Israel had fought three wars of necessity: its 1947–1949 struggle for independence, the "war of attrition" between Israel and Egypt in the Sinai Peninsula during the late 1960s, and the October 1973 Israel-Arab war. He described the 1956 Suez war (in which Israel, France, and Great Britain acted jointly against Egypt) as a war of choice. More surprising was his decision to describe the 1967 "Six Day" war as one of choice. "The Egyptian army concentrations in the Sinai approaches do not prove that [Egyptian president Gamal Abdel] Nasser was really about to attack us. We must be honest with ourselves. We decided to attack him." He even anticipated the argument that Egyptian actions left Israel with no alternative. "While it is indeed true that the closing of the Straits of Tiran was an act of aggression, a *casus belli*, there is always room for a great deal of consideration as to whether it is necessary to make a *casus* into a *bellum*."

What characterizes wars of necessity? The most common situation involves self-defense. More generally, wars of necessity involve the most important national interests, the absence of promising alternatives to the use of force, and the certain and considerable price to be paid if the status quo is to stand. Wars of necessity do not require assurances that the overall results of striking or resisting will be positive, only the assessment that the results of not so doing will be unacceptably negative and large.

Wars of choice tend to involve stakes or interests that are less clearly "vital," along with the existence of viable alternative policies, be they diplomacy, inaction, or something else but still other than the use of military force. One result is that wars of choice tend to increase the pressure on the government of the day to demonstrate that the overall or net results of employing force will be positive, that is, that the benefits outweigh the costs. If this test cannot be met, the choice will appear to be ill-advised and in fact most likely is.

The distinction between wars of necessity and wars of choice is obviously heavily subjective, inevitably reflecting an individual's analysis and politics. I introduced the phrases into the Iraq war debate in an op-ed in the *Washington Post* on November 23, 2003, five months after I left the administration. The piece argued that the first Iraq war was a classic war of necessity, the second a classic war of choice. Not surprisingly, President George W. Bush did not share my views. Asked by Tim Russert on NBC's *Meet the Press* on February 8, 2004, about my contention, the president protested, arguing that the second Iraq war was in fact a war of necessity. The full exchange merits quoting. Russert began with a question. "In light of not finding the weapons of mass destruction, do you believe the war in Iraq is a war of choice or a war of necessity?" The president seemed perplexed and had clearly not thought about the war in these terms. "I think that's an interesting question. Please elaborate on that a little bit. A war of choice or a war of necessity? It's a war of necessity. We—in my judgment, we had no choice when we look at the intelligence I looked at that says the man [Saddam Hussein] was a threat." History, I believe, will show otherwise.

As it turns out, the concept of wars of necessity and wars of choice was less original than I thought. (Note to self: Just because something appears new does not make it so.) Maimonides, one of the great scholars in the annals of Judaism, wrote more than eight centuries ago of wars he judged to be obligatory and those he termed optional. The former were those waged by the king for narrowly defined religious causes and in self-defense, i.e., "to deliver Israel from the enemy attacking him." He distinguished such necessary wars from those discretionary conflicts undertaken by a king against neighboring nations "to extend the borders of Israel and to enhance his greatness and prestige."

The two Iraq wars also constitute two fundamentally different approaches to American foreign policy. The first represents a more traditional school, often described as "realist," that sees the principal although not sole purpose of what the United States does in the world as influencing the external behavior of states and relations among them. It is the external actions of others that most directly affect U.S. interests, while U.S. power is more suited to affect what others do rather than what they are. What goes on inside states is not irrelevant, but it is secondary. This is a U.S. foreign policy that focuses on foreign policy, and was the bias of the country's founders, of FDR and Harry Truman, of Dwight Eisenhower and Richard Nixon, and of Gerald Ford and George H. W. Bush.

The second Iraq war reflects an approach to foreign policy that is at once more ambitious and more difficult. It believes the principal purpose of what the United States does in the world is to influence the nature of states and conditions within them, both for moral and ideological reasons as well as for practical ones in the sense that mature democracies are judged to make for better and more peaceful international citizens. This is the foreign policy of Woodrow Wilson, to some extent that of Jimmy Carter and Ronald Reagan, and clearly that of George W. Bush.

The difference between a foreign policy designed to manage relations between states and one that seeks to alter the nature of states is critical, and constitutes the principal fault line in the contemporary foreign policy debate. The two Iraq wars are of great import, both for what they were (and are) and for what they represent: the two dominant and competing schools of American foreign policy. They thus constitute a classic case study of America's purpose in the world and how it should go about it.

For me, all this is as personal as it is political. I have been contemplating writing a book about the United States, Iraq, and the broader Middle East for some three decades now. My interest goes back to the summer of 1974, when I first went to Washington, D.C., as something other than a tourist. I had just completed my first year of graduate school in England and was looking for a summer experience that would bring me back to the United States and, if all went well, provide me with an idea for the thesis required for an Oxford graduate degree. Thanks to an introduction, I got a job as an intern in the office of U.S. senator Claiborne Pell, a liberal Democrat from Rhode Island and a member of the Senate Committee on Foreign Relations. Against the backdrop of the final days of Richard Nixon's presidency, I was assigned the issue of Diego Garcia, a small Indian Ocean island owned by Great Britain that the U.S. Navy wanted to develop for ships that would be spending time in and around the Persian Gulf. Although the money at stake was small by Pentagon budget standards—only some $26 million for a modest logistic support base, subsequently reduced to a limited communications facility in the face of congressional resistance—the request triggered a surprisingly intense debate. Many in the Senate saw this request as the proverbial camel's nose in the tent, fearing it would only be a matter of time before the Defense Department would be back asking for much more. However, what made the debate so heated was not so much the funds per se but rather what they symbolized. Many believed that what was at stake was nothing less than the course of U.S. foreign policy after Vietnam, where U.S. involvement was fast approaching its inglorious end. Following debate and votes, the coalition opposing the new commitment lost, and the Navy got its funds for the facility. And I had my thesis topic.

I went back to Oxford to complete my doctorate and, in 1977, joined the staff of the first of many think tanks at which I would work over the years, the International Institute for Strategic Studies, located in London. There I wrote about U.S.-Soviet naval arms limitation talks in the Indian Ocean, one of a number of arms control initiatives launched by President Jimmy Carter. By 1979 I found myself back in Washington, in this case the Department of Defense, where I was one of several relatively junior civilians (working in a windowless office in the bowels of the Pentagon) tasked with developing contingency plans and U.S. capabilities for crises in the Persian Gulf. Much of our time was taken up with planning how best to stop a Soviet offensive across the Zagros Mountains of northern Iran; in the wake of the Iranian revolution that ousted the Shah and brought Ayatollah Khomeini to power, the Soviet invasion of Afghanistan, and the taking of the American hostages in Tehran, the focus of the planning shifted and the urgency increased.

With the election of Ronald Reagan, I shifted from the Department of Defense to the Department of State. Although Iraq and Gulf-related issues constituted only a small percentage of my job (first in the Bureau of Politico-Military Affairs, later in the Bureau of European Affairs), at times they dominated the administration I worked for and, in the case of Iran-Contra, almost brought it down. Following nearly five years at State, I moved to Harvard University's Kennedy School of Government, where I spent three and a half years teaching graduate students about decision making and American foreign policy. Little did I realize that I was about to become my own case study.

This book is the result of all these experiences, but principally those that came after and were associated with my time working for George H. W. Bush, the forty-first president, and George W. Bush, the forty-third. I was the principal Middle East hand on the staff of the National Security Council for the initial President Bush, and for the first time, I had a significant role in shaping significant history—or, in this case, histories, as I was heavily involved in the making of U.S. policy toward Iraq before and after the 1990 Iraqi invasion of Kuwait and toward Israel and its Arab neighbors both before and after that crisis.

I departed government in January 1993—along with others working for the forty-first president of the United States, I received, in the immortal words of Winston Churchill, "the Order of the Boot" upon the inauguration of Bill Clinton. I returned to government eight years later, in January 2001, and once more a good portion of my time was devoted to Iraq and the Gulf region. It was a very different experience, though: I was at the State Department, not the White House; I was on the periphery rather than at the center of policy making; I was uncomfortable with the policy, not one of its principal champions. I stayed for two and a half years, until June 2003, when I took up my current position as president of the Council on Foreign Relations, an independent, nonpartisan membership organization, think tank, and publisher based in New York.

The Iraq war, which had begun just months earlier, was still very much going on when I left government, with results all too much in line with my pessimistic predictions. I was increasingly unhappy with the policy, one that I believed was threatening to undermine a rare moment in which the United States could reshape the world, an idea that informed a general book on U.S. foreign policy that I published in 2005, *The Opportunity*. Some of my frustration with Iraq policy surfaced in a chapter in that book, some in the op-ed already mentioned. Called "Wars of Choice," the piece argued that the Iraq war was a manifestation of an imperial foreign policy, in that the United States went to war for reasons other than vital national interests. "The debate can and will go on as to whether attacking Iraq was a wise decision, but at its core it was a war of choice. We did not have to go to war against Iraq, certainly not when we did. There were other options: to rely on other policy tools, to delay attacking, or both."

I have written hundreds of op-eds over the years, and few generated the reaction or garnered as much attention as this one. It was this combination of concern on my part and interest on the part of others that led to my decision to write this book. It is the first time I have ever written a book of this sort. Most of my previous work could be described as foreign policy analysis, about the ends of

American foreign policy, how it is made, or the military, diplomatic, and economic tools used to implement it. This is different. It is foreign policy analysis and history to be sure, but also personal reflections and recollections. I was one of only a few individuals, along with such disparate people as Colin Powell, Dick Cheney, and Paul Wolfowitz, to be involved at relatively senior levels of government with both Iraq wars. I want to give a sense of why things happened and their consequences. My intention, however, is not to settle scores or to say "I told you so" on those occasions when I may have been more correct than others. It is not simply that it is too soon to make confident judgments as to who was right, but also that I made my share of mistakes and then some.

Last, I am well aware that events in Iraq are still unfolding as I write this. My own thinking continues to evolve as well. My late dear friend David Halberstam said it best: "A book like this does not have a simple, preordained linear life. A writer begins with a certainty that the subject is important, but the book has an orbital drive of its own—it takes you on its own journey, and you learn along the way." This has been quite a journey, and I have learned a great deal.

2. THE WINDING ROAD TO WAR

NOTHING IN THE history of the United States and Iraq suggested that the two countries would one day fight two wars and become so central to each other's modern narrative. The best place to pick up the story, though, is with the U.S. response to the gradual and often lurching British withdrawal from "East of Suez," which gained pace in the 1960s. C. L. Sulzberger, one of the leading columnists of his day, wrote in 1967 that "the ultimate implication to our foreign policy east of Suez of Britain's decision is bound to be as significant as the ultimate implications west of Suez were when London shed Greek responsibilities twenty years ago." Few observers at the time shared his view that what would happen in the Persian Gulf would prove as important as the events that had led to the Marshall Plan, NATO, and the Cold War. A half century later, however, Sulzberger looks more than a little prescient.

The British withdrawal came to a head in the late 1960s and was resisted by the United States, then concerned with possible Soviet and Chinese expansion into the oil-rich Persian Gulf and preoccupied with and burdened by its own vast commitment in South Vietnam. But no amount of American persuasion could dissuade the British, who could only reach a sustainable equilibrium between overseas commitments and available resources by reducing the former. Something of a debate ensued in Washington. The State Department, after noting "regret" with the British decision, added that "the United States has no plans to fill the gap." Senate majority leader Mike Mansfield remarked, "I am certain we will be asked to fill the vacuum east of Suez. I don't know how we are going to do it because I don't think we have the men or resources for it." It was simply inconceivable then that two decades later a half-million American troops would be dispatched to the region to protect Saudi Arabia and liberate Kuwait. It was just as difficult to predict that events in this region would come to materially affect the legacies of four of the modern presidents of the United States.

With its hands full in Southeast Asia and with both communist powers, the incoming administration of Richard Nixon and his national security advisor, Henry Kissinger, accorded little attention to the part of the world dominated by Iraq, Iran, and Saudi Arabia. Kissinger recounts in his memoirs a meeting in December 1968 between the then president-elect and the visiting emir of Kuwait:

"I assumed that the Arab-Israeli conflict would be at the forefront of the Amir's [sic] concern and prepared an erudite memorandum on the subject. Unfortunately, the Amir wanted, above all, to learn what plans the new administration had for the Persian Gulf after the United Kingdom vacated the area, as it had announced it would do in 1971. What were America's intentions if, for example, Iraq attacked Kuwait? Nixon gave me the glassy look he reserved for occasions when in his view the inadequacy of his associates had placed him into an untenable position. Manfully he replied that he would have to study the matter, but that, of course, we were interested in the territorial integrity of all states in the area; what tactical measures we would adopt would of course depend on circumstances. The Amir seemed content with this Delphic utterance."

In July 1969, as a means of preparing for the British retreat, Kissinger ordered a review of U.S. policy toward the region. He asked that the review include a discussion of the problems created by the British withdrawal, "including the possibility of an Arab-Iranian confrontation in the region," and consider options for U.S. policy and naval presence. The now declassified interagency study rejected 1) trying to reverse the British decision, 2) cutting a deal with the Soviets in which both superpowers would stay aloof, or 3) ignoring the region. Instead it looked closely at taking over the British role, choosing one local country to be America's "chosen instrument," fostering Saudi-Iranian cooperation, and creating a regional security pact. In the end, the centerpiece of what emerged from National Security Study Memorandum 66, "Future U.S. Policy in the Persian Gulf," was the "twin pillars" policy. A heavily burdened United States would strengthen Iran and Saudi Arabia so that they could take the lead in looking after the stability of the oil-rich region. Billions of dollars of the most advanced conventional (nonnuclear) arms were sold to the two, in part to absorb petrodollars they were accumulating after the Arab members of the OPEC oil cartel brought about the first oil price increases in the context of the 1973 Middle East war, and in part to offset the gathering strength of "radical" Iraq, which in 1972 had signed a friendship treaty with the Soviet Union.

Iran and Saudi Arabia effectively became the poster children of the new foreign policy doctrine, announced by Richard Nixon in late July 1969. Nixon and Kissinger were flying to the Philippines when, during a stop in Guam, the president talked about how the United States, heavily obligated militarily, economically, and politically because of the Vietnam War, could maintain order and bolster its allies at one and the same time. The comments were later codified into a three-part doctrine. First, the United States would keep all of its treaty commitments. Second, it would provide a shield if a nuclear power, that is, the Soviet Union or China, threatened the freedom of an ally or a nation whose survival was deemed vital. And third, "in cases involving other types of aggression we shall furnish military and economic assistance when requested and as appropriate. But we shall look to the nation directly threatened to assume the primary responsibility of providing the manpower for its defense." The doctrine was devised as a means of maintaining stability and American influence at a time when the United States (and the U.S. Army in particular) was stretched thin in Southeast Asia. It was thus a foreign policy based on indirectness, in which favored allies would assume the immediate burden of maintaining order and the United States would limit itself to ensuring they had the means and providing backup should they appear overwhelmed. As Kissinger later wrote in his memoirs, the Nixon Doctrine provided a coherent answer to domestic critics who feared U.S. overextension at the same time as it reassured friends in Asia and elsewhere who feared American withdrawal not just from Vietnam but the entire region.

In the Persian Gulf, the twin-pillar policy remained U.S. policy so long as the pillars remained stable and pro-American. Indeed, the policy largely worked for a decade following the British withdrawal, through the Nixon, Ford, and early Carter years. The Carter administration continued the flow of substantial amounts of modern arms to both countries (and Iran in particular) despite its own declared bias against arms transfers to developing countries.

Iran appeared to be stable. The possibility of the monarchy's collapse was not on the horizon when Jimmy Carter assumed the presidency in January 1977. Months later, on a visit to Iran, Carter publicly described Iran as "an island of stability in one of the more troubled areas of the world." A year later, the Shah was gone. It is not clear that any U.S. policy could have saved him at that point, given his weakness and vacillation, his deteriorating health, and the depth and breadth of domestic political opposition that had developed over the years. His political prospects were not enhanced, though, by divisions within the Carter administration and the split between those who sought to cobble together some sort of coalition government with a reduced role for the monarchy and those who advocated firm backing of the Shah and a pro-Shah military coup if need be. By 1978, when it became clear just how bad things had become, National Security Advisor Zbigniew Brzezinski was correct when he argued "a policy of conciliation and concessions might have worked, had it been adopted two or three years earlier, before the crisis reached a politically acute stage. . . . But once the crisis had become a contest of will and power, advocacy of compromise and conciliation simply played into the hands of those determined to effect a complete revolution."

In January 1979, the Shah gave up what little power he retained and fled the country. One of the twin pillars of American policy was gone. Brzezinski was not exaggerating when he described this as the administration's greatest setback and a political calamity. But it was only the first of several strategic setbacks for the United States that year. Ten months later, in November, U.S. diplomats in Tehran were taken hostage. And in December, the Soviets invaded Afghanistan.

The three events galvanized the Carter administration and led the president to articulate a new doctrine in his January 1980 State of the Union address. "Let our position be absolutely clear: An attempt by any outside force to gain control of the Persian Gulf region will be regarded as an assault on the vital interests of the United States of America, and such an assault will be repelled by any means necessary, including military force."

These events combined to form a watershed. Traditionally, Europe and Asia were the two great theaters that drew the bulk of the attention of U.S. policy makers, since those areas had dominated the twentieth century's two world wars as well as the Cold War. These were also the two regions that were home to the other great powers of the day. But with the events of 1979, the Persian Gulf had emerged as the third theater of American strategic preoccupation, a reflection of both its inherent importance (largely a result of energy resources) and the multiple threats to its stability.

Amid this transformation, there were still elements of continuity. The declared focus of the new Carter Doctrine was on an outside threat, that is, the Soviet Union. This was understandable, given the recent Soviet invasion and subsequent occupation of Afghanistan. This tendency to view events through a Cold War lens was widely shared; writing about the world of 1981, Alexander Haig, Ronald Reagan's first secretary of state, noted, "The Persian Gulf was now threatened by a theocratic regime in Teheran that seemed to have abandoned reason, and the moderate Arabs wondered who would protect them if the Soviets gained control of the fundamentalist movement." But this perspective was also too narrow and backward looking, for as time would quickly demonstrate, the emerging threats to U.S. interests in the region were local, namely Iran and Iraq, both of whom were increasingly beyond the ability of either Moscow or Washington to control. Although it was anything but obvious, elements of what would come to characterize the post–Cold War world were already beginning to emerge.

I had no role in the decision making surrounding any of these events, since I only joined the Defense Department, and in a relatively junior position at that, in September 1979. My formal position was to work with Daniel Murphy, a retired admiral who held one of the longer job titles I can recall: the Deputy Under Secretary of Defense for Policy Review. (Murphy later ended up as chief of staff for Vice President George H. W. Bush.) He essentially oversaw intelligence policy issues for Secretary of Defense Harold Brown. I mostly worked directly with Murphy's boss, Under Secretary of Defense Robert Komer, as part of a small office of civilians and midlevel military officers who were given license to get involved in virtually every aspect of defense policy. Komer, known as "Blowtorch" from his Vietnam days, was one of the more difficult people and bosses I ever knew. But he could get things done. Confidence and energy count for a lot. In this case, he spearheaded work on creating a capacity to intervene in the Persian Gulf, work that led to the March 1980 creation of the Rapid Deployment Force, established at Mac-Dill Air Force Base outside Tampa, Florida. At the time, it seemed a modest innovation, an empty shell of a command without dedicated forces at its disposal, but years later it morphed into the Central Command, the military organization that oversaw both Iraq wars as well as the war in Afghanistan.

THE REAGAN YEARS

I somehow survived the transition from President Carter to Ronald Reagan; being junior has its advantages. I spent the first eighteen months of the Reagan administration heading up the regional security affairs office of some fifteen people in the State Department's Bureau of Politico-Military Affairs. Given Haig's military background and his preference for working closely with a few favored staffers, this position actually brought me into fairly regular contact with the secretary of state on important policy issues, including countering what Cuba and Nicaragua were doing in Central America; Libya; the Falklands war; and the Middle East. I then spent three years in the State Department's Bureau of European Affairs (which then covered all of Europe as well as Canada and the Soviet Union) heading up ties with Europeans on issues falling outside Europe (in particular Lebanon and elsewhere in the Middle East) and overseeing U.S. policy toward Greece, Turkey, and Cyprus in addition to being the U.S. envoy to the Cyprus negotiations. The first position tracked with the tenure of Haig as secretary of state, the second with that of George Shultz.

Interestingly, the first item of business facing the new administration involved Iran. I remember being tasked to write a memorandum to Secretary of State Haig that provided the background to the subject of one of the first National Security Council meetings of the Reagan administration. The question was whether to honor the agreement negotiated by the Carter administration with Iran that resolved the hostage crisis. Most in the room voiced opposition to the agreement or were silent. My own view was that it would be folly to reject the accords. The hostages had already been released. Abrogating the agreements would make the United States look like the party acting illegally and would encumber the president and U.S. foreign policy with an issue that was a sideshow. It is important for a major power to demonstrate continuity, since predictability is reassuring to friends and can restrain others. Haig was onto something when he wrote, "Of the many destructive effects of Vietnam and Watergate, none is worse than the tendency for a new administration to believe that history began on its inauguration day, and its predecessor was totally wrong about everything, and that all its acts must therefore be canceled." It was Haig, the new secretary of state who came to be much ridiculed in some quarters, who carried the day on Iran. It was also Haig who averted a crisis between the United States and its closest allies in Europe by insisting the administration see through both dimensions of the two-track policy of countering Soviet "Euro-missile" deployments and supporting an arms control proposal that would place a ceiling on the competition. And it was Haig who preserved the budding and still fragile U.S. relationship with China in the face of calls to expand the U.S. relationship with Taiwan.

Iraq surfaced in an unanticipated way: the result of a surprise Israeli preventive attack on the Osirak nuclear facility in June 1981. The reactor designed to produce nuclear fuel that could be used to generate electricity but also fill bombs was about to be activated, something Israel sought to avoid. This was a classic preventive attack, one undertaken to interrupt a gathering threat. It is to be contrasted with a preemptive attack, which is an action designed to interrupt an attack judged to be imminent. The difference is significant, both legally and politically, as only the latter (preemptive) is recognized as a form of self-defense and enjoys considerable legal and political support. More than two decades later, the administration of George W. Bush described and tried to justify the attack on Iraq as preemptive, but in fact it was nothing of the sort. Like the Israeli attack on Osirak, it was preventive. Preventive attacks are by their very nature wars of choice; preemptive attacks by their nature almost invariably are wars of necessity.

The U.S. reaction to the Israeli strike on Osirak was quite negative. In addition to public and private criticisms, the Reagan administration delayed the shipment of additional military aircraft sought by Israel that were similar to those used in the Osirak attack. My reaction at the time to the U.S. stance was one of some surprise. I didn't see what was so wrong about Israel's limited and precise use of military force to destroy the Iraqi nuclear facility before it could manufacture bomb material, particularly in light of Iraq's decision a year before to attack Iran and its close ties to the Soviet Union. In the end, Israel dismissed U.S. criticism, while the military sanction imposed by the U.S. government didn't last for long: a far greater number of high-performance aircraft were provided to Israel in order to win congressional acceptance of the controversial sale of AWACS (warning and battle management) aircraft to Saudi Arabia.

The Reagan presidency coincided almost exactly with the Iran-Iraq War, which began some four months before Ronald Reagan became president and ended some six months before he left office. The war was initiated by Saddam Hussein in an apparent bid to assert his and Iraq's primacy in the region at a time when Iranians were consumed with the domestic political aftermath of the ouster of the Shah. Saddam may also have been motivated by Iranian-sponsored terrorism in Baghdad, but if so, he both overreacted to and misjudged his adversary. Initially, Iraq gained the upper hand, but by 1982 the Iraqi assault had stalled. Iran went over to the offensive, gaining control of significant portions of Iraqi territory. This development triggered alarm in the United States, a reaction captured well by George Shultz in his memoirs: "Iraq's retreat as the numerically far greater Iranian forces swept forward was all too apparent. If Iraq collapsed, that could not only intimidate but inundate our friends in the Gulf and be a strategic disaster for the United States."

The war itself, which lasted some eight years, was costly by any measure to both sides. Estimates are that half a million or more Iranians and as many as several hundred thousand Iraqis lost their lives. Iran spent more than $50 billion on the war and Iraq some $80 billion. Indirect economic costs were several times those amounts for both protagonists. What could not be known at the time was that it sowed the seeds of war between the United States and Iraq in two ways. First, the effort left Iraq, if not impoverished, at least far from able to fund Saddam's ambitions. This was the root cause of his intimidation and subsequent invasion and absorption of Kuwait. Second, the fact that Iraq emerged from its long war with Iran as depleted as it did lulled many American analysts and policy makers into concluding that Iraq would opt for years of tranquility (in order to regain its strength) rather than initiate yet another potentially costly military adventure.

Henry Kissinger probably came close to capturing the privately held view of many U.S. officials at the time when he wryly commented that it was a pity both sides couldn't lose. In reality, the United States sought to stop the war, both through diplomacy and through denying weapons to both protagonists. Diplomacy would not bear fruit until July 1987, when the U.N. Security Council unanimously passed Resolution 598, which called on Iran and Iraq to "observe an immediate cease-fire, discontinue all military actions on land, at sea and in the air, and withdraw all forces to the internationally recognized boundaries without delay." The U.S. attempt to thwart arms transfers, Operation Staunch, was at most a partial success, one reason being that the United States violated its own policy.

Beneath this official posture was the realization that the war would likely go on for some time and that revolutionary Iran was the more dangerous of the two protagonists. Shultz was characteristically honest about this. "While the United States basically adhered to the policy of not supplying arms to either side, our support for Iraq increased in rough proportion to Iran's military successes: plain and simple, the United States was engaged in a limited form of balance-of-power policy. The United States simply could not stand idle and watch the Khomeini revolution sweep forward." The memories of the hostage crisis, together with Iran's role in bolstering Hizbollah, the group behind the 1983 bombing of the marine barracks in Lebanon, reinforced the inclination to make sure that Iran did not emerge victorious from its struggle with Iraq. It is interesting to note that members of the preceding administration, in this case National Security Advisor Zbigniew Brzezinski, were prepared to signal Iran that the United States was inclined to provide military aid to Iraq if it were necessary to pressure Iran to release the American hostages.

What emerged was a U.S. tilt toward Iraq. Donald Rumsfeld, then a former secretary of defense brought into the Reagan administration as the president's special Middle East envoy, was dispatched to Iraq to float the idea (one put forward by Israel) of building an oil pipeline that would run from northern Iraq to Haifa. Iraq turned it down. More seriously, the United States took only limited diplomatic action after receiving reports in 1983 that Iraq had used chemical weapons against Iran; a year later, in November 1984, following a White House visit by Iraqi foreign minister Tariq Aziz and an Iraqi decision to close the Baghdad headquarters of the Abu Nidal terrorist group, the United States and Iraq reestablished diplomatic relations after a break of seventeen years.

Establishing diplomatic relations was the right thing to do despite Iraq's bellicose behavior toward its neighbors and Saddam's repressive behavior toward Iraqi citizens. As a rule of thumb, diplomatic ties and talking with other governments should not be judged as a favor or, more broadly, as a sign of approval or endorsement of another country's nature or its policies. Rather, relations and talking should be premised on a judgment that communication is preferable to the alternative and that the other government has the capacity to modify its behavior if it so chooses. Not talking and not having a diplomatic presence denies the U.S. government the opportunity to observe and influence developments inside another country—and should only be U.S. posture in rare circumstances when the government's behavior is so extreme as to render communication useless.

The most significant manifestation of the pro-Iraqi bias of U.S. policy was the reaction to a Kuwaiti request in late 1986 that outsiders protect its tankers from the threat posed by Iran. After months of diplomatic back-and-forth, including a Kuwaiti invitation to the Soviet Union that it take on a major role in deterring Iranian attacks on local shipping, the United States agreed to place American flags on eleven Kuwaiti tankers. The U.S. Navy would beef up its presence and activity in the region commensurate with that action. The Reagan administration went along with the "reflagging" of tankers (Operation Earnest Will) in May 1987, but only after months of debate and in the face of considerable congressional opposition. Shultz explains why. "I did not want to let the United States get drawn into the Iran-Iraq War. But it was critical that Iran not come to dominate the Gulf and therefore the Arabian Peninsula." Ironically, the event that may have sealed the deal stemmed not from Iran but from Iraq. On May 17, the USS *Stark* was struck by two Iraqi missiles, with some three dozen U.S. sailors dying as a result. The Iraqis apologized and years later paid fair compensation, although whether it was in fact accidental remains unclear.

This attack by Iraq was soon followed up by intentional attacks on shipping by Iran. The United States responded forcefully, by boarding a vessel laying and carrying mines, by sinking a number of Iranian gunboats, and by destroying an Iranian oil rig. An American naval cruiser (the USS *Vincennes*) shot down a civilian Iranian airplane (killing all 290 civilians on board) when crewmen confused it for a warplane, an explanation rejected by many in Iran. These actions, coupled with setbacks on the battlefield and a decaying economy, led Ayatollah Khomeini to reluctantly accept peace in July 1988, an action he described as "more lethal for me than poison."

Another aspect of U.S. support for Iraq was economic and largely involved two programs. The first, involving Commodity Credit Corporation (CCC) guarantees, was designed to promote sales of agricultural products by U.S. farmers to Iraq. Some $4 billion in credit guarantees were approved by the Department of Agriculture during the Reagan years. These guarantees were extended to U.S. exporters as a form of protection in the event Iraq did not pay them for items (wheat, rice, soybeans, etc.) received. No U.S. government money was provided to Iraq under this program, and, as it turned out, Iraq tended to pay its bills in full and on time, so the credit guarantees did not have to be converted into cash.

The second economic program introduced during the Reagan years involved licensing the sale of so-called dual-use items to Iraq. *Dual-use* refers to any product that could have a military in addition to a civilian or nonmilitary use. Dual-use items can range from trucks to transport aircraft to communications systems. Prior to 1989, approximately $1.5 billion in licenses for dual-use exports were approved, although less than $500 million worth was actually exported to Iraq. Even assuming the worst, that all of these items were diverted for military use, it was a tiny percentage of the billions and billions of dollars Saddam spent on military procurement during this decade.

It is worth going into some detail on all this to make clear that while the United States did in fact tilt toward Iraq during the Reagan years, the degree of the incline and the scale of the relationship should not be exaggerated. This was a limited relationship, one that was mostly diplomatic and commercial. It did involve the provision of some useful military intelligence to Iraq, but not the sale of arms—other than, that is, two revolvers and one pistol, worth $913, purchased from an American source by Saddam's son Qusay. On balance it was a justified relationship, one that got things about right: on one hand, sufficiently pro-Iraqi to help offset Iran given the reality that revolutionary Iran constituted the greater threat at the time to U.S. interests in the region; on the other, sufficiently limited so that the United States did not get too close to a government that was clearly repressing its own people and had a history of working against regional stability.

It is also impossible to write about the Reagan years without noting one other dimension of U.S. policy toward the region, namely, the U.S. decision to provide arms to Iran as part of what became known as "Iran-Contra." Even with the advantages of two decades of hindsight it is a baffling, jaw-dropping episode. In direct contravention of both U.S. counterterrorism policy and Operation Staunch (the commitment to block arms reaching either Iran or Iraq), the Reagan administration provided arms to Iran via Israel in (depending upon whom one believes) an effort to win the release of American hostages being held in Lebanon or to achieve a diplomatic breakthrough with Iran that its advocates argued would compete in significance with the opening to China some fifteen years before. What is more, the "profit" earned on the sales to Iran of various systems was used as an off-the-books means of financing the "Contras" fighting the government in Nicaragua. No legal means of financing was available owing to congressional fiat. These actions came close to bringing about the impeachment of Ronald Reagan and the unraveling of his presidency. If anyone ever needed a case study showing the dangers of a National Security Council staff becoming overly operational, this was it.

This strange episode should not be allowed to obscure the prevailing pattern of a U.S. preference for Iraq over Iran. The United States was correct in the main (if not in all the details) to do what it did to deny Iran a victory over Iraq. Not coming down hard on Iraq for using chemical weapons to stave off waves of Iranian troops, while arguably deplorable, was at least understandable; allowing Iraq to use chemical weapons to repress its own citizens with impunity was something quite different. At a minimum, significant sanctions against Iraq were warranted. As history would later show, however, the U.S. tilt toward Iraq and away from Iran was not enough to change Iraq's fundamental orientation; my first rule of the Middle East is that the enemy of your enemy can still be your enemy.

THE GEORGE H. W. BUSH YEARS

George H. W. Bush was inaugurated as the forty-first president of the United States on January 20, 1989. As is often the case, history unfolded in ways that were far from what people were thinking that day. It was impossible to predict that over the next few years the world would witness the conclusion of the Cold War and the unification of Germany within NATO, the end of apartheid in South Africa, the outbreak of a major war with Iraq, and a conference that for the first time brought Arabs and Israelis face-to-face to negotiate peace.

My own role in the Bush administration was anything but a sure thing. I came to be involved in the Bush presidential campaign in 1988 as a foreign policy advisor only after I crashed and burned with the Bob Dole campaign in New Hampshire. Soon after, Bush campaign chief Jim Baker got in touch with me and before long I was a member of the foreign policy team of George H. W. Bush. I divided my time between Harvard University's Kennedy School of Government, where I was teaching public policy and international affairs, and the campaign, where I wrote position papers, worked on speeches, and often debated those individuals (in some cases my fellow professors) performing similar functions for Democratic candidate and Massachusetts governor Michael Dukakis.

Once Bush won that November, I got involved in transition work, which was clearly dominated by Baker when it came to the future State Department. Brent Scowcroft would be the national security advisor, a position he had held under President Gerald Ford. John Tower would get Defense if he could survive all the questions about alcohol and alleged womanizing. (In the end he could not, which paved the way for Dick Cheney, then in Congress, to return to the executive branch, where years earlier he had been chief of staff to President Ford.) It wasn't clear what if any job I would end up with. For a while it looked like it would be the assistant secretary for Latin America post at State, but then a story appeared in the Miami papers about how a Bush advisor was anti-Contra. In fact I was not anti-Contra, but had argued in a paper that the United States would be unwise to predicate its policy upon the notion that the Contras would win a military victory over the Nicaraguan government. In Washington, however, analysis is often equated with advocacy. Baker made it clear to me that I was too controversial for the Latin America job. I was getting antsy, as I had promised the dean at the Kennedy School that I would let him know by January 30 if I would be around to teach in the second semester. I was also getting frustrated, since I was ready to leave academia and this administration seemed a natural fit for me given my centrist political leanings. Above all, I was hungry for more government experience. Baker and Brent Scowcroft were looking at me for several other posts, including the European position at either State or the NSC. Finally, on January 25, Brent called and offered me the position of special assistant to the president and senior director for Near East and South Asian affairs on the National Security Council staff, in part because (he later told me) he wanted someone who was not "declared" on the Arab-Israeli issue. We never had a substantive exchange about my views on the region. I asked for two days to think it over, but after only one called Brent back to accept. I flew up to Boston, packed several dozen boxes (mostly of books), flew back, and started work on Monday, January 30.

There is a good deal of confusion about the structure and role of the National Security Council and its staff. The NSC was established in 1947 with only four statutory members: the president, vice president, secretary of state, and secretary of defense. This formal NSC rarely if ever meets. Instead, each president creates his own NSC, one that tends to include such others as the chairman of the Joint Chiefs of Staff, the head of the intelligence community (formerly the director of central intelligence, now the director of national intelligence), selected other cabinet secretaries, the White House chief of staff, and the assistant to the president for national security affairs, usually known as the national security advisor. This individual— Brent Scowcroft under George H. W. Bush—is both a counselor to the president and the traffic cop overseeing the process by which the executive branch makes foreign policy. Wearing that second hat, he must make sure that the executive branch addresses the essential issues, the necessary agencies are involved in the decision-making process, all policy options are developed and vetted, and presidential decisions are communicated clearly and implemented faithfully. The trick is to make sure that the role of counselor does not get in the way of the guarantor of due process; if it does, the system breaks down as everyone does end runs to get to the president. Brent managed this balance of advisor and coordinator better than anyone who has held this job before or since.

To help him do this, the national security advisor oversees the NSC staff, which varies in size from administration to administration but always includes a number of more senior aides responsible for a part of the world such as Latin America or Asia or some functional area, such as arms control or nuclear proliferation. Each of these senior aides then has a few persons assigned to them to share the work. I was responsible for the stretch of countries from Morocco in the west to Bangladesh in the east, or more simply North Africa, the Middle East, the Persian Gulf, and South Asia. I had two assistants: David Welch, a young but experienced and tough-minded foreign service officer who more than a decade later would be the U.S. ambassador to Egypt and then the principal Middle East advisor to Condi Rice during her tenure as secretary of state, for North Africa and the countries directly involved in the Arab-Israeli equation, and Sandra Charles, an experienced and hardworking civilian who had served in the Pentagon, for the Persian Gulf and South Asia.

The national security advisor and his deputy (initially Bob Gates, who went on to head the CIA under Bush 41 and the Defense Department under 43) occupied offices on the ground floor of the West Wing; actually, the deputy's office was closer to a closet. The rest of us were in the Old Executive Office Building, or the OEOB as it was then known. (It is now the Eisenhower EOB.) The OEOB was and is one of the grand buildings of Washington, with its high ceilings and marble floors and history. It once housed the departments of state, war, and navy; the fact that all three departments could easily fit into one modest-sized building underscores just how much the size and role of government has changed. The OEOB was also where Richard Nixon kept his hideaway office as president and where Oliver North devised and carried out his plans to trade arms for hostages and use the profits to fund the Contras.

What was missing was any manual on how to do the job. I can still remember showing up on my first day of work, just a few days into the administration, and making my way past the security guards and metal detectors and door locks to my office on the third floor. Bill Burns, then a midlevel foreign service officer who had served in the Middle East directorate of the Reagan NSC and who years later would go on to be the U.S. ambassador to Russia and undersecretary of state for political affairs, was about to leave. The bank of four-drawer metal files was empty, as all the Reagan memos and documents had been carted off, presumably for sorting en route to their final resting place in the future Reagan presidential library. Bill and I spoke for a short while, after which I was pretty much alone. If this was the handoff between two Republican administrations, it was hard to imagine what one would be like between those of different parties.

I began by putting together a list of issues that needed attention: Pakistan's nuclear program and whether the U.S. government could certify (as required by law if Pakistan was to continue receiving foreign aid) that it did not possess a nuclear explosive device; what to do about Afghanistan once the last Soviet troops departed as scheduled in mid-February; Libya; the Persian Gulf; arms sales; Lebanon; hostages; and the Arab-Israeli peace process. My strong sense was that the last of these issues, the relationship or lack of one between Israel and most of its Arab neighbors, would consume the bulk of my time and energies given its domestic and international political importance. I was right, but only when it came to the first eighteen months of the administration and then again for the last eighteen months. In between, there was the year dominated by Iraq's invasion of Kuwait and the U.S. reaction to it.

Starting a new job is always difficult, requiring among other things establishing a relationship with and the trust of one's new bosses. I knew Brent a bit, but not all that well, and mostly in the context of issues dealing with arms control. I did not know Bob Gates other than by reputation. What complicated things was a call early on from syndicated columnist Rowland Evans to Gates in which Evans suggested that some of my writings rendered me unfit for my new position. What made him particularly unhappy (in addition to rumors that I was "too much of a Zionist," code for being Jewish and overly sympathetic to Israel) was one piece I had written for *Commentary* and another I had done for the more academic journal *Survival* suggesting that diplomacy premised on a return to the 1967 borders and the "territory for peace" formula was not an immediate option given the absence of local leaders both able and willing to compromise. So I sent Gates a sampling of my published pieces with a cover note that explained that a few years back, diplomatic prospects did in fact appear bleak, but that owing to changes in Palestinian politics as well as in Israel there was now a somewhat greater chance to advance peace. This must have been enough, as Evans and his partner Robert Novak then published a column claiming I had privately recanted my earlier views, suggesting I was now an acceptable choice for this sensitive position. What makes all this more than a little ironic is that before the four years were over I had earned considerable enmity from some on the other side of that issue for being too hard on Israel and too sympathetic to the Palestinians. Another rule of the Middle East is that it is just about impossible to win.

The big issue in the first weeks of the administration turned out to be Afghanistan. The last Soviet troops were due out February 15,

1989, and the United States needed a policy for what would soon be a new situation. I am not sure we got it right. The United States never quite moved from the anti-Soviet era, in which support was channeled to those Afghans who had proved their mettle at fighting Soviets, to the post-Soviet era, when we needed to think more about strengthening the hands of those Afghans we wanted to favor in order to shape the new political order in that country. There was an understandable aversion about getting overly involved in internal Afghan politics and playing favorites, but by avoiding them and granting the Pakistanis as much influence as we did, the United States may have unintentionally contributed to the sorry history that characterizes so much of modern Afghanistan.

The first stirrings about the Persian Gulf during the opening weeks and months of the administration tended to emanate from the Pentagon, where the U.S. Navy was anxious to reduce the size and pace of its presence in the area now that the Iran-Iraq War was over and the threat to shipping was mostly a thing of the past. I was reluctant to go back to the status quo ante when we had precious little presence, but figured these and other issues would be hashed out in the policy review that would get under way in the spring.

Iran also garnered some notice, mostly because of the mention in the inaugural address that "goodwill begets goodwill," a clear reference to the American hostages in Lebanon and a signal to Iran that its help in getting them freed would redound to Iran's advantage. But any chance of a quick improvement in ties was nipped in the bud by the fatwa issued against Salman Rushdie following the publication of his novel *The Satanic Verses*. The surprising good news was the robust nature of the European response, as many European Union countries withdrew their ambassadors from Tehran as a sign of protest.

Even with the passage of time and the release of several American hostages held in Lebanon, the improvement in U.S.-Iranian ties suggested in Bush's inaugural address never materialized. Although Iran clearly was behind the decision to free these individuals, the taking of new hostages by Iran-backed groups and evidence of Iranian-sponsored terrorism undermined the case for building a better relationship. This didn't stop the Iranians from feeling that we had moved the goalposts and that they had been misled. Years later, I met the Iranian foreign minister at a conference. Hearing my name, he smiled as he extended his hand, saying, "Ah yes. Mr. Goodwill begets goodwill."

Ninety percent of my time and energies were focused that first spring on the Middle East and trying to get a diplomatic process going between Israelis and Palestinians. There was a succession of Israeli visitors: cabinet secretary Eli Rubenstein, Foreign Minister Moshe Arens, finally Prime Minister Yitzhak Shamir himself. It was clear even before the visits that the situation did not lend itself to—or, using the term I developed in one of my first books, the situation was not "ripe" for—a major diplomatic undertaking on the scale of the 1982 Reagan plan or the earlier Rogers plan, named for Richard Nixon's decent but oft-ignored first secretary of state, William Pierce Rogers. Solving the Israeli-Palestinian dispute was not in the cards at this time. As is often the case, this was not because of the absence of reasonable formulas so much as it was the absence of political leaders on either side of the impasse who were inclined to make meaningful compromises and were sufficiently strong politically to sell them to a reluctant public. But neither was there reason to believe that doing nothing would help matters; neglect would likely be malign, as actions inevitably would be taken by both sides that would pose additional obstacles to peace if and when a promising moment arrived to pursue it with greater intensity. The decision, therefore, was to think small, to try to demonstrate some progress on the ground, and to establish momentum so that we could avert the worst and conceivably create conditions where more ambitious diplomacy might be possible.

What made things particularly difficult was the situation on the ground: the Palestinian intifada was raging, and the conservative Israeli government was in no mood to sit down and talk with the Palestine Liberation Organization (PLO) even though the United States in the final weeks of the Reagan administration had opened up a direct dialogue with the PLO once the organization had at long last forsaken the use of terror to advance its political agenda. The interlocutor for the U.S. side was our ambassador in Tunis, where the PLO had set up shop after it had been exiled from Lebanon a few years before. Israel, however, was still not prepared to deal directly with the PLO. A good deal of time was thus devoted to finding Palestinians whom Israel would talk to and whom Palestinians would see as credible. Israeli hopes that the moderate government in Jordan could speak for the Palestinians was a nonstarter given the strength of Palestinian nationalism and identity. Another more promising idea was to hold elections in the West Bank and Gaza that would produce an "alternative" leadership that would be acceptable to the PLO but not formally part of the PLO.

Matters came to something of a head in early September 1989 when Israeli prime minister Shamir visited Washington in the wake of a visit by Egyptian president Hosni Mubarak. Both visits included black-tie White House dinners, my first. The Mubarak visit also included a trip to Baltimore for opening day of the baseball season. I can't remember whom the Orioles were playing, much less who won. What I do recall is feeling silly showing up at the stadium in a suit and tie, sacrilegious about leaving after five innings, getting an autographed ball from Ted Williams, and being amused by the announcer's introductions before the game: "The president of Egypt, Hosni Mubarak, a baseball legend . . . Ted Williams." The pause made it sound as if Mubarak was the legend, which must have confused the Egyptians almost as much as the game itself.

Going to the game turned out to have an unanticipated effect. It made the Israelis angry at the special treatment for Mubarak. Israeli cabinet secretary Eli Rubenstein complained to me, "You hug Mubarak like your bubalah [little grandmother], take him to a game, and us you treat like shit." Also unhappy with what we planned to say in public during Shamir's upcoming visit, the Israelis demanded that the president do something equally "friendly" with Shamir. So I asked the Israeli ambassador if the prime minister, someone who had spent his entire life either fighting or in politics, had any hobbies. Neither he nor anyone else could think of any. In the end, the president and the prime minister took a walk around the Rose Garden.

More serious (although none of us realized it for months) was the breakdown of trust between Bush and Shamir. It stemmed from their initial conversation in the Oval Office. It was just the two of them, along with Israeli ambassador Moshe Arad and me. The president raised the matter of Israeli settlements in the occupied territories, long considered an "obstacle to peace" by every U.S. administration and inconsistent with international law by some. Shamir waved his arm and waved away the president's concerns, saying in English, "no problem." Bush thought he had an understanding from Shamir that the Israelis would not cause any problems with their settlement activity, meaning that they would cease building new ones. Shamir, I later learned, thought he was telling the president that the settlements were causing and should not cause any problem and that all the debate was much ado about nothing. Shamir thus continued authorizing them; Bush thought the Israeli leader had broken his word. When Arad and I unraveled all this and I explained the misunderstanding to the president, I met with a reaction that fell somewhere between skepticism and disbelief. It was a good if painful lesson that a lack of clarity can cause real harm; contrary to what is often alleged, not all diplomatic ambiguity is constructive. All this history made the ability of these two leaders to work together during the Persian Gulf War a year later all the more remarkable.

Israeli-Palestinian issues continued to dominate my attention that spring, although my colleagues elsewhere in the administration were focusing on a deteriorating security situation in Panama and problems with West Germany over whether to modernize nuclear forces in Europe. In May I took my first trip to the region in my new capacity, along with Dennis Ross (head of the State Department's Policy Planning Staff, and who also oversaw the Middle East for Jim Baker) and several others. Much of the focus remained on how to structure elections to choose a Palestinian leadership that was credible and acceptable. There was (appropriately enough) a theological element to all this, as everyone knew that the Palestinian leadership would have to be supportive of and blessed by the PLO even if they could not be formal members of the organization. We went to Israel, the West Bank, Cairo, and Amman, and then I returned through Europe to brief the European allies on what we'd learned.

During the trip, Dennis and I, along with Dan Kurtzer (a respected foreign service officer who would become ambassador to Egypt and then Israel) and Aaron Miller (an academic who would work these issues in government for some two decades), drafted the speech Secretary Baker was slated to give on May 22 to the annual meeting of the American Israel Public Affairs Committee (AIPAC), the core of the so-called Israeli or Jewish lobby. The end result was crisp and clear. Baker called upon the Arab world to end its economic boycott of Israel, stop its challenges to Israel's standing in the United Nations, and repudiate the outrageous notion that "Zionism is racism." He asked Palestinians to renounce all violence. But what garnered the bulk of the coverage was his calling on Israelis "to lay aside, once and for all, the unrealistic vision of a greater Israel" and both "forswear annexation" and "stop settlement activity." In retrospect, it was a mistake to have the secretary of state say this, since the speech was not linked to any policy initiative and was not given against the backdrop of a strong relationship between the United States and Israel. It is one thing to pay a political price to achieve diplomatic gain, quite another to pay a price for no obvious purpose.

The rest of the world was not standing still while the protagonists in the Middle East pursued their familiar struggle. The Chinese government cracked down hard on the students and others gathered and protesting in Tiananmen Square; in so doing the government forfeited sympathy and legitimacy alike. As much as anything else, what the confrontation highlighted was the disparity between China's economic dynamism and its political stagnation. At some point China would either have to slow its economic development or accelerate its political reform. Either would entail risks for social and political stability and above all for the continued position of the Communist Party.

The contrast with the Soviet Union could not be greater. There, with Mikhail Gorbachev, we were seeing political change that was far outstripping economic developments. For me the question at the time was whether Gorbachev could prosper if his country did not— and whether he could manage change within bounds, that is, without losing control of the Soviet empire or the country itself. Clearly, he could not.

In the greater Middle East, there was the death of Iran's Ayatollah Khomeini. He was a living contradiction: the medieval figure who came to power thanks to modern cassettes of his sermons and who arrived in Tehran from Paris on a jet plane. It was not clear whether his death would present any opportunity for an improvement in U.S.-Iranian ties. I was somewhat skeptical, thinking it more likely that we would face a period of contested leadership in which the various claimants would likely compete for who could be the most rabidly anti-American. As it turned out, there was a relatively smooth transition to the new leadership "team" of President Akbar Hashemi Rafsanjani and Supreme Leader Ali Hoseyn Khamenei. U.S. options remained limited and essentially what they were. Regime change, however desirable, was not attainable, which tended to leave us with containment. The question was whether we would be willing to leaven that basic approach with some signals of a willingness to enter into a more positive relationship. A number of possibilities existed: offering compensation for the accidental U.S. Navy shoot-down of an Iranian civilian airliner, continuing to deal with each side's financial claims, restrained public rhetoric. My own view was that it made sense to keep some lines out to a country that, for better or worse, would likely continue to be a major regional actor for years to come.

I took a few days off around Labor Day, but returned feeling less than refreshed. It is not easy to work hard day in and day out on a set of issues that never seem to show signs of progress. The Middle East was getting lost in numbers: a 21-point election proposal, an Egyptian 10-point plan, a Mubarak 4-point letter, a May 14 Israeli plan, a 5-point Baker proposal. Unfortunately, they added up to nothing. Conversations between Bush and Shamir tended to make matters worse. It was difficult to avoid comparing the Middle East with how things were going in South Africa. There, with Nelson Mandela and F. W. de Klerk, the sides were blessed with one leader prepared to forgo violence and move beyond the injustices of the past and another who was willing to make the case to his public about why they should be willing to give up many of the advantages that for decades had defined their lives and instead accept a very different relationship with South Africa's blacks. Such people can create ripeness and the potential for diplomatic accomplishment. The contrast with the combination of PLO leader Yasir Arafat and Shamir could hardly have been more stark—or depressing.

My interest was also focused on Afghanistan. I traveled that fall to India and Pakistan and came back anything but reassured. Six months had passed since the Soviet withdrawal, and the regime in Kabul was still in place and the war was continuing. Predictions of a rapid transition to something new and better had not been realized.

History is likely to record that the most significant moment in 1989 came on November 9, with the dismantling of the Berlin Wall and, with it, the Cold War. The president was restrained in his reactions, limiting them to answers to questions at a press conference and even then doing all he could to drain the moment of import and impact. Partially this was his style, partially it was a conscious decision not to say or do anything that would undermine Gorbachev. Over the next eighteen months this approach would pay substantial dividends as Gorbachev and the Soviet Union were remarkably supportive of U.S. policy during the Iraq crisis.

At the time, though, there was no thought of an Iraq crisis. Nineteen eighty-nine was drawing to a close with the president and others heading off to Malta for a summit with the Soviets. I did not go; my role was limited to preparing papers on regional issues. I was feeling somewhat sorry for myself, wondering why I had allowed myself to move away from European issues just when they were getting interesting and immersing myself in the Middle East when it seemed more hopeless than ever.

I have gone on at considerable length here in order to provide a relatively developed picture of what constituted the backdrop to the making of U.S. policy toward Iraq. It is important to make this clear, for all too often historians, journalists, politicians, and others focus on a particular issue and take it out of the context in which policy involving that issue was made. The reality is that policy makers have to juggle issues competing for their time and attention. Often it is only in retrospect that the relative importance of an issue emerges with any clarity. For the first year and a half of the Bush administration, the president and his senior aides focused for good reason on the fall of the Berlin Wall and the peaceful end of the Cold War, Germany's unification and its entry into NATO, political repression in China, challenges to the U.S. position in Panama, and the risk of war in South Asia. Iraq was barely on the radar (literal or figurative) of any midlevel much less senior official.

This even applied to me for much of the eighteen months. Within the part of the world for which I was responsible, I spent most of my time dealing with efforts to find Palestinians whom Israel would talk to and who were worth talking to; working with Afghans on a post-Soviet government; keeping Indians and Pakistanis from going to war with one another; and trying to get the American hostages out of Lebanon. Iraq was not a top priority.

Still, the Bush administration reviewed policy toward Iraq, Iran, and the Persian Gulf much as it reviewed many policies. Such comprehensive assessments are typical of new administrations since they allow officials to get up to speed on issues and provide a basis for officials to get to know one another better and to learn to work with one another. Responsibility for writing the review itself fell to my directorate on the NSC. Sandy Charles and I did the drafting. It was then subjected to interagency review. Virtually all administrations over the past half century have embraced some version of a three-tiered layer cake for interagency policy making. The bottom tier involves those at the assistant secretary level and below. The intermediate tier, normally called the deputies, involves the number two or three person at participating departments and agencies; the most senior level involves the principals (cabinet level) and on occasion the president himself, when it becomes an NSC meeting.

The Iraq-Iran policy review was completed that June and then, as if to underscore the lack of priority, sat unchanged in the president's inbox for several months until it was signed by him on October 2, 1989. National Security Directive 26, "U.S. Policy Toward the Persian Gulf," began by setting forth U.S. policy toward the region in broad brushstrokes:

> *Access to Persian Gulf oil and the security of key friendly states in the area are vital to U.S. national security. The United States remains committed to defend its vital interests in the region, if necessary and appropriate through the use of U.S. military force, against the Soviet Union or any other regional power with interests inimical to our own. The United States also remains committed to support the individual and collective self-defense of friendly countries in the area to enable them to play a more active role in their own defense and thereby reduce the necessity for unilateral U.S. military intervention. The United States also will encourage the effective support and participation of our western allies and Japan to promote our mutual interests in the Persian Gulf region.*

The document also provided more specific guidance regarding Iraq. What it said was fully consistent with the policy inherited from the Reagan administration, namely, it called for a limited attempt to build a more normal relationship with Iraq in an effort to shape Iraqi foreign policy. It was thus a classic case of constructive engagement, a policy of trying to build bridges with a country that was an adversary or at least a problem in the hope of moderating its behavior. But it was also an example of conditional engagement, since it emphasized that normalization would not go ahead if Iraq acted in ways contrary to U.S. interests. Indeed, the U.S. commitment to defend American interests in the region, including with military force if need be, is underscored. The document is clear on all of this:

Normal relations between the United States and Iraq would serve our longer-term interests and promote stability in both the Gulf and the Middle East. The United States government should propose economic and political incentives for Iraq to moderate its behavior and to increase our influence with Iraq. At the same time, the Iraqi leadership must understand that any illegal use of chemical and/or biological weapons will lead to economic and political sanctions, for which we would seek the broadest possible support from our allies and friends. Any breach by Iraq of IAEA [International Atomic Energy Agency, the U.N.'s watchdog in this area] safeguards in its nuclear program will result in a similar response. Human rights considerations should continue to be an important element in our policy toward Iraq. In addition, Iraq should be urged to cease its meddling in external affairs, such as in Lebanon, and be encouraged to play a constructive role in negotiating a settlement with Iran and cooperating in the Middle East peace process.

We should pursue, and seek to facilitate, opportunities for U.S. firms to participate in the reconstruction of the Iraqi economy, particularly in the energy area, where they do not conflict with our non-proliferation and other significant objectives. Also, as a means of developing access to and influence with the Iraqi defense establishment, the United States should consider sales of non-lethal forms of military assistance, e.g., training courses and medical exchanges, on a case-by-case basis.

In many ways Directive 26 did not represent a departure; to the contrary, it mostly codified both the thinking and the policy already in place. Even with the Iran-Iraq War over, Iraq was still seen as something of a foil to more dangerous Iran. Iraq was also seen as becoming less radical: it had moved away from the Soviet Union (which in any event had become much less of a factor given internal developments there), it had moved away from support for terror, and it had moved away from the radical Arab rejectionist bloc that did all it could to frustrate Israeli-Arab normalization. Iraq had joined (along with Egypt, Jordan, and North Yemen) the new "Arab Cooperation Council," a coalition of "moderate" and mostly pro-Western Arab states. Also, it looked as if the United States and Iraq would be able to reach a fair settlement reflecting American claims relating to the Iraqi attack on the USS *Stark*. In addition, the general view of Iraq (one supported by a National Intelligence Estimate issued in late 1989) was that it, like Iran, was too drained from its eight-year war to cause much trouble for some time to come and would want to devote its time and energy to rebuilding its economy. Nonetheless, no one had any illusions about Iraq—Saddam was clearly a bad guy, Iraq had started the war with Iran, and it had used chemical weapons against not only Iran but its own Kurdish citizens. Again, though, there was the widely held view that continued diplomatic and commercial engagement might prove beneficial in the same way that we had been able to work with Syrian leader Hafiz al-Assad. There was also the realization that a more confrontational tack toward Iraq would fail since neither the Arab states nor the Europeans were prepared to support such an approach.

The Bush administration thus continued to extend CCC credit guarantees to American exporters to facilitate Iraq's continued purchase of agricultural commodities from the United States. In the fall of 1989, Iraq requested $1.03 billion in new CCC credit guarantees for the coming fiscal year. Given questions that had arisen about how the Iraqis were administering the program, the Department of Agriculture recommended establishing a phased approach to the CCC program in which any new credit guarantees would be divided into two roughly equal tranches. The administration authorized the first tranche of $500 million in guarantees, but repeatedly delayed the second tranche. In the end, only about $400 million in agricultural commodities were actually shipped to Iraq prior to the imposition of sanctions. In addition, $75 million in dual-use exports were licensed by the Commerce Department during the Bush presidency, although there is no way to know how much if any of this was illegally diverted to military use.

Years later, allegations regarding the improper administration of the CCC and dual-use export programs were cited as "proof" of a scandal dubbed "Iraqgate." The charge was levied that the Bush administration had secretly armed the Iraqis through these programs and had in part created the threat that the first Iraq war had to combat. However, more than four years of hearings and investigations by various executive branch, congressional, and judicial bodies during the Bush and Clinton administrations made clear that these charges were false. No U.S. funds were ever transferred to Iraq under the CCC program, no U.S. arms were exported, and the amount and significance of the dual-use exports were minimal. If there was a scandal, it was in the behavior of the Congress, in particular Henry Gonzalez, the chairman of the House Banking, Finance, and Urban Affairs Committee, who made dozens of speeches and held several hearings in which he launched one unsubstantiated accusation after another. Then senator Al Gore also deserves special criticism, for unlike Gonzalez, Gore was a serious and respected member of the Congress. Yet Gore, too, seemed unable or unwilling to understand the limited nature of U.S. interaction with Saddam's Iraq.

The mainstream media was hardly better. *U.S. News*, the *Los Angeles Times*, and the *New York Times* among others ran dozens of news stories, columns, and editorials that got the facts wrong and hurled charges with little or no justification. What made all this serious was the congressional investigations that absorbed hundreds of hours. I remember putting in full twelve-hour days and then along with my staff having to spend several more hours responding to various congressional requests for documents. I was concerned not over anything we had done but over the possibility we might miss locating and handing over some document in a file drawer and be charged with obstruction of justice. Policy differences are legitimate and unavoidable, but this was something else. What made it all worse was the lack of accountability. None of the members of Congress or journalists paid any price as best I can tell for their inaccuracies. But for those of us in the executive branch, it was demoralizing and exhausting and, in some cases, costly. People who complain about why it is so difficult to attract the best people to public service could get some of their answer from this episode and others like it.

Gradually, however, the rationale for continuing even limited programs with Iraq and the policy of constructive engagement more generally began to weaken. Saddam's behavior at the February 1990 summit of the Arab Cooperation Council in Amman, Jordan, caused some consternation, both for the way he pressured and threatened other Arab governments to forgive Iraq's considerable debt and for his call for the U.S. Navy to leave the area. Then, in March, the Iraqis charged British journalist Farzad Bazoft with espionage, condemned him to death, and went ahead with his execution despite a lack of evidence and international calls for clemency. Weeks later, customs officials at London's Heathrow Airport seized electronic devices bound for Iraq that could be used as triggers for nuclear weapons. In April, British customs officials stopped another illegal shipment bound for Iraq, in this case elements of an artillery system or super gun (we dubbed it "big Bertha") that in principle could have been used for launching a chemical munition over a significant distance. Saddam made matters worse by his rhetoric, threatening to use chemical weapons to "eat up half of Israel" if it were to attack Iraq.

Anyone could see that our Iraq policy was not working. I convened an interagency Policy Coordinating Committee (PCC) meeting at the assistant secretary level in March that turned out to be fairly inconclusive. Again, no one was defending Saddam. The question was tactical: Should we shut down (as some in Congress argued) what little there was of the U.S.-Iraq relationship, or was it smarter to keep at least something in play (call it constructive engagement lite)? The inclination was not to shut down the relationship and to keep open the possibility of influencing Iraq's trajectory.

Around the same time, a bipartisan group of senators led by prominent Republican Robert Dole and including Ohio Democrat Howard Metzenbaum traveled to Baghdad. They got an earful from Saddam, who, in the way of many from his part of the world, saw a vast conspiracy being mounted against him. Saddam was unhappy with news reports of the investigation that an Italian bank (Banca Nazionale del Lavoro, or BNL) had laundered money used for Iraqi arms purchases, with the congressional push for sanctions, and with a Voice of America editorial in February that was critical of him and his regime. The senators did their best to reassure Saddam of American interest in an expanded bilateral relationship. In so doing, they went too far—a transcript later released by the Iraqis did them no favor—although even so it seems Saddam came away unpersuaded.

It soon became clear that the Department of Agriculture was coming down with a severe case of cold feet. Officials there circulated a draft press release suspending the second $500 million tranche of CCC credit guarantees, a political decision that I felt strongly they had no right to make. Commerce was likewise getting uncomfortable with the dual-use export program. I convened another PCC in mid-April to review the situation in Baghdad and Washington, after which I bucked up the issue to a deputies committee meeting chaired by Bob Gates. The bias there was against continuing the CCC program, more because of concerns with how it was being implemented than due to Iraq's behavior writ large. No decision was taken, but the handwriting was on the wall.

What we had in effect decided was that the second tranche of CCC credit guarantees, which was about all that was left of the attempt to build a relationship, would not go ahead. The question was whether we would simply let it lie there or whether we would make a formal, public announcement of the suspension, an action that would communicate a more negative message to Baghdad. Scowcroft and I spoke, and he decided that it made sense for me to go to Baghdad to see what if anything could be done to alter the political momentum.

First, however, there was the matter of considerable intelligence suggesting that India and Pakistan were moving toward war, less out of calculation than out of a loss of control over events. So Bob Gates, John Kelly (my counterpart at the State Department), and I flew over to both New Delhi and Islamabad in an effort to get both governments to reassess their behavior and convey how much they had to lose from another round of fighting given the likely inconclusive results and the risk that any conventional war could cross the nuclear threshold. We succeeded, although as is almost always the case our success in that arena drew considerably less notice than our collective failure to avert war between Iraq and Kuwait ten weeks later.

I returned to Washington, but days later took off for Baghdad, arriving in late May. I stayed at the residence of U.S. ambassador April Glaspie, a respected Arabist and foreign service officer. If she had been British and born a century earlier, she would likely have been one of those intrepid Englishwomen in the mode of Gertrude Bell. My Iraqi host for the trip was Nizar Hamdoon, formerly their ambassador in Washington, now the number two in their Foreign Ministry. Nizar was a decent, moderate, and articulate man, one who was committed to building a bridge between Iraq and the United States. During his years as ambassador to the United States, he did more than anyone else to create the possibility of an improvement in U.S.-Iraqi ties; in my experience, he was one of the few diplomats posted to Washington who figured out how to insert himself into the policy process. My first night in Baghdad, he and I went out for dinner in a downtown restaurant. A fifth of Johnnie Walker Black Label was brought to the table; it was near empty by dinner's end, with Nizar doing the lion's share of the drinking. His tone was one of sorrow, not anger, as we discussed how relations had deteriorated and what might be done about them.

I met with several members of Saddam's cabinet, but not with Saddam himself, who was busy preparing for an Arab summit he would soon host. My main meeting was with Tariq Aziz, Saddam's recognizable and urbane English-speaking foreign minister. (I always thought that Aziz was the one piece of evidence that Saddam possessed a sense of humor. Saddam enjoyed sending Aziz, a Christian, to represent Iraq at the meetings of the Organization of the Islamic Conference. It was one more way Saddam could show contempt for his fellow Arabs.) The meeting was in Aziz's office at the ministry and lasted for more than two hours. The coffee was strong, the Havana cigars we each smoked top-of-the-line, and the conversation combative, almost debatelike. My basic theme was that the relationship could evolve in any direction, that we had not written off Iraq nor made up our minds that it was a threat or adversary, although what Iraq was saying and doing was a source of growing concern, and that it was Iraq that would determine how things would evolve between us by what it said and, more important, did. Aziz would cite specific Iraqi grievances and kept returning to the theme that much of what we were doing was anti-Iraqi in origin and nature. He placed particular emphasis on our naval presence in the vicinity, saying it must be anti-Iraqi because there was no longer a justification for it given that the Iran-Iraq War and the threat to shipping were over. I reminded him that the presence had existed for four decades and was there as an expression of support for U.S. interests in the region. The presence was not aimed at Iraq or any other country unless it threatened U.S. interests. I drew a parallel with the U.S. presence in Europe now that the Berlin Wall had come down: we maintained armed forces there despite the absence of a particular threat. This last argument seemed to have some effect, because for once Aziz had no comeback and the Iraqis never leaked the transcript of a meeting I assume they secretly taped.

I returned to Washington believing that we ought not shut down commercial contacts unless there was evidence Iraq had violated the terms under which goods or services had been provided. I argued as much in a cable I sent in from Baghdad. I didn't want to increase the paranoia of those in Baghdad who saw a conspiracy against them. Nor did I want to give up on trying to build a relationship with Iraq in the hope of moderating its behavior. And I was skeptical of what unilateral American sanctions could accomplish. But another deputies committee meeting in late May found the CCC program without any backers. There were more than enough legal questions to warrant placing the program on ice. We did, however, agree to soften the message sent to Iraq by getting authorization to explain that the decision to hold back the second tranche of credit guarantees was only temporary, pending the results of the CCC and BNL investigations. There was more consensus on the desirability of further limiting exports of dual-use technologies. New, tougher guidelines were developed. But before they were in place, word reached us that a New Jersey–based company called Consarc was trying to export high-temperature furnaces to Iraq that could process titanium and other metals. The license request stated the furnaces were for the purpose of fabricating artificial limbs, but U.S. intelligence agencies suspected they were far more likely to be used to fabricate aircraft, missile, and nuclear weapons components. All this information reached me, along with the fact that there were only some twenty-four hours to act before the furnaces set sail. There was no way the new more restrictive guidelines would be in place in time, so I asked if there was any other legal way to stop this shipment. Someone suggested an obscure provision in the Nuclear Non-Proliferation Act of

1978 could be employed. It worked for me. I signed the necessary documentation and the furnaces were seized on the docks literally hours before they were to be loaded on a ship. For the first and only time in my career, I was extolled on the floor of the U.S. Senate for service to my country by none other than Jesse Helms, the archconservative senator from North Carolina.

Still, the attempt by Iraq to acquire the furnaces was yet another reminder that Saddam's agenda was incompatible with our own. Saddam's statements at the Arab League meeting he hosted in late May also contributed to our judgment that engagement was not working and that Iraq was a growing although not immediate problem. At the Arab League meeting, Saddam was heavy-handed in his treatment of the Kuwaitis, accusing them of stealing oil from fields that were he alleged were Iraq's and demanding that they forgive Iraqi debts racked up in the war against Iran, a war that Saddam argued he had fought on behalf of all Arab states.

By mid-July, Iraq started to back up its threats with actions, mobilizing troops across from its border with Kuwait. My own view then and for the next two weeks was that Saddam was unlikely to invade Kuwait (much less occupy all of it) and that this was instead a crude means of pressuring Kuwait to forgive debt and support a higher price for oil, something that required Kuwait and others to produce less so that supply would not overwhelm demand. Behind all this was Saddam's increasingly desperate drive for money to fund rebuilding and rearming. The challenge for intelligence is almost always to discern both capabilities and intentions. That Iraq possessed the ability to overwhelm Kuwait if it chose to attack was not in doubt. But its intentions were far less certain, and the betting was that Iraq sought to intimidate, not invade.

There was much back-and-forth within the administration in mid-July about how to further reduce the odds (generally judged to be low) that Iraq's mobilization would lead to an outbreak of fighting in late July. The State Department declared on July 18 that the United States remained "determined to ensure the free flow of oil through the Strait of Hormuz and to defend the principle of freedom of navigation. We also remain strongly committed to supporting the individual and collective self-defense of our friends in the Gulf with whom we have deep and longstanding ties." What made it particularly difficult to take a tougher line toward Iraq (in addition to skepticism about Saddam's real intentions) was pressure on us from Arab governments not to do too much to warn Baghdad or prepare for the worst lest such actions on our part actually contribute to a momentum toward war. Kuwait turned down the U.S. offer to participate in a military exercise that would demonstrate its ties to the United States and U.S. willingness and ability to work with it. The only exception to this reticence came from the United Arab Emirates, which on July 22 asked that the United States dispatch aerial refueling tankers and exercise with its air force. Over the objections of the Saudis and others, we quickly agreed, although a week later I found out that the exercise had not taken place as designed because the U.S. tankers and UAE planes could not "mate."

Then, on July 25, U.S. ambassador Glaspie received word that she had been summoned to meet Saddam. This had never happened before, and the short notice made it impossible for her to receive formal instructions. She was widely criticized for her performance but much of this criticism was unfair. In particular, people took one item out of context, that the United States took "no position" on the territorial dispute between Iraq and Kuwait, and interpreted it to mean that we didn't care if Iraq used force against Kuwait. Her point (one that was clear from the transcript of the entire meeting) was to underscore that the United States did not hold a position on where borders ought to be drawn but that the United States "can never excuse settlement of disputes by other than peaceful means." What is more, amid a rambling monologue filled with bluster, Saddam did communicate his agreement to sit down with the Kuwaitis and find a peaceful settlement to the crisis.

This last point was the bottom line of her reporting cable back to Washington. It was consistent with the message being communicated to us from Egyptian president Hosni Mubarak and others, and was consistent with our own reading of the situation, namely, that Saddam was engaging in a modern-day form of gunboat diplomacy to get Kuwait to abide by OPEC oil production quotas (which would likely lead to an increase in the price of oil, something desperately sought by a cash-starved Saddam) and forgive some or all of what Iraq owed Kuwait. Ambassador Glaspie's cable reporting on her meeting with Saddam came in at the same time the CIA issued a warning of possible war and just as we were deliberating what sort of a message to send Saddam in order to get him to stand down. We were leaning toward something quite muscular. I had sent a memo through Brent for the president that suggested three possibilities in descending order of likelihood: that Saddam was bluffing, that he was about to grab a piece of Kuwait to trade for financial help, or that he was actually contemplating an invasion and possible conquest. The memo went on to urge that the president send the sternest of warnings to Saddam and back up those words with high-visibility military actions. But after reading the report from Baghdad, I pulled the memo back, believing it was no longer necessary and risked being counterproductive given the apparent shift in the crisis in the direction of a diplomatic resolution. Things looked good enough that Ambassador Glaspie left Baghdad on a long-scheduled vacation.

The message we did send from the president to Saddam on July 28 was meant to be calming but with an underlying message of strength:

I was pleased to learn of the agreement between Iraq and Kuwait to begin negotiations in Jeddah to find a peaceful solution to the current tensions between you. The United States and Iraq both have a strong interest in preserving the peace and stability of the Middle East. For this reason, we believe that differences are best resolved by peaceful means and not by threats involving military force or conflict. I also welcome your statement that Iraq desires friendship rather than confrontation with the United States. Let me reassure you, as my ambassador, Senator Dole, and others have done, that my administration continues to desire better relations with Iraq. We will also continue to support our other friends in the region with whom we have had long-standing ties. We see no necessary inconsistency between these two objectives. . . .

Both Ambasssador Glaspie and the administration were criticized after the fact for not having done more to convince Saddam Hussein not to attack. I do not believe that there was more under the circumstances we could or should have done or, more fundamentally, that anything we might have done would have made a difference. Saddam was a selective reader of history, and it is clear from his July 25 meeting with Glaspie that he viewed the United States as soft. This was the lesson he took from Vietnam and, more recently and closer to home, from the American withdrawal from Lebanon in 1984 following the bombing of the marine barracks there the previous year. To be sure, statements by various administration officials that we had no formal alliance commitment to Kuwait were unfortunate and may have reinforced these perceptions. And nearly all of us were wrong in discounting the possibility that Saddam might invade Kuwait as he did. Still, on any number of occasions the United States signaled its commitment to its friends, and U.S. forces remained in the region to underscore that commitment. There was no way the ambassador or anyone else could have credibly threatened Saddam with a response of the scale of what the United States and the world ultimately did in the Persian Gulf War. It is also important to keep in mind Saddam's lack of respect for his fellow Arabs. He almost certainly dismissed the possibility that they would rally around widely disliked Kuwait and stand up to him. I am also reminded of the small sign that Bob Gates kept on his desk: "The best way to achieve complete strategic surprise is to take an action that is either stupid or completely contrary to your self-interest."

Three days later, the Saudi-hosted meeting between Iraq and Kuwait produced nothing. Over those same days, the Iraqi buildup and mobilization continued unabated. On the morning of August 1, Charlie Allen, the national intelligence officer for warning, again came to see me. This time I was persuaded the Iraqis were doing more than intimidation; military action looked highly likely. The intelligence community sounded the alarm, upgrading its "warning of war" to a more imminent "warning of attack." We hastily convened an interagency meeting on the State Department's seventh floor. By late afternoon, I returned to the White House with the mission of persuading Brent and the president to make one last attempt to dissuade Saddam Hussein from making good on his threat to attack Kuwait. Saddam did just that while we were discussing the mechanics of how best to reach him.

3. DESERT SHIELD

IT WAS THE evening of August 1 in Washington, the morning of August 2 in Baghdad and Kuwait. Iraqi forces, encountering little in the way of resistance on the ground, moved quickly to consolidate their control of Kuwait. Brent Scowcroft and I hastily arranged a late interagency meeting, one that would run until the early hours of the morning, on the secure closed-circuit video system. We still didn't know the full extent of Iraq's intentions—that wouldn't become apparent for a few more days—but we knew we had to take steps quickly to prevent the new situation from becoming the new status quo.

Improvisation was the order of the day. There was no playbook and no contingency plan for dealing with this scenario or anything like it. Agreement was reached to freeze not only Iraqi assets in the United States (the president was awakened in the middle of the night by Brent to sign the necessary papers) but also those of Kuwait to make sure the new puppet government installed by the Iraqis could not lay claim to what was rightfully Kuwait's. We also decided to go to the United Nations right off the bat to get on the books a Security Council resolution calling for the withdrawal of all Iraqi forces from Kuwait. Resolution 660, which demanded that Iraq "withdraw immediately and unconditionally" from Kuwait, was passed 14-0-1 on

August 2 with no real opposition (only Yemen, then occupying the rotating "Arab seat" on the Security Council, abstained) and little delay. The fact that the Soviets and Chinese lined up with us was a good sign. The Soviets then went a step further by agreeing to a joint statement that backed up the U.N. resolution. This sent a powerful signal to Saddam that he could not count on Soviet support to somehow balance U.S. opposition, as might well have been the case during the Cold War. Indeed, it is worth noting that for Secretary of State James Baker it was this action, more than the earlier crumbling of the Berlin Wall or anything else, that signified the end of the Cold War.

The first formal NSC meeting of the crisis was convened the morning of August 2 with President Bush in the chair. The president, Brent, and I spoke beforehand and agreed we would take the unusual step of inviting the media into the Cabinet Room at the outset. I quickly drafted a statement summarizing the U.S. position and steps that had been taken that the president read aloud. The president caused problems for himself, though, when in answer to a question from Helen Thomas of UPI he seemed to rule out the possible use of military force down the road. Bush was simply trying to say that it was premature to signal U.S. readiness to liberate Kuwait by force and that we had not given up on achieving Kuwait's liberation by other means. Although he clarified his stance later that day in a press conference, the general perception was one of a lack of certainty and commitment.

As was always the case when I attended such White House meetings, I was a backbencher and sat in one of the chairs against the wall. The meeting itself was unfocused and a sharp disappointment. Several people opined about Iraqi intentions and our military and diplomatic options; what worried me (and, as I soon learned, Brent and the president as well) was the apparent readiness of some in the room to acquiesce in what had taken place. They seemed to suggest there was nothing we could do about it and that instead the focus of U.S. policy ought to be on making sure Saddam did not go any farther and do to Saudi Arabia what he'd done to Kuwait.

As soon as the meeting ended, the president left for Aspen, Colorado, to give a long-scheduled speech on U.S. military strategy now that the Cold War was winding down and to meet with British prime minister Margaret Thatcher. I walked out of the room and expressed my unhappiness to Brent with how the meeting had unfolded. He agreed and said he would raise it with the president on the plane. He also told me to write up something that he could give to the president upon his return. The memo summarized what it would require to get Iraq out of Kuwait and to discourage it from moving against Saudi Arabia. The conclusion was that the strategic price of allowing Iraq to keep Kuwait would be enormous, and that evicting Iraq would likely require the use of military force on our part. "I am aware as you are of just how costly and risky such a conflict would prove to be. But so too would be accepting this new status quo. We would be setting a terrible precedent—one that would only accelerate violent centrifugal tendencies—in this emerging 'post–Cold War' era."

The second NSC meeting on the crisis, on Friday, August 3, could not have been more different. All crises have a rhythm, and this was no exception. People had had time to find their bearings and collect their thoughts. The president wanted to set a fundamentally different mood. Before entering the Cabinet Room, we huddled in the Oval Office, where Brent and Larry Eagleburger persuaded him to hold back, fearing that once he had spoken no one would be prepared to argue for a different course. It was decided that Brent would give the Churchill speech, that is, a rousing call for the imperative of resisting and, in the end, reversing Iraqi aggression. That is exactly what he did to kick off the meeting. "My personal judgment is that the stakes in this for the United States are such that to accommodate

Iraq should not be a policy option" is how he began. Brent could be a good deal more forceful and opinionated than people realized; his soft-spoken manner, slight appearance, and almost ascetic manner masked a powerful intellect, a developed view of history, and a strong philosophy of American purpose. Larry echoed Brent, emphasizing not only how our response would shape the era but that allowing Saddam to keep Kuwait would give him sway over Saudi Arabia, OPEC, and Israel. Defense secretary Dick Cheney then echoed Larry. Again, there was no decision, but the future direction of U.S. policy was there for all to see.

The difference between the first and second NSC meetings highlights a fundamental truth. People matter. It was anything but axiomatic that the United States would decide to deploy half a million troops halfway around the world to rescue a country that few Americans could find on a map. A different president and set of advisors might have tolerated Iraqi control of Kuwait and limited the U.S. response to sanctions so long as Saddam did not go on to attack Saudi Arabia. What is more, this was not something the American people could have known one way or the other when they elected George H. W. Bush. The question of how the United States would react to an Iraqi invasion of Kuwait was for understandable reasons never raised during the campaign or in the first year and a half of the Bush administration. Often the most fateful decisions of a presidency are those that are made without much in the way of foreshadowing. It is why basing one's vote on judgment and character might be best.

The third NSC meeting was held up at Camp David that Saturday morning. I assembled with the others—Vice President Dan Quayle, Brent, Jim Baker (back from Mongolia), Chief of Staff John Sununu, spokesman Marlin Fitzwater—at the vice president's home off Massachusetts Avenue and we helicoptered up. Cheney and the military leaders flew up separately from the Pentagon. The meeting was divided into two parts: an initial briefing by General Norman

Schwarzkopf, head of Central Command, followed by a principals-only conversation.

The meeting itself went quite well. Our military options were better than expected. Colin Powell, then chairman of the Joint Chiefs of Staff (JCS), was effective and reassuring in highlighting Iraq's weaknesses: low-quality forces, vulnerable lines of communication, U.S. advantages in airpower. Powell described the scene as a target-rich environment about which every twenty-four-year-old fighter pilot dreams. Powell estimated maybe a hundred thousand troops, some reserves, and host nation support would be required to repel any Iraqi attack on Saudi Arabia. The big concern was over Arab and in particular Saudi reluctance to invite U.S. forces in and work openly with us.

A strategy was beginning to emerge. U.S. and other forces would be dispatched to the region to deter further Iraqi aggression against Saudi Arabia—Desert Shield—and to provide a backdrop to economic sanctions so that Iraq would either have to capitulate and leave Kuwait or get pounded. A blockade of Iraq would add teeth to the sanctions. This would require a new U.N. resolution if we were to get others on board. I was skeptical of the Saudis and pushed that we come up with military options, such as using bases in Turkey, which did not depend entirely on the Saudis making available facilities for hosting a liberating force. I also suggested we send a high-level emissary to both Turkey and Saudi Arabia. Dick Cheney, one of those around the table who despaired of ever getting the Saudis to invite us in, was ready to attack Iraq without Riyadh's approval or involvement.

The meeting, as was the case with the others before it, ended without a decision. This was not a problem, since the basic idea was only to have an initial discussion on military planning. After two hours, we broke up and left the cabin. Standing there with the president along the path were tennis greats Chris Evert and Pam Shriver, who had been invited to come up to Camp David long before the crisis materialized. The president knew I liked to play tennis and asked if I wanted to stay, since they needed a fourth. I was sorely tempted and turned to Scowcroft, who simply shook his head and laughed at me. So I trooped to the helicopter with the others. It would be my last chance to play tennis for nearly a year.

For the rest of that day the big issue was how to get the Saudis to work with us. We were prepared to send someone out there to talk with King Fahd and others, but only if we knew in advance they would cooperate with us. It would be a terrible signal for us to send a presidential envoy only to have him come back empty-handed. There was also the matter of whom to dispatch. The initial idea was to send Brent, someone close to the president and who knew the Saudis well. Cheney quickly objected, saying it was more appropriate for the secretary of defense, in other words, himself, to go, given that what was at stake was a major U.S. military deployment. Brent, who more than anyone I have ever met in a high position is not a prisoner of his own ego, put all this to the president, who quickly said he needed Brent here and that Cheney should go and take Bob Gates with him. Bob, just returning that Saturday night from vacation, was told to pack his bags so that he and Cheney could leave the next day if in fact we had a Saudi commitment in hand. I told Bob I was about to teach him his first word of Hebrew. It was *shalom*, hello and good-bye. The third meaning, peace, did not seem to apply.

Brent, Chief of Staff Sununu, and I then arranged to meet with the Saudi ambassador Sunday morning. Prince Bandar bin Sultan bin Abdul Aziz al-Saud, the son of the Saudi defense minister and a nephew of the king, prided himself on being able to navigate the worlds of tradition and modernity alike. He could arrive in traditional robes and show deference to his seniors—or he could be the scotch-drinking, cigar-smoking, trash-talking former fighter pilot, if somewhat graying and thicker around the middle. Bandar had been the Saudi ambassador for years—for so long, in fact, he had achieved the status of dean of the diplomatic corps, an honorific reserved for the longest-serving representative in Washington. It was hard to avoid the irony in this, as Bandar spent less time in Washington than any other ambassador. He was regularly jetting off to one or his palaces, escaping to his 55,000-square-foot "cabin" in Aspen, or undertaking some assignment in his role as Saudi Arabia's diplomatic troubleshooter.

Bandar was under instructions to get a U.S. envoy to come and visit the kingdom to discuss what might be done. Brent said no, that there would be no envoy unless we knew the Saudis were prepared to work with us and stand up to Iraq. Bandar sought to keep things open. He was reflecting Saudi nervousness. Some of it stemmed from doubts about American reliability, something Bandar attributed to the 1979 U.S. decision to send an emergency shipment of jet fighters to reassure Saudi Arabia, then unnerved by the Iranian Revolution. The action had precisely the opposite effect when the Carter administration revealed the planes were unarmed. The rapid U.S. withdrawal from Lebanon in 1984 after the marine barracks were bombed was another bad memory that raised doubts about U.S. staying power. The Saudis realized full well that inviting in the U.S. military was to choose sides and to antagonize Saddam and they were reluctant to do so. Nothing less than the future of the royal family was at stake.

This backdrop meant that we had some ways to go to reassure the Saudis. Meetings involving Cheney, Powell, and Bandar went a long way toward achieving this objective. The defense secretary and the chairman of the JCS gave Bandar a good preview of the scale of the military deployment being contemplated. "You're serious" was the Saudi envoy's reaction. But just as important was getting the Saudis off the fence. During the conversation, Bandar went so far as to ask Scowcroft point-blank why the Saudis should want to be defended by the United States. Brent was equally straightforward in his response, telling Bandar that the Saudis had a choice between being defended and being liberated. In the course of several meetings and phone calls Brent and I made clear to Bandar that we would not budge: no Saudi commitment, no U.S. envoy, no U.S. deployment. Bandar was clearly taken aback when he finally understood that there was no give on our part and that the Saudis needed to decide now. He was persuaded to pick up the phone and call his uncle the king, which he did from Brent's office. There was clearly great unease halfway around the world, but after some minutes Bandar told us his uncle and the Saudi government were ready to accept the Cheney delegation and that they understood this meant they had accepted military cooperation with us. They asked only that this not be announced until after so it appeared to be a decision reached as a product of the Cheney mission.

We had scheduled a fourth NSC meeting that afternoon, mostly to review where things stood. Cheney, Bob Gates, Schwarzkopf, and others had taken off earlier that Sunday. The NSC meeting would take place after the president arrived back from Camp David. I was in the basement of the West Wing, where the NSC secretariat had its offices, just off the Situation Room. With the advent of the crisis, I had moved my operation there for what turned out to be a month; I simply did not have time to move back and forth between my office in the OEOB and the West Wing since I was frequently being called to see Scowcroft or the president. By then I was working sixteen hours or more each and every day, and the minutes saved by not having to walk back and forth were precious. I also did not have time to read much less respond to the thousands of emails coming in; several weeks into the crisis, the computer people came to me and said I was responsible for slowing down the entire NSC system and that something had to be done. The solution was simple:

we erased all the messages that I was never going to have time to read.

A call came for me from Scowcroft's office. Brent came on the line, saying he had just gotten off the phone with the president, who would be returning from Camp David in about an hour. Brent could not be there to meet his helicopter—I believe it had to do with his wife, who was quite ill at the time—and told me to be there to brief the president when he got off the helicopter so that he'd be ready to speak to the waiting media. I said fine, but after hanging up I got a bit uneasy. I had been home for only a few hours the night before, and was dressed quite casually. The consensus around the office was that I didn't need a tie but I did need a blazer. The only problem was that I didn't have one with me. I borrowed one from one of the guys working there. The sleeves were several inches too short but there was nothing to be done. There was clearly no time for a haircut.

The bigger challenge was getting something ready for the president, as it meant digesting all that had taken place that day. I sat down at the computer to type out the state of play and what was going on militarily and diplomatically. The lack of sleep was clearly taking its toll, as my normally modest typing speed had slowed to a crawl. Standing there next to me was Condi Rice, my colleague on the NSC staff responsible for the Soviet Union, who happened to have stopped by that day. Condi couldn't take it. She ordered me to get up, yanked me out of my chair, and told me to dictate what I wanted the note to the president to say. I did so as Condi typed away with impressive speed, taking down my summary of the messages received from King Hussein of Jordan and others in the region telling us yet again not to overreact. I also summarized the intelligence, including the situation on the ground in Kuwait.

With the president about to arrive, I was running out of time. The immediate problem was that I couldn't recall how to get out to the White House lawn. Again, the lack of sleep was having the predictable effect. It is worth noting that crises are by definition the moments that count the most, where the stakes are greatest, as are the challenges and opportunities. Judgment and sound reasoning are at a premium. Yet it is precisely during crises when those making policy are closest to their physical limits and in many ways not at their best. In such circumstances, there is nothing to be done other than to suck it up. Not surprisingly, historians and academics who have never experienced government and its pressures tend to overlook or discount physical strain as an influence on those making policy.

Again, though, Condi came to the rescue, and pointed me in the right direction. I was there when the president's helicopter landed. He got off and quickly motioned for me to come over. I handed him a sheet of paper with the highlights and, as he scanned it, we talked about the latest developments. He was clearly frustrated with the lack of diplomatic progress and the absence of a strong Arab response. Asked by the waiting journalists how he would prevent the installation of a puppet government, Bush could barely contain himself. "Just wait. Watch and learn." His parting words were even stronger. "This will not stand. This will not stand, this aggression against Kuwait." Baker later described it as "arguably the most famous—and courageous—line of his presidency."

The picture of me standing there next to the president got a lot of play and drew some potshots from then reporter Maureen Dowd in the *New York Times*. "Each international crisis also puts the spotlight on a different member of the scrupulously faceless staff members of the National Security Council. This time it is Richard N. Haass . . . who was the aide who rushed out onto the White House lawn on Sunday afternoon and thrust a secret memo into Mr. Bush's hand that seemed to spark the President's irritation. . . . 'He seems pretty happy about it,' an administration official said of Mr. Haass's Andy Warhol moments of fame. 'After all, he's getting a lot of face time on national television.' " That in turn led William Safire to dedicate one of his language columns to the expression "Face Time." Looking back at the picture, I find it a tad worrisome that I appeared in worse shape than the president, who had a good thirty years on me. Colin Powell, who I later learned was watching it all on the television in his home study, was taken aback, realizing that he might well have just received a new mission. Brent Scowcroft got a call soon afterward from Powell, who kiddingly chided him, saying, "That's what happens when we leave you alone with the president." I was told later that Powell saw me as pushing the president to say what he said and commit the United States to a policy of not just deterring further Iraqi aggression but reversing what had already been done. For a while, I was referred to as the teenage ninja warlord at the White House by some in the inner circle of the chairman of the Joint Chiefs of Staff.

By August 6 we had received word from the traveling party led by Dick Cheney that the Saudis were on board. What apparently did it was the realization by King Fahd that this was one of those rare, truly decisive moments in life. Some of his fellow royals were reluctant to put their future in our hands and preferred that the Saudis somehow hedge their bets and not oppose Saddam so starkly. Fahd shut them down, pointing out that Kuwait's ruling family (the Sabahs) had been reduced to living in hotels in a remote corner of Saudi Arabia, and that a similar fate might await them unless they acted decisively.

August 6 was also the day of the fourth NSC meeting of the crisis (one mostly devoted to energy-related concerns) and the first face-to-face meeting between a U.S. official and Saddam Hussein since the invasion. With April Glaspie out of Iraq and unable to return, it was Joe Wilson, the number two person at the American embassy (in his capacity as acting ambassador or chargé d'affaires), who was summoned. Saddam wanted to send the message that Kuwait was now a permanent part of Iraq, that he did not intend to attack Saudi

Arabia, and that any U.S. military action would be costly and futile. "I will tell you how you will be defeated. You are a superpower and I know you can hurt us, but you will lose the whole area. You will never bring us [Iraq] to our knees. . . . We will never capitulate."

That same day also saw the visits of British prime minister Margaret Thatcher and NATO secretary general Manfred Woerner to Washington. Thatcher was all worked up over the fact that the new Security Council resolution (661) that imposed comprehensive economic sanctions on Iraq did not include any provision for using force to make sure they had the intended effect. Her fear was that by having gone to the U.N. and arranged for such a resolution we would now be required to go back and get another resolution authorizing us to enforce sanctions before we could in fact act to enforce them. She thought going the U.N. route tied our hands, and that we should have simply done everything we wanted pursuant to asserting the fundamental right of self-defense, in this case on behalf of Kuwait. She browbeat me and Undersecretary of State Bob Kimmitt for a good half hour while the lightning and rain made it impossible for her helicopter to take off from the White House. To say we failed to bring her around to our position would be something of an understatement. The only compensation was that Woerner got his solo meeting with the president, which reinforced NATO's participation in the crisis.

Prime Minister Thatcher's objections to our approach raised a larger point. She did not want to go to the U.N., both because she thought it unnecessary and because she saw it as constraining. She was partly right, in that it wasn't necessary. But it did not turn out to be constraining in any meaningful way. And even when it did slow us down or cause us to change tack, it was worth it. Many Americans might not respect the United Nations, but for most people around the world and their governments the U.N. is an important and at times essential source of authority and legitimacy. Its endorsement can constitute a prerequisite for the participation of others, be it to make sanctions effective or to lend support to U.S. military efforts or to introduce forces of their own. The U.N. does not hold a monopoly on legitimacy but it is a significant force in the world of diplomacy.

The next few days of the crisis were the most worrisome, as it was the time of greatest disparity between the capabilities of several divisions of deployed Iraqi troops and the few thousand American forces in place and operational. If the Iraqis had so chosen, that was their moment for gaining control of some or even all of Saudi Arabia. They also could have made life miserable for us if they had used chemical munitions at airfields and ports so as to make it difficult for the United States to introduce troops and equipment in large numbers. Wearing chemical suits in Saudi Arabia in August dramatically increases the need for water and dramatically decreases efficiency. Saddam did not move against Saudi Arabia or use chemical munitions, which reinforces my sense that he thought he would get away with absorbing Kuwait without encountering significant resistance given Kuwaiti unpopularity, Saudi weakness, and, in his mind, American softness. Saddam also realized that taking Kuwait was all he needed. Not only would he control its great wealth and oil, but the Saudis and the other much smaller Gulf states would essentially be under his sway. He would dominate the Arab world and OPEC, the global oil cartel, something that would make him a force to be reckoned with not just in the region but worldwide.

Pressing events made it difficult to dwell on such considerations. Brent called to say the president had decided the Cheney group should stop in Morocco as well as in Cairo on their way back. I was instructed to tell the party to alter their plans. So I got Bob Gates on the phone. It was one of those hard-to-hear-and-understand calls. We were forced to speak very slowly and overenunciate and then insert "over" after each thought. "Bob, this is Richard. Over." "What's up? Over." "You need to go to Morocco. Over. "You are shitting me. Over." "Afraid not. Over." "You are shitting me. Over." "You'll like Morocco. Over." "Whose idea was this? Over." "The commander in chief of the free world. Over and out." For my sins, I had to wake the president up at about 3 A.M. to call King Hassan of Morocco, a task Scowcroft was only too happy to delegate. It was the first time I ever did that, and I remember pacing around my bedroom, going through the White House switchboard, and getting the president on the line, who despite the hour was gracious and agreed to call the king to make sure the delegation was welcome.

The substantive work involved drafting the president's Oval Office address for August 8. This would be the first time he spoke about the crisis to the country and the world in a formal way from a prepared text. Brent and the president and I met with John Sununu and press secretary Marlin Fitzwater for an hour up in the residence. I turned down several offers of a drink from an always polite president, knowing that if I had even one I was as good as finished. I completed a draft within two hours, which was then sent to the speechwriters, who got it back to us around 12:30 A.M. Brent and I were waiting for it in his office, both of us fighting sleep. We then went through the draft line by line and word by word for the next few hours, finally comfortable with it as the clock neared 3 A.M.

The address underscored the four principles at the heart of U.S. policy: immediate, unconditional, and complete Iraqi withdrawal from Kuwait; restoration of Kuwait's legitimate government; U.S. commitment to the security and stability of the region and to Saudi Arabia in particular; and U.S. determination to protect the lives of American citizens abroad. Acceptance of the new status quo, that is, appeasement, was ruled out; the comparison with the 1930s was clear for all to see. So too was the call for a collective response under U.N. auspices. "We agree that this is not an American problem or a European problem or a Middle East problem. It is the world's problem."

This was one of the better experiences I had with the speechwriters, then headed by David Demarest. The policy maker–speechwriter relationship is filled with friction. Speechwriters believe, not surprisingly, that they should be the ones writing the speeches. Policy makers generally believe that the role of speechwriters should be limited to polishing and "speechifying" the prose provided on those occasions when policy is at the heart of a speech. As you might expect, speechwriters had about as much enthusiasm for what they saw as my encroachment as I did with what I viewed as their interference. I took it as something of a badge of honor some months later when William Safire, a good friend despite our deep differences over what he termed "Iraqgate," wrote a column warning incoming speechwriter Tony Snow (someone as talented as he was decent) about me. "Up to now, the most pellucid prose to come out of Mr. Bush's mouth has been by the National Security Council's Richard Haass, in a news conference statement of war aims; he also drafted the powerful letter to Saddam Hussein. But Professor Haass is merely a policymaker, not a card-carrying speechwriter; insist that NSC stuff be routed through the writing shop, lest you wind up in a domestic backwater." I felt even better after I looked up *pellucid* in the dictionary and saw it was a compliment.

The president's Oval Office speech went well. I remember standing in the Oval Office as it was put on the teleprompter. The president had provided his changes and we finished getting everything ready with maybe a minute to spare. He delivered it well after only an awkward few seconds at the outset. It made for a powerful moment. When he finished there was silence. Several of the few staffers and technicians standing there in the Oval quietly applauded. It was the first time in days I had stopped moving, and the stakes sank in on me in ways they had not up to that point. A few days later, the Arab League condemned the Iraqi action and endorsed the idea of member states responding favorably to Kuwaiti and Saudi requests for assistance. Again, Saddam had misjudged. We were clearly on something of a roll.

In normal times, but even more so amid crises, it is never enough to do the right thing. It is also necessary to go out and explain what you are doing and why and, in so doing, build domestic and international support for the policy. The Oval Office speech was one such effort: necessary, but hardly sufficient. That Sunday, some ten days after Iraq's invasion, the administration decided to fan out on the morning talk shows. Just to make sure we were all on the same page, I prepared some themes and sent them around to Baker, Cheney, Wolfowitz, and Scowcroft. Early Sunday morning we convened a conference call to go over the themes and the Sunday papers and discuss what people would say later that day on television. A number of commentators were particularly hard on us, making the argument that our motive was to make America safe for gas guzzlers. We were going through my list of potential questions that could be raised. Toward the end of my list was "Why does the United States not have in place an energy policy?" There was dead silence, followed by some awkward laughter, and a chorus of voices saying "good question."

The good news for us was that no one was confronted that day with the question, but the reality was that the United States did not have much of an energy policy. It was nearly two decades since the oil shocks associated with the 1973 Middle East war, and U.S. dependence on imported oil (as well as consumption of oil from all sources, foreign and domestic) had grown. In 1973, the United States consumed approximately seventeen million barrels of oil a day, of which imports (some six million barrels every day) constituted just over one-third. By 1990, consumption was roughly the same but imports had jumped by almost two million barrels each day to nearly half of what was consumed. It was a scandal, eclipsed only by the fact that the situation had been allowed to grow far worse by the

time the next Iraq war materialized a little more than another decade later, in 2003. By then, consumption had reached more than
twenty million barrels a day; imports had grown to over twelve million barrels a day or more than 60 percent of what was used. People
often complain, with considerable justification, that American politics suffers from too little bipartisanship. But this was an area of too
much, in that Democrats and Republicans, in Congress and the
White House, had all shied away from doing what could and should
have been done to curb America's thirst for oil and to develop viable
alternatives. It was and is simply untrue that sound energy policy
threatens economic growth. The result has left the United States vulnerable to supply interruptions and price spikes. It has also channeled enormous flows of dollars to some dubious and in some cases
hostile regimes, contributed to global warming, and weakened the
dollar and the U.S. economy.

    None of this is meant to suggest that U.S. interest in Iraq or the
Persian Gulf more broadly could (or, for that matter, can) be reduced
to oil. This oil-centered explanation of U.S. policy motives is a favorite theme of many on the political left and right alike. Alan Greenspan wrote in his memoir that "the Iraq war is largely about oil." He
was speaking of the second Iraq war, but many have put forward a
similar argument about the first. To be sure, oil and gas matter, and
the principal reason the region matters as much as it does stems
from its resources and their relevance to the world economy. Iraq
alone controls some 10 percent of world proven oil reserves. But the
region would also matter if oil did not, for reasons to do with terrorism, Israel, nuclear proliferation, and humanitarian concerns, although absent oil and oil's importance it would count for much less.
Saying this, however, does not support the contention that either
war was about oil. The U.S. interest in the region's oil is strategic,
one of ensuring American and world access to adequate supplies,
not tied in any way to gaining financial advantage. The United States

did not seek or gain any special control or ownership of Kuwaiti or Saudi or Iraqi oil as a result of all that it did in 1990–91 or in 2003. U.S. and international energy companies control a small and diminishing share of the region's and the world's oil and gas.

A week after the Oval Office speech, the president visited the Pentagon for a briefing in the "tank" (the secure conference room of the chairman of the Joint Chiefs of Staff) and then delivered a speech that made me uncomfortable. The president kept inserting and insisting on references to the 1930s. I of course agreed with the need not to repeat the folly of appeasement, but I was less than comfortable with his many references. My discomfort had little to do with historical subtleties, but rather with the concern that making the comparison would add pressure on us to go beyond our mission and remove the regime lest we appear to be failing when in fact we were not. There was at least one lighter moment, though. One of the speechwriters had inserted a line critical of Saddam for taking money away from Iraq's poor and giving it to the generals. I suggested this might not go over all that well at the Pentagon. It was deleted.

A complication quickly arose with Jordan's King Hussein, who wanted to come visit at short notice. It is hard to say no to a king, especially for someone such as the president. Yet King Hussein was a major disappointment throughout this crisis. Whether out of fear of Saddam, the pro-Saddam loyalties of his own mostly Palestinian populace, or hopes of political and economic gain, he had thrown in his lot with Saddam. It emerged that he might be carrying some sort of message from Saddam, something we had no interest in given our insistence that we would accept nothing short of complete implementation of the U.N.'s demand for Iraq to leave Kuwait and for Kuwait's sovereignty to be restored. A further complication arose when the Saudis also asked to send envoys (the foreign minister and Prince Bandar, their ambassador to the United States) to see the president. Nothing less would suffice. So we decided to invite them all up to Kennebunkport, Maine—the Jordanians for lunch, the Saudis for tea—on August 16. It had to be Kennebunkport because that is where the president insisted on being. He was adamant that he not make the same mistake as Jimmy Carter and become a prisoner of the White House so long as the crisis continued. Bush thought it essential that he take a vacation and signal that Saddam could not change how Americans went about their lives. He was right on the policy, but it didn't always make for good politics or photos.

Brent and I flew up from Andrews Air Force Base that morning, but when we met with the president in the living room of his country house, none of us had a good idea as to what King Hussein was bringing. Based on Brent's meeting the day before with his majesty's chief of staff, it was far from clear that they knew what their agenda was. The king and his delegation arrived, but most of us (Baker, Sununu, Gates, Fitzwater, and I as well as the Jordanians, including the prime minister and foreign minister) milled around on the porch while the president and the king, with only Brent and the king's chief of staff, went into a small meeting that seemed never to end. There was much awkward conversation on the porch, as we all skirted the issue of the day given that we had no idea what was being said over in the other cabin. The four finally returned after more than an hour and we immediately sat down to a lunch. The conversation would have been a letdown had we entertained any expectations. King Hussein was tired and dispirited, seemingly overwhelmed by events. He felt it necessary to tell us how much he had done to avoid war and how close he had come to succeeding. None of us believed this, but there was no reason to challenge him, so we did not.

I thought we should have pressed him harder on Jordan's failure to comply with U.N. sanctions designed to penalize Saddam for his occupation of Kuwait and bring about Iraq's withdrawal. I favored a deal: full Jordanian compliance in exchange for financial compensation for any lost trade and security from any Iraqi retribution. I also wanted the president to be undiplomatically direct in setting down some markers on Jordan's behavior vis-à-vis Iraq. I was concerned Hussein might ally with Iraq and thereby make the second great error of his life, the first being his decision in 1967 to enter the war against Israel, a decision that cost him half his country when Israel emerged from the conflict in control of the West Bank and Jerusalem. But the president was uncomfortable in being too hard on the king. Like many Americans, he liked the modest and polite and always respectful monarch. The meeting came and went, doing little to clear up the mistrust in the relationship and even less to affect events.

We had little time to get ourselves ready for the Saudis. As advertised, it was Foreign Minister Saud (like Jim Baker, Princeton-educated) and Bandar. On our side it was the president, Baker, Sununu, Brent, Bob Gates, and me. We opted for the living room, one filled with pale pastel colors, worn furniture, and lots of family photos and wooden ducks. Coats and ties came off. This was a consultation among friends, not a negotiation. But it quickly became clear that if the Jordanians lacked a real agenda, the Saudis had one and then some. They began by making clear they were speaking not just for themselves but for Egypt and Syria as well. Their message was blunt: "Our assessment is that it will take more than economic sanctions to liberate Kuwait." What they wanted was for us to do whatever was necessary to liberate Kuwait by force, preferably under U.N. auspices, in the process destroying enough of Saddam's war-making machine so that they wouldn't have to continue to live in fear and in Saddam's shadow. Consistent with this, if Saddam did withdraw from Kuwait with the bulk of his forces intact, they wanted some sort of permanent international peacemaking force along the Iraq-Kuwait border.

In short, the Saudis wanted more than a return to the status quo ante; strict fulfillment of the U.N. resolution calling for Iraq's complete withdrawal from Kuwait, as unlikely as it was, was no longer good enough. I thought all of this made sense. It would have been more impressive if they had made clear just what they were prepared to do to bring it about. What also emerged was their impatience, stemming from a mix of a lack of confidence in our staying power and their fear that the Arab street would with time turn against governments standing up to Saddam. As Brent put it after they'd left, they seemed to be offering to hold our coat while we got into the ring with Saddam. For our part, we told them we were not yet prepared to give them a formal response, that we wanted to give sanctions some more time to work, and that we would use that time to explore the possibility of cobbling together a multinational military coalition that included significant Arab participation. It all took maybe an hour and a half, after which the president did a mini press conference that broke no new ground.

The Saudis flew off, and we trooped back to the house for what turned out to be a critical conversation. Our nightmare was the emergence of a situation in which economic sanctions were not enough to convince Saddam to get out of Kuwait but we couldn't garner the domestic and international support to use military force to bring about that same end. The consensus was that we needed some mechanism or new development to use force and that we couldn't just one day announce we'd grown tired of waiting. What this trigger would be was not clear, especially if Saddam played it smart and did not do something new that provoked outrage. We also believed it would be difficult to get an explicit U.N. mandate to use force. We did not have unlimited time, though, since whatever military stability our presence in Saudi Arabia provided would gradually be offset and more by the political instability it could generate. We kicked all this around for more than an hour and finally ran out of gas. The president had had enough, and so had we. Brent, Baker, and I drove off for the airport and the short flight back to D.C.

The three of us continued the conversation at a higher altitude, although the thinner air did nothing to improve the quality of the policy options. At one point Baker turned to me and asked how old I was. "Thirty-nine," I told him. "A good age. I remember where I was twenty years ago. It was a rough time. My four children had just lost their mother. I didn't know if I could make it. Men just aren't equipped to provide kids what it is they need." We went back to talking about the crisis, until there was again a pause. I pointed to a story in that day's *New York Times* and asked Baker if, as rumored, he could have been commissioner of baseball. He said yes, the job was his if he'd wanted it. I then asked if he regretted the decision. He said no, that only George Will had told him he'd chosen wrong. He then added, "I've been secretary of the treasury and now secretary of state. That's not bad."

It was a rare personal moment for the two of us. Today, more than fifteen years later, I would describe us as friends who tend to agree on most things. Jim Baker is someone for whom I have the greatest respect. We can and do kick back and share candid opinions. Then we didn't know each other nearly as well and we didn't quite click. It didn't help that someone close to him had poisoned the well by telling him that I often leaked things that made him look bad. I never did—I do not believe in doing this as a matter of principle—but it is the sort of accusation that is impossible to disprove and often lingers.

There was also the reality that some friction was inevitable, in that I worked for Scowcroft and not Baker and was not shy about pushing my own views and disagreeing with him and State when I thought the president needed to get a second opinion. Such independence tends to be appreciated in the abstract. Brent told me that Baker more than once complained to the president about me, a revelation I took as something of a compliment, at least until July 1992, when I was with Baker when he became the first senior U.S. official to visit Lebanon in nearly a decade. Security was understandably high. The night before the visit, I was surprised but pleased to learn that I would be riding in the secretary's vehicle. Well, I thought to myself, Jim and I have come a long way. Finally he wants to spend some time with me and get my advice. My satisfaction was short-lived, however, when it became clear the next morning that Baker was riding in another car in the motorcade and I was simply a decoy, riding uncomfortably in the backseat of a limousine on one of the world's most dangerous roads.

The Iraq crisis was at times difficult for Baker; during such crises, power and action inevitably flow to the NSC and the president. The reason is twofold: on one hand, government-wide coordination is at a premium, and only the NSC can provide it. This meant a larger role for Brent, Bob Gates, and me. Second, by definition crises involve bigger stakes, and the president inevitably wants and needs to get involved personally given the consequences for all he holds dear. Crises such as this one that involve military matters also bring the Defense Department to the fore. State had an important role, but it was just that: a role. The NSC and the White House were at the center of decision making.

It would be wrong, however, to convey the sense that there was tremendous friction within the administration. I have worked for four presidents, and there was considerably less infighting and associated dysfunctionality in this administration than in any of the others. Presidents set a tone, and this one made it clear that intense bureaucratic infighting would not be tolerated, much less rewarded. It also helped that both the principals and their senior lieutenants knew one another well and got along fairly well. Bush, Powell, Scowcroft, Baker, and Cheney had all gotten to know one another during the Ford or Reagan administrations. They had a good deal in common and had come to trust one another. Disagreements existed but tended not to be so large that agreement was made impossible. Brent's personality and operating style also played a large and constructive role. He was fair, intellectually open, and did not use his close relationship with the president to undermine others or prevent them from making their case. Indeed, he would often make it for them just to make sure the president knew what everyone was thinking.

Disagreement between the secretary of state and the national security advisor can paralyze an administration. Both the Carter and Reagan presidencies suffered from just this. Brent told Jim Baker at the outset that he would not give speeches or go on television without first discussing it with him. After three months, Baker essentially told Brent just to do what he thought correct. It helped that Baker took Larry Eagleburger, a career foreign service officer who was one of Brent's closest friends, as his number two. On numerous occasions Larry served as an informal but invaluable bridge between Baker and Scowcroft. Brent also understood and accepted Jim Baker's special friendship with the president. Clearly, Baker and State counted for a lot, as a decision early on in the Iraq crisis made apparent. Sanctions were in place, but we were having difficulty in securing U.N. endorsement for military enforcement. Ships carrying cargo were heading toward Iraq. We were about to be faced with the awful choice of having to let them go through, which would break the embargo and set a terrible precedent, or use force without a U.N. blessing, which could lead to the loss of support from the Soviets and possibly others not just for sanctions enforcement but for the entire effort to undo what Saddam had done. Not surprisingly, it was Thatcher who was leading the charge to act without the U.N. This was precisely the situation she had warned about. Baker pleaded for more time, and the president gave it to him. In the end, U.N. Security Council Resolution 665 was passed, which meant not just that sanctions would be enforced but that international solidarity would be sustained. It was a critical milestone.

The episode matters for another reason. The phrase "Don't go wobbly" has entered into the political lexicon, and for good reason. Standing firm is often what is required of a president. Many people believe it was spoken by Thatcher early in the crisis in an effort to encourage an allegedly vacillating President Bush to stand up to the Iraqis. This is wrong. He didn't require any such encouragement, as he was there from the outset. "Don't go wobbly" was said by Prime Minister Thatcher, to be sure, but it was several weeks later and in the context of not giving the U.N. a say over whether the sanctions would be enforced. She wanted to act without waiting for the Security Council to vote; Baker and the president made the right call to push back and go the extra mile to get international support.

With all this sorted out, we returned to the basic question of how to cope with the reality of Iraqi occupation of Kuwait and the uncertainty about how best to reverse it. We also devoted considerable time to pondering what else might develop (or go wrong) and what we could do about it. It was possible to imagine a wide range of futures: stalemate; the Iraqis taking hostages and attacking foreign nationals; Iraqi-sponsored terrorism somewhere in the region; an effort to undermine the monarchy in Jordan; an attack on Saudi Arabia. There was also the difficult question of what to do if Saddam actually complied with what was being demanded of him. This latter question reflected the Saudi concern that containing a muscle-bound Iraq might prove too much for them. Again, it was becoming clear that "succeeding" in getting the Iraqis to comply with international demands might be a mixed blessing, since the intrinsic Iraqi threat would remain.

One additional concern was what to do about the American citizens in Iraq being held there against their will. We had consciously avoided using the word *hostages* lest we raise their value to Saddam, something that might induce him to keep the Americans and others being prevented from leaving. But it was increasingly clear these several thousand people from the United States and other countries were in fact hostages. So on August 20, in a speech in Baltimore to the Veterans of Foreign Wars, the president used what we had come to call the "H-word." "We've been reluctant to use the term 'hostage.' But when Saddam Hussein specifically offers to trade the freedom of those citizens of many nations he holds against their will in return for concessions, there can be little doubt that whatever these innocent people are called, they are, in fact, hostages." The president also declared he would hold the Iraqi government responsible for their safety and well-being, something he and we hoped would make Saddam think twice before causing them physical harm.

Crises tend to have peaks and valleys, and this one was no exception. There was the constant one step forward, one step backward, of gaining support in the U.N. for robust action. There were on-again, off-again reports of Americans and others being taken hostage. At home, the naysayers were beginning to be heard. On the left, Jesse Jackson was about to travel to Baghdad to do who knows what; on the right, Jeane Kirkpatrick criticized us for assuming too large a role compared to our interests. King Hussein, meanwhile, continued to be his unhelpful self by saying that we exaggerated the Iraqi threat to Saudi Arabia; his tilt toward Saddam was fast depleting his stock of goodwill in the United States. Saddam, for his part, staged a grotesque scene with British hostages, awkwardly patting some English boy on the head. Oil had reached $32 a barrel, up from $21 when the crisis erupted; the Dow had fallen below 2500, down from 2900.

Nevertheless, by the end of August, we seemed to have the basics of our policy in place, something we codified in National Security Directive 45. The world was on record demanding a full and unconditional Iraqi withdrawal from Kuwait. Sanctions were in place along with the means to enforce them. Oil producers had increased their output to make up for lost Iraqi crude. Thanks to the presence of U.S. forces, Saudi Arabia was increasingly in a position to repel an

Iraqi attack. The real question was what came next and when. My argument to the president and others was straightforward: "If we believe what we have said, then the status quo is unacceptable, and if sanctions do not succeed, then we will have no choice but to use force to liberate Kuwait." The question was whether to work through the U.N. I proposed a secret exploration to determine the potential to get U.N. backing; if we could secure it, great; if not, we would back off and put together a narrower and less formal grouping that would pressure Iraq.

A recurring matter was Israeli anxiety. David Ivry, a senior official in Israel's defense ministry and the individual who a decade before had planned the attack on Iraq's nascent nuclear program, led a small Israeli delegation to Washington to discuss scenarios. A few officials, including Paul Wolfowitz and me, met with him. I ended up playing something of the heavy, making clear that U.S. stakes were enormous and that we had accomplished a great deal by amassing an international coalition of dozens of countries that included substantial Arab participation. I argued that Israel should not take it upon itself to act unilaterally even if threatened by Iraqi missiles or instability in Jordan. Ivry was clearly not prepared for this, although the discussion was not in vain given that the U.S. and Israeli governments would have to manage just this contingency in the early days of the war. What also emerged from the Israeli side was a concern not unlike that of the Saudis, namely, that containment of the Iraqi threat was not a sustainable proposition.

It was becoming increasingly apparent that whatever we did and no matter how it turned out, we were going to run up a sizable tab. The United States was prepared to bear the lion's share of the effort, but there was no reason it should bear the lion's share of the cost. Members of Congress were insistent on this—burden sharing is always a popular refrain on Capitol Hill—and they had a point. So we devised the "tin cup" missions, in which Jim Baker and treasury sec-

retary Nicholas Brady essentially divided up the world and flew off
to raise funds. In the end it proved wildly successful. More than once
I worried we would raise too much. It was impossible not to think
of Mel Brooks in *The Producers,* promising more than 100 percent
of the proceeds to unwitting investors. To be sure, some money went
the other way, too, as we forgave some $7 billion in debt to Egypt,
an important inducement to a pivotal Arab state.

The immediate priority, though, in early September was the Helsinki summit. It would be the first face-to-face meeting between Bush
and Gorbachev since the crisis erupted more than a month before.
The president wanted the meeting to signal Saddam that he could
not play off the two superpowers against one another to Iraq's advantage and to make sure this was in fact the case, that is, to make
sure the Soviets were prepared to stay the course, which meant using
force if need be. Condi and I did most of the pre-trip briefing for the
president and others. Soviet behavior up to that point was not bad.
They still had some advisors in Iraq, but they had gone along with
us in the U.N. Security Council, although in each instance it took
some time and work to get them to vote for the resolution at hand.
Clearly, there was a strong pro-Iraqi faction within the Soviet government. There was also some suspicion that we were using the crisis
for narrow ends, including institutionalizing a U.S. military presence
in the region.

The flight over was notable mostly because it was the maiden
voyage of the new *Air Force One.* NSC types such as me sat in the
equivalent of business class. Senior White House aides got first class.
The traveling press got stuck in coach. The food was generous in
portion and heavy on the starch. I briefed the press en route and
spent the rest of the time trying to sleep and working on what the
president should say to Gorbachev on regional issues and what
should go into a joint statement. The meetings began on Sunday, the
day after we arrived. I was supposed to sit in on the bilateral with

Gorbachev, but the scheduled fifteen-minute "pre-meeting" with the two presidents lasted for three hours. I cooled my heels by spending time with Dennis Ross and our Soviet counterparts working on a joint statement. The Soviets pressed hard for a call for an international conference on the Middle East. The president had long wanted one, but most of his advisors thought this was the wrong context in which to agree to hold such a gathering lest it appear that Saddam's aggression was being rewarded. I complicated matters somewhat by introducing the notion that the sanctions ought not to cover food and medicine. It required some extra time to work out the precise wording of this exception, but it was the right thing to do, not just morally, but practically, since there would have been no way to sustain domestic and international support for sanctions if they had appeared to deny the basics to average Iraqis.

In a matter of hours it all came together. The two countries declared on September 9, "We are united in the belief that Iraq's aggression must not be tolerated. No peaceful international order is possible if larger states can devour their smaller neighbors." (I thought there was more than a little irony in this given Soviet history, but this was not a time for nitpicking.) The statement also communicated a clear readiness to resort to military force if need be. "Our preference is to resolve the crisis peacefully. . . . However, we are determined to see this aggression end, and if the current steps fail to end it, we are prepared to consider additional ones consistent with the UN Charter." The statement was another message to Saddam that he had miscalculated and another sign that reflexive Cold War hostility between Washington and Moscow was a thing of the past.

Two days later the president spoke to a joint session of the Congress. I wrote the foreign policy sections of the draft and went along to be there when he delivered it. It was a thrill. The speech itself was something of a camel: half Gulf crisis, half budget crisis. I succeeded in getting the language regarding the latter toned down so it didn't look as if we were accusing Democrats of being unpatriotic if they didn't support the president on the budget. I also left out any references to the Cold War being over, lest that become the lead. What was left was a good recapitulation of our policy and what was for Bush a rare moment of high-minded prose linked to his and Brent's notion of a new world order. "A hundred generations have searched for this elusive path to peace, while a thousand wars raged across the span of human endeavor. Today that new world is struggling to be born, a world quite different from the one we've known. A world where the rule of law supplants the rule of the jungle. A world in which nations recognize the shared responsibility for freedom and justice. A world where the strong respect the rights of the weak."

More and more of my time was being spent with members of Congress, whether in large meetings or in one-on-ones over breakfast or in their offices. Burden sharing remained a frequent concern. Representative Les Aspin, the chairman of the Armed Services Committee and who a few years later would be Bill Clinton's first secretary of defense, voiced a concern that we might be getting overly multilateral and find ourselves unduly constrained! Senator Rudy Boschwitz was helpful, indicating a willingness to forgive Egypt's multibillion-dollar debt and agreeing to additional arms sales to the Saudis. But as later events would prove, we underestimated congressional reluctance to support what we were doing, especially when it came to transitioning from the threat to the actual use of force.

If there was a recurring question, it was how long to stick with sanctions and how to persuade people that the time had come to use military force. We wanted to avoid the impression that we were somehow the side doing the escalating. This argued against allowing the current situation to harden as the new status quo. There was another reason for not allowing too much time to pass: before long, there would not be much left of Kuwait to save. A distraught Kuwaiti ambassador came to see me in mid-September with simply awful stories of a country being ravaged and depopulated. This aspect of the crisis dominated the small White House lunch hosted by the president in late September for the emir of Kuwait. (This turned out to be my last meal before fasting for twenty-four hours for Yom Kippur, the Jewish day of atonement. There were ironies everywhere.) The deteriorating situation on the ground in Kuwait bolstered the argument put forward by the British and others that we not go back to the U.N. but rather launch a military action predicated on Article 51 of the U.N. Charter, which enshrines the basic right of self-defense. I still favored at least exploring whether we could garner international support for a formal resolution authorizing the use of force to liberate Kuwait, an outcome that would provide us with far more regional and international support (political, economic, and military) and help create a useful international precedent. That said, the Iraqis might at any time confront us with a need to act, be it by taking action against foreign nationals or sponsoring some terrorist action. Absent such a provocation, it was our aim to control the timing and keep the focus on the Iraqi aggression against Kuwait.

Again, though, this was a period characterized by uncertainty. Congress and the media (abetted by some of my colleagues around the administration) seemed intent on going over recent history and engaging in "Who lost Kuwait?" recriminations. Some military leaders seemed less than enthusiastic about the entire enterprise. Israel and its supporters were unhappy with all the attention being focused on Arab members of the coalition and constant calls for Israel to lie low. Many on the right thought we were being too multilateral; many on the left believed we were overly bellicose. The French wanted more emphasis on pressuring Kuwait's leaders to accept democratic reforms as the quid pro quo of being liberated. We sent a tough message from Bush to French president François Mitterrand reminding the French that the resolutions they'd supported called for restoring

Kuwait's legitimate government. There would be a time later to debate the desirability of promoting internal political reform.

As if all this were not enough, the United States faced three other immediate challenges in October. One involved Pakistan. For years we had continued to provide economic and military assistance to Pakistan despite its interest in developing nuclear weapons. In order for aid to continue to flow, Congress required that the executive branch certify annually that Pakistan "does not possess a nuclear explosive device." It was odd wording, because we had to be confident of a negative. The problem was that making such a certification was no longer possible. There was simply too much evidence indicating Pakistan had in fact developed nuclear devices for us to look the other way, although the desirability of maintaining a good relationship with Pakistan made it tempting to do so. Many inside the administration also believed the credibility of U.S. policy opposing the spread of nuclear weapons was at stake. So we made the decision not to certify, with the result that the United States cut off much of its military relationship with Pakistan, a development that angered virtually everyone in Pakistan. They felt their country was being discarded now that its help was no longer needed to confront the Soviet army in Afghanistan. In so doing, we may have inadvertently reinforced the determination in Pakistan to develop nuclear weapons.

A second challenge involved the tinderbox that was (and is) the Middle East. On October 8, Jewish zealots tried to build a "Succoth" (booth) on the Temple Mount, one of the holiest sites for both Judaism and Islam. Palestinians gathered and started throwing rocks at Jewish worshippers praying at the Western Wall, and the Israeli security forces stepped in. Before long, some twenty-one Palestinians were dead. There was a powerful international outcry at what was widely viewed as an excessive use of force. We were anxious not to be put in a position in which we had to veto some outrageous anti-Israeli move at the U.N. As a result, the United States introduced a resolution critical of Israel at the U.N. Security Council. Although this proved to be controversial, it was the right thing to do on the merits, and it helped to keep the anti-Saddam coalition intact.

The big story, though, and one that overshadowed not just Pakistan but the Middle East and the Gulf crisis, was the budget battle. After months of gridlock, the Bush administration and the Democratic leadership reached agreement on a budget for the coming fiscal year. For many Republicans, the devil truly was in the details, as the president agreed to a tax increase as part of the pact. I thought this the right and necessary thing to do, although many people disagreed strongly on economic grounds or politically, it being at odds with Bush's "No New Taxes" campaign pledge. But it was easy to disagree with how the White House announced the deal. A statement was issued that buried the news of the tax increase. This was a huge mistake. If I had been asked, which for understandable reasons I was not, I would have advised the president to speak to the nation from the Oval Office, explaining what he had done and, more important, why. This was a big policy reversal, and as much as anything else cost him reelection. As the cliché goes, if you have lemons, make lemonade. The president should have gone out and sold lemonade. He would have convinced at least some of the critics and earned points for being presidential. By not presenting the package himself, he let his critics put their face on the deal, which made him look weak and unprincipled when in fact it took considerable courage and a commitment to what he genuinely believed was in the best long-term interests of the country.

My principal preoccupation that October was how to move U.S. strategy toward Iraq and Kuwait from containment phase to liberation. I spent a good deal of time working on a memo that would first be discussed in the "small group," the subset of the deputies committee that we had created for handling the most sensitive aspects of the crisis. There were six members, with no substitutes and no additions.

Bob Kimmitt represented State; Paul Wolfowitz, Defense; Admiral David Jeremiah, the Joint Chiefs of Staff; and Dick Kerr, the intelligence community. Kimmitt and Wolfowitz, while technically the number three people in their respective buildings, were both senior policy aides to their respective secretaries. Both Jeremiah and Kerr were the actual deputies. Bob Gates chaired the group, and I was the sixth and the one who did the drafting.

Bob Gates ran a meeting as well as anyone I have worked with. This is worth noting because meetings are so prevalent and so few people know how to conduct them. Beforehand he and I would sit down to review what needed to be discussed, what was likely to come up, and where we wanted things to come out. People got the chance to say their piece but not to filibuster. We would get through the agenda in the allotted time, and at the close of the meeting everyone understood what had been decided and what was expected in the way of follow-up. Bob was also able to hold strong views yet still capable of weighing the positions of others fairly. In my experience he was fair, rigorous, and nonideological, in important ways still resembling the boy who grew up in Kansas and made it to Eagle Scout. He was never far from Brent's side, and as a result he became the crucial link between the president's inner circle and the rest of the government.

The small group became a venue for true policy planning. I outlined in considerable detail the three basic options available to us: sticking with sanctions in the hope that they would pressure Saddam to vacate Kuwait; giving an ultimatum (ideally, U.N.-backed) to Iraq to leave Kuwait by a date certain or be forced out; or waiting until Saddam did something new and then using that provocation to oust him from Kuwait. There was also a stopgap option of sending in a small force to extract embassy personnel and foreign nationals being held in the country against their will. I wanted this paper to be the basis of discussion, so while it laid out the pros and cons of each option, I did not make a recommendation. My preference may have seeped through nonetheless. I had little confidence that sanctions would ever provide enough leverage and even in the highly unlikely event they did, it would take so long that Kuwait and its population would be essentially gone. The idea of requiring a new provocation would leave the initiative with Saddam and put us in the odd position of responding militarily to what would seem to many to be a lesser offense than the taking over of Kuwait. A forced extraction was precisely the sort of military operation that would get messy and put U.S. troops in the middle of an urban battlefield. The ultimatum was best. It addressed the concerns of those at home and abroad who opposed what they saw as a rush to war; at the same time it placed a time limit on how much longer the status quo could endure. In so doing, it was preferable to Thatcher's inclination to just attack, an approach that would have left the administration largely isolated. And given that there was a chance the ultimatum would work and Saddam would withdraw, I introduced the idea of placing new limits on what he could possess and import in the way of technologies that could increase his ability to produce weapons of mass destruction (WMD).

This conditional approach to the U.N. Security Council gradually emerged as the preferred position of the administration, but only after some time and many more meetings. The president was the most impatient, perhaps because he was greatly affected by reports about human suffering inside Kuwait and concerns about what Saddam might do to American citizens trapped there. Brent and Bob Gates were totally on board with the ultimatum approach. So too was Jim Baker, although he appeared uneasy at times with putting so much at stake and was more open to a diplomatic outcome. The military seemed the most wary. U.S. force levels in the region had reached approximately two hundred thousand, but the Pentagon wanted at least twice that.

October ended much as it began. The Soviets were still searching for a diplomatic solution. Their envoys would go too far for our taste in what they put to Saddam, but Saddam would not take it in any event, thereby easing the difficulty of maintaining the coalition. At home, much of the Congress opposed moving from sanctions to armed force. At a meeting with the leadership in the Cabinet Room in October, Speaker of the House Tom Foley was explicit in saying the president would risk losing the Congress and the country if he changed tack. This position was held by virtually everyone else, with only a clear minority prepared to support the use of force and then only if specifically authorized by the U.N. Security Council. The president was equal parts sobered and frustrated by what he'd heard. He rejected having policy dictated by public opinion yet understood how important public and congressional support would be if he took the country to war. The president was in a bind.

The next day, Baker, Scowcroft, Gates, Kimmitt, and I met to discuss Baker's upcoming trip to the capitals of U.N. Security Council members. The plan was to pitch the ultimatum without calling it one and without leaning so far forward that we couldn't pull back if it became obvious there was no way we could get Security Council support. It was coming down to the wire, since November was the best chance for us to get such a resolution. It was fortuitously the month the rotating presidency of the Security Council came to us. We would then have just enough time to let the ultimatum play out and launch an attack if it came to that. We could not put off an attack much beyond January given the problem of keeping hundreds of thousands of troops parked in the desert, the advent of the Muslim holy month of Ramadan in mid-March, which could weaken support in the Arab and Muslim world for any military action on our part, and the approach of warmer weather, which would reduce the efficiency of offensive military operations.

Brent and I sat down for lunch in his office the next day. The policy choices had come down to two: sticking with sanctions (as many in Congress, the media, and around the world favored) or giving Saddam an ultimatum followed up with force if he failed to act in time. One risk in the latter approach was the possibility we would try to get a formal ultimatum approved by the U.N. and we would fail. As a result, I started toying with the idea of simply issuing an ultimatum on behalf of as many members of the coalition as would support it. This would be our fallback, since getting a U.N. authorization would be so advantageous as to be worth the time and risk. I was to go with Baker on his tour of relevant capitals.

It was not until the second week of October that we received the first comprehensive military briefing of what was being developed. The plan was unimaginative, essentially calling for an Army-led ground offensive into the heart of Saddam's forces. This is where Brent's being national security advisor became particularly significant, as he (being a retired Air Force lieutenant general) was in a far better position to challenge the Joint Chiefs and the Central Command leadership than those of us who lacked military experience. Some in the room concluded the plan was designed to get the president to rethink the entire strategy of using military force to liberate Kuwait. A less political but probably more accurate interpretation was that the planners were rushed and more concerned at the time with defending Saudi Arabia. What planning there was for Kuwait's liberation focused on the air campaign. Whatever the explanation, Brent spoke to the president, who sent the Pentagon back to the drawing board.

Colin Powell was a reluctant warrior. His formative years were in Vietnam, and he took with him a suspicion of civilians who cooked up ideas that got a lot of young men and women in uniform killed. We clashed at times over his caution, but all things being equal, I much prefer the notion of cautious generals to cocky ones who over-promise and underdeliver. The price for winning Powell's support for military intervention was agreeing to his marshalling enormous manpower and firepower, to assign the military objectives they could readily understand and carry out, and to refrain from micromanaging them in the field. It seemed a fair price and good policy to boot.

The Air Force shared little of this caution. To the contrary, its leadership was letting it be known that they had a better idea: use airpower to decimate Iraq's command and control and with it their ability to deploy and employ their forces. If some in the Air Force had had their way, the war would have lacked a ground phase altogether. Nevertheless, Central Command with the support of the JCS carried the day and made the case that the roughly two hundred thousand troops then in Saudi Arabia were enough for defending the kingdom but not enough to take on the added mission of liberating Kuwait. At least twice that many forces would be required. This was consistent with one of the basic tenets of the so-called Powell Doctrine, which argued that overwhelming force should be used for military tasks. (The second and less well-known basic tenet of the doctrine, that military forces should be assigned missions that they are suited to carry out, also applied here. Powell articulated his thinking in the wake of the Lebanon debacle in the early 1980s, when U.S. forces were too few in number and were not given a military mission that was clear and doable.)

The president made the decision to double troop levels at the end of October. The announcement of the decision was to be delayed, however, until after the midterm elections. Many in Congress were arguing that any such troop increase would be tantamount to making a decision to use force, and the president did not want this issue to be central to the political campaign.

This change in military planning coincided with the diplomatic effort to build international support for the ultimatum option. This turned out to be less than ideal. Baker was on his odyssey rounding up support from Security Council members and didn't want any announcement about a doubling of troop levels lest it appear we had given up on diplomacy, something that he feared would work against his chances of succeeding. I agreed, but neither of us knew that the Pentagon was pressing the White House for authority to begin implementing the increase so as not to interrupt the flow of troops and equipment to the theater. Brent and the president were inclined to go along, which I duly reported to Baker. He exploded—at me! The PG version of events was along these lines. "Why the hell do I have an NSC guy here with me if the White House is going to do things that undermine my trip?" He leaned on me hard to weigh in and delay the decision, which was what happened after I made the case over the phone to Brent. The formal announcement was made by the president on November 8, during Baker's trip but at least after he had completed the meetings with the Saudis, who would have to host the lion's share of the additional troops. It was important that the decision be made to look like one we had reached with them and not imposed on them.

Baker's diplomatic efforts were extraordinarily successful. Modern secretaries of state (and national security advisors, for that matter) tend to come from one of three backgrounds. The most common is the legal: Acheson, Dulles, Rusk, Rogers, Vance, and Warren Christopher come to mind. There is also the soldier-statesman (Marshall and Powell) and the policy intellectual (Kissinger, Albright, Rice). Baker was of the first category, and like the others of this background, could master the most detailed brief and negotiate for hours if that was required. But what distinguished Baker from other lawyers who became secretary of state was his strength of personality, his political skills, and the closeness of his ties to the president. He was better pursuing a brief than anyone I have encountered. Baker was not a foreign policy intellectual in the sense of Kissinger or Brzezinski, but he brought several enormous strengths to the position. To begin with, he used trusted staff to the maximum. He recognized talent in others and made the most of it. He did not let his ego get involved. Second, Baker was a master of the tactics of negotiating. He knew when to hang tough and when to add a sweetener. He also had great political skills, calculating what was doable both in the sense of what his counterpart could do and in the sense of what he could sell at home. Indeed, his political antennae only deserted him once during this trip. It came when he was asked to explain why the administration was so intent on forcing Saddam to vacate Kuwait: "jobs jobs jobs." The fallout was immediate. The secretary was panned for shifting the rationale for the policy, and worse yet for reducing it to a level that appeared unworthy. This was the clear exception, however; as a rule, Jim Baker stayed on message.

As was the case before I left with Baker, the challenge was how best to sustain domestic support. We again met with the congressional leadership and went to great lengths to argue the troop increase decision did not constitute any crossing of the Rubicon but rather a necessary move that would raise the chances that sanctions would succeed in persuading Saddam to leave Kuwait and give us options if this failed. Baker briefed the congressional leaders on his trip and on the strong international opposition to partial solutions. I remember more than one member of the leadership arguing that we should not turn to using force unless we were provoked, a strange argument, I thought, given what Saddam had already done. The president also found it a bit much to take, at one point exclaiming, "Hell, I've been provoked."

Clearly we were not winning over all of the Congress or the public. There was a dilemma at work here. If we repeated what we'd been saying, people would get tired of hearing it and turn us off. If we added new arguments, the papers would be filled with articles that the administration had changed its policy or its rationale or both. Forced to choose, I opt for the former. If real estate has three laws—location, location, and location—then public diplomacy has its three: repetition, repetition, and repetition. (This is in contrast to private diplomacy, whose three laws are consultation, consultation, and consultation.)

The midterm election results came in, and as tends to be the case, the party of the president (in this case, the Republican Party) lost seats in both the Senate and the House. Attention then shifted back to diplomacy, private and public. The president decided he would attend the European security meeting in Paris, in part to make sure Gorbachev was on board with the U.N. Security Council resolution we hoped to pass before the end of the month. The president would then leave Paris to visit the troops in the field, which he had wanted to do for months.

These plans created some complications for me. On one hand, I was expected to travel with the president. At the same time, the previous spring I had gotten engaged, and November 17 had seemed like a date far enough in the future to allow my fiancée and me to fence off the necessary time. Even after the invasion in early August, it was far from clear just how big and enduring this crisis would be, so we went ahead with all the preparations and commitments, from printing up and mailing invitations to renting a place for the ceremony and party.

In the end, we made a decision that, if not quite Solomonic, at least worked. The president and Brent and the others went off to Eastern Europe and then to Paris, and I went off to Boston to get married. I made it in time for the rehearsal dinner Friday night. Susan and I got married Saturday night in the city's North End, and on Sunday night I flew to Paris. The only problem was that I flew off without my bride, who stayed behind not far from the proverbial altar in Boston with her parents and her maid of honor. Brent suggested that she come with me to Paris and that she and I could celebrate a brief honeymoon with him and the president before everyone (sans Susan) flew off to the Gulf, but for some reason that didn't quite appeal. (My wife disputes this account, saying she never would have turned down even a short trip to Paris.) We finally got our honeymoon some six months later, but by then my wife was also pregnant and nothing she'd bought for the honeymoon fit. I am still paying for this.

I met up with the presidential party in Paris. Gorbachev was a much-weakened leader presiding over a country and an empire fast coming apart. Thatcher had just lost her job, as the Conservative Party opted for the new face of John Major. From there we went to the Middle East. There were opulent feasts with Saudi leaders followed by emotional meetings with American soldiers in the Saudi desert, where we carried gas masks in case Saddam launched a missile in our direction. The president, tired and sweating through his blue workshirt, nevertheless derived great strength from the soldiers. On board the USS *Nassau*, we participated in a poignant prayer service.

On the way back, the president learned I had just been married and this had become my honeymoon. He immediately penned a note: "Dear Susan: Richard was with me in the desert today—honest. Please forgive both of us. Great Happiness. George Bush." That note, framed, hangs in our home to this day. We stopped in Egypt for a meeting with the always confident President Hosni Mubarak. We also added a last-minute stop in Geneva to meet with Syrian president Hafiz al-Assad. There was more than a little criticism of doing this, given Assad's record of repression at home and his years of confrontation with Israel. But it was the right thing to do. Syria was, along with Iraq, a center of Arab radicalism, and how better to highlight Saddam's lack of support than to have an Arab radical on our side? We thought this would make it much less difficult to win over hearts and minds throughout the Arab world. The fact that Syria's military contribution was marginal was secondary. What mattered was that it was in. Reaching out to Damascus also paid

off in the war's aftermath, when Assad was the first Middle East leader to accept our invitation to attend the peace conference in Madrid.

There was and is a larger point involved here as well. Foreign policy must be about priorities, and priorities require a willingness to choose and make trade-offs. The priority was to defeat Saddam; if this meant associating ourselves with some unsavory regimes in the process, so be it. (As is so often the case, Churchill said it best: "If Hitler invaded Hell I would make at least a favourable reference to the devil in the House of Commons.") It is for this reason that I am not attracted to calls for a caucus or coalition of democracies; in many cases, we will need to work with nondemocratic governments if we are to succeed in stemming proliferation, thwarting terrorism, promoting trade, or slowing climate change. There is also the possibility that by including less than perfect governments in what we do, we increase the chance that they will come to appreciate their own stake in maintaining a good relationship with us. Also possible is that some of what is best about us—protection of basic freedoms, respect for the rule of law, etc.—will rub off on them.

We returned home in late November to a domestic political scene that was if anything worse than before we left. A front-page story in the *New York Times* was headlined "The Collapse of a Coalition." The subhead—"Hawk and Dove Join in Criticism of Bush"—was no more reassuring. Former president Jimmy Carter was writing the leaders of the other countries then on the U.N. Security Council and advising them not to support us! Senator Sam Nunn, normally something of a hawk on matters of war and peace, was holding hearings on the crisis in which witness after witness testified before the Senate Armed Services Committee that the misguided policy of the Bush administration would lead to massive American casualties and expensive oil. (I found it noteworthy that years later Nunn publicly regretted his stance against the war.) With few exceptions (Henry

Kissinger stands out) the witnesses and the senators favored giving sanctions more time to work. The president was moved to write an open letter to the American people titled "Why We Are in the Gulf" to shore up domestic support for U.S. policy.

The month ended on both a strong and an uncertain note. The former was the passage on November 29 of U.N. Security Council Resolution 678. The United States had beaten back Soviet attempts for multiple resolutions on the grounds that this required too much time and diluted the impact of any signal to Saddam. The text came out much as envisioned by Bob Kimmitt and me some months before. This latest resolution authorized U.N. member states (under Chapter VII of the U.N. Charter, the chapter linked to military action) to use "all necessary means" to oust Iraqi forces from Kuwait if all Iraqi forces were not withdrawn and Kuwait's government restored by January 15, 1991. We now had in place the deadline and the backing we wanted.

The cause for concern was the surprise announcement by the White House that the secretary of state would be prepared to meet one or more times with Tariq Aziz, his Iraqi counterpart, in one last push for peace. It was a surprise to me, cooked up by the president and John Sununu. Brent shared my view that it was a bad idea, since it looked as though we were searching to give Saddam a way out short of full compliance with the U.N. resolutions. It also looked as though we were blinking after passage of the resolution saying that the United States and others were authorized to use all necessary means—military force—to oust Iraqi personnel and equipment from Kuwait. The Saudis in particular were unhappy, both over the substance of the announcement and over not being informed in advance. (I had to scrape an incensed Bandar off the ceiling. The president had to place a number of calls to reassure others.) Brent was somewhat sheepish, but what was done was done. In defense of those who made the decision, it should be pointed out that there was

considerable domestic and international pressure to go the proverbial extra mile for peace. In the end, it turned out fine, and the entire
episode did buttress the argument that the administration had done
all that could be expected and then some to avoid the resort to military force. It helps when one has an adversary as blind and as stub-
born as was Saddam.

Another surprise came a week later when the State Department
announced that we would be pulling our diplomats out of Kuwait
once all the hostages were released. I thought this was a bad idea; it
would look like a concession to Iraq and that we were giving up on
Kuwait's independence. What made it worse was the lack of interagency review and consultation with our allies, with the British in
particular feeling betrayed given that we'd asked them to hold off
doing just what we did. Months of crisis were beginning to take
their toll since tired people tend to be prone to make poor decisions
that are then implemented badly.

This was the context for a visit by Israeli prime minister Yitzhak
Shamir. I briefed the president beforehand, emphasizing the importance that Shamir be reassured that we were not trading off Israel's
interests to maintain the coalition. That said, the president pressed
him hard to talk with us before undertaking any military action if in
fact Iraq threatened or attacked Israel. The president also promised
to give Shamir a heads-up before we attacked Iraq. All in all the
meeting went fairly well, in part because Shamir needed U.S. economic assistance to help absorb the flood of Soviet Jews arriving in
Israel and to demonstrate (as all Israeli prime ministers must) that he
could manage Israel's most important bilateral relationship.

Two days later (on December 13) there was the welcome news
that the hostages were to be released. (One of my favorite moments
of the entire crisis was the president's reaction to a question of
whether the United States would give something in return for their
freedom. "Hell, no! Not one thing! You don't reward a kidnapper.")

Amid all this I headed up to New York City for some public diplomacy. I had lunch at the *New York Times* with the editorial board. I
made no headway in arguing that sanctions were unlikely to do the
trick and that waiting had costs that were immediate (Kuwaiti suffering) and long term (time for Iraq to develop unconventional
weapons). I then headed over to meet with the Conference of Presidents of Major American Jewish Organizations, which is sort of the
AFL-CIO of Jewish leadership. Unlike the AFL-CIO, however, in recent years it had grown quite conservative, hewing closely to the
thinking of those Israelis who tended toward a hard line when it
came to compromising for peace. There the focus was very much on
how the administration was not doing enough to ensure that Israel's
needs and interests would be protected. My last stop was at the
Council on Foreign Relations, the influential, independent, and nonpartisan New York–based foreign policy membership organization
that hosts speakers, maintains a think tank, and publishes *Foreign
Affairs* (and where I am now president). There I made the case for
what we were doing and might have to do and why. I got off easier
there than I expected, although one member who was clearly against
any recourse to force on our part did come up to me after I spoke to
warn me of the dangers of hubris and to suggest I read (which of
course I had) David Halberstam's *The Best and the Brightest.*

What came home to me in the aftermath of these and other similar sessions is the difficulty in managing three very different audiences simultaneously: the coalition, Iraq, and the home front. We did
not have the luxury of sending signals or messages to one and not
have it reach the others. There is no narrowcasting in today's world.
However, it was all but impossible to be simultaneously tough toward Baghdad, reassuring toward the coalition, and flexible toward
Congress. Making matters even tougher was that little stays private
and what is communicated is heard not just widely but often instantly. News cycles have been compressed. The Iraq crisis came to

be the first 24/7, CNN conflict, something fundamentally different from Vietnam, when television was mostly limited to several minutes on the nightly news programs using material filmed one or more days prior to the broadcast. Still, we had done all right overall. We had won the debate over the stakes and why this was a vital national interest. Where we were still falling short was on debate as to why we could not just wait longer for sanctions to work.

I also engaged in what might generously be termed unintended public diplomacy. That same month Susan invited over to our home for dinner the Washington bureau chief of a major U.S. newspaper and his wife, old friends of Susan's who could not make it to our wedding. As might be expected, conversation turned to the Iraq crisis, and I explained how we felt a strong sense of urgency, why we opposed waiting, and how the president was totally comfortable with using force if need be. He seemed incredulous that we were as serious as we were saying; when I tried to make clear that we were, he himself said "this is just between us." After they'd left, Susan commented that I had come on strong and that I'd given them more than a little insight into administration thinking. I said that I thought that what I had said was pretty well-known, and that in any event we were not on the record or even on background. She said I should call him to make sure, but I demurred, saying it was unnecessary and insulting; this was with friends at our home over dinner and anything but a working lunch.

Susan, a former television news producer, was right to be concerned. Friday dawned with a front-page story quoting senior administration officials (one of whom was clearly me) saying that the president had decided to go to war sooner rather than later. This was technically wrong, although the essence of the piece was on the mark. Needless to say, it became a big story. I was teed off. So much for off the record. I was also unhappy because I didn't want us to be seen as simply going through the motions in the upcoming

Baker meeting with Aziz. If war came, it was important that it be widely viewed to have been thrust on us by Saddam. So after telling Marlin Fitzwater what had happened, I was authorized to go tell CNN that the newspaper had gotten it wrong and that the president hadn't made up his mind on whether or when to go to war. If Saddam was confused at times as to our intentions, it is hardly any wonder. (A postscript: Some weeks later, the bureau chief in question and I had a "bark off the tree" conversation, during which he apologized. So you can imagine my surprise when, many months later, I turned on the television only to see him recount the entire episode as his most interesting moment of 1990 and say that he may have lost a friend and a source but that it was worth it given the size of the story.)

Much of my and our focus, though, was on preparing for the possibility of a Baker-Aziz meeting. There was much to-ing and fro-ing over the proposal to bring them together, including how many meetings and where and when they would be held. I was uneasy with multiple meetings and anything close to mid-January since I feared an outcome that suggested any sign of possible progress would have the effect of tying us in knots. In the end, it came down to one meeting, in Geneva on January 9.

Even one meeting worried me. I feared that the diplomat's natural proclivity to go for a deal would prompt Baker to be too flexible. It was also human nature to want to succeed. And no one was better at closing a deal than Jim Baker. There was as a result some concern at the White House about the Geneva meeting. The parallel that came to mind was the Cuban Missile Crisis, when President Kennedy agreed in private to withdraw intermediate-range Jupiter missiles from Turkey if Soviet premier Khrushchev withdrew missiles from Cuba. The difference was that Kennedy was correctly prepared to pay a high price to avoid a nuclear confrontation with the Soviets; we were not in a parallel situation in that we were confident we could prevail in a war with Iraq at a relatively modest cost. We were also concerned about managing the threat posed by an Iraq that withdrew from Kuwait but kept all its military might. An additional factor was the reality that we had half a million troops deployed to the desert and we could not park them there forever. To many in the administration, a war now seemed preferable to one down the road against a more capable Iraq.

Brent and I talked about my going to Geneva, but both of us concluded I would have little influence there and that it made more sense for me to stay in Washington and work. We instead sent one of my deputies, Sandy Charles, on the trip. We did, however, draft a cable to the secretary of state (who otherwise had no formal instructions) on what we wanted out of the talks and on the limits to our flexibility. The cable emphasized that Saddam should not be given rewards or face-savers in exchange for complying with Security Council demands. Baker, though, thought it was important to give the Iraqis every chance to avoid war, and told them that, in addition to staving off a coalition attack, if they were to fulfill the requirements of the relevant U.N. resolutions, no U.S. ground forces would remain in the region, economic sanctions would be relaxed, and there would be an active U.S. effort on behalf of the Middle East peace process. Still, the Iraqis would not withdraw. What all this reveals is that Saddam either believed we would not actually follow through on our threats to attack or thought that once we began he could somehow weather the onslaught and manipulate the diplomacy to leave himself better off.

I also drafted a letter from President Bush to Saddam Hussein. It was an attempt to make sure that Saddam understood what we sought and the consequences of refusing to agree. The tone was measured. "I write this letter not to threaten, but to inform." We had some reason to believe Saddam thought we were bluffing, and we wanted to disabuse him of this. "You may be tempted to find solace in the diversity of opinion that is American democracy. You should resist any such temptation. Diversity ought not to be confused with division. Nor should you underestimate, as others have before you, America's will." I doubted it would have any effect, but it was necessary to try. In the end, Aziz read but refused to accept the original, signed version of the president's letter to Saddam. We were forced to find another means of getting it to Baghdad.

The January 9 meeting between Baker and Aziz in Geneva ran over six hours, considerably longer than anticipated. Back in Washington, there was a good deal of looking at watches and clocks. We got word of how things were going when, during a meeting with a group of congressional leaders, the president got called out to take a call from Secretary Baker. The talks had reached an impasse. Many in the room had mixed reactions to this news. On one hand, there was a sense of relief, since it was clear that we had not compromised any of our core objectives and would not have to contend with any of the diplomatic half-loaves that we feared Saddam might put forward; on the other, there was a strong sense of sobriety because it was 99 percent certain there would be war within a week.

The Baker-Aziz meeting hardly took place in a vacuum. For months there had been an ongoing conversation within the administration and between the administration and Congress over the role of the latter and in particular over whether its approval was necessary before any use of military force could be decided upon or undertaken. Congress demanded a role, although what exactly that role would be was unclear. Leaders were adamant, though, that the support of the international community as expressed through the United Nations, however desirable, was not sufficient.

Inside the administration, there was a recognition that having Congress on board was wise. The only exception to this was Secretary of Defense Dick Cheney, ironically enough one of the very few people in the room who had ever served in the Congress. (Not for the first time, familiarity bred contempt.) Most of the others believed congressional support would be a good thing, but were clear that Congress was expressing its approval, not providing authority. The president felt he had all the authority he needed to employ military force in Article 51 of the U.N. Charter (that contains the right of self-defense), in the various U.N. resolutions, and in the inherent power of the office. That said, his reading of LBJ's travails during Vietnam convinced him that he would be much better off with a declaration of congressional support. The obvious risk in going to Congress was that we might not succeed. We would be much worse off if this were to happen. Nevertheless, I thought going to Congress was the right thing to do and argued as much. It was desirable not just politically but also philosophically. Conservatives are meant to use traditional procedures and institutions not just when they prove to be convenient. In the end, we decided to take the risk, because we thought it was smart to have this support and were confident we could get it once we had the U.N. resolution in hand. We did not think the Congress would want to appear less resolute when it came to standing up to Iraqi aggression than would the bulk of the international community. We were almost wrong; the Senate vote in particular was a cliffhanger. But after much nail-biting, the House and Senate both voted in favor of authorizing U.S. participation in the implementation of U.N. Security Council Resolution 678, which effectively endorsed the use of force to restore Kuwait's independence.

Some of the friction between the administration and the Congress was over policy. Nearly half of those in the Congress opposed going to war, or at least opposed turning to military force in January 1991. Whether they ever would have moved off sanctions and favored force is an open question. There is more than a little irony in all this; I never thought sanctions had more than a 10 percent chance of succeeding if success was defined as persuading Saddam to vacate Kuwait. (The history of sanctions suggested some modesty in what they could be expected to accomplish, especially in a relatively short period of time, and even with considerable international backing.) Their value to me was that we needed to do something right away to show we were serious in our opposition to Iraq's occupation of Kuwait and were committed to bringing about what the U.N. resolutions called for, namely, a full and unconditional Iraqi withdrawal. Also, there was no military option available in the initial months following Iraq's aggression, and none would be available for perhaps half a year while we built up a military presence. So sanctions filled the gap. Most important, we needed to demonstrate to domestic and international audiences that we had tried lesser remedies if we could expect to receive support for or at least tolerance of escalating to the use of military force. There are times when you can succeed even when you fail, and this was one of them. What we hadn't counted on was that so many people in the Congress and beyond would fall in love with sanctions and come to see them as the ultimate U.S. policy rather than as a way station.

I found it difficult to understand (and still do for that matter) why so many in Congress, among the pundits, and in the nation writ large were so opposed to this war. What the Iraqis did in their invasion and absorption of Kuwait violated several of the most basic building blocks of international order, including the primacy and essential sanctity of the nation-state and the idea that force is not to be used to settle disputes except in the most narrow of circumstances, which clearly did not apply to Iraq's action. No principles are more widely accepted. This was the biggest improvement of the modern era over the Middle Ages. A world in which states regularly used force to settle their disputes and realize their ambitions would be a Hobbesian world of never-ending violence. The fact that this challenge to order took place at the close of one historical era (the Cold War) and the emergence of a new one (still unnamed) only increased the stakes because what was done here would go a long way toward defining the character of the new era.

But the rationales for supporting the use of force went beyond such arguments of principle. The United States had vital national interests at stake. A Saddam who controlled Kuwait would dominate the oil-rich Middle East, given the value of Kuwait's oil and the likelihood that other Arab states would fear standing up to him lest they suffer Kuwait's fate. It would only be a short while before he gained nuclear weapons. Israel's security would be badly compromised. At the same time, there was little in the history of sanctions that suggested that they alone would provide enough leverage to force Saddam to change so large a policy. Nor was there reason to conclude that time was on our side.

For me it was not even a close call given the stakes and the policy choices. This was a war of necessity if ever there was one. The stakes were enormous, and we had tried and exhausted the alternatives to employing military force. So how could so many, including a number of individuals I truly respected, come out so differently and in my view get it so wrong? For some, especially in the Democratic Party, it was politics plain and simple, in that the safer political position was to oppose a Republican president using force. But others simply misread the situation, wildly exaggerating how difficult it would be to accomplish our aims and underestimating both the costs of not acting and the benefits of succeeding. By the time, more than a decade later, when Americans were asked again to decide on war with Iraq, just as many if not more got it wrong, but in the opposite direction, underestimating the difficulty and costs of succeeding and exaggerating the benefits of going to war while dismissing the alternatives.

To be sure, not all of the friction with Congress was over particular policy. Some was also over the principle of whether the executive branch could take the country to war by itself or whether Congress needed to be involved and, if so, how. This is the classic debate over war powers. The Constitution has little to say about it, other than that Congress alone has the right to declare war. The problem is that war has been declared formally for only five conflicts in more than two hundred years of American history. The most recent occasion was World War II. Korea, Vietnam, and literally dozens of other situations involving the use of deadly force were not wars in the formal sense.

At stake was more than semantics; the debate was over the power to make policy and commit troops. Those in the executive and legislative branches alike had their reasons for avoiding formal declarations of war: no president wanted to have his hands tied, and many in Congress did not want to give the president all the powers that accrue to him if war is formally declared. But neither did Congress want to give presidents a free hand. The "solution" thought up a quarter of a century ago was the War Powers Resolution, which allows the president to commit troops to combat without first getting congressional approval but allows him to continue the policy beyond sixty or ninety days only if Congress explicitly authorizes him to do so. Presidents have uniformly rejected this constraint, so the dispute continues in a sort of legal and political limbo that is unlikely to be resolved.

What would have happened in early 1991 had Congress not supported going to war? President Bush would have done it regardless. He says as much in the book he co-authored with Brent Scowcroft. "In truth, even had Congress not passed the resolution I would have acted and ordered our troops into combat. . . ." I do not believe this was after-the-fact bravado; he would have done just that. What he said in various meetings and conversations and, more importantly, how he said it made it clear. Had he gone ahead in the face of a no vote by one or both chambers of Congress, there would have been bills of impeachment introduced, which then would have gone nowhere given politics and, perhaps just as important, how quickly and successfully the battle unfolded.

The key to understanding George Herbert Walker Bush and what made him tick was his sense of decorum. It came through on matters big and small alike. Bush was genuinely offended by the Iraqi invasion and then absorption of Kuwait. It was simply not how civilized countries behaved toward one another. It harkened back to a cruder era of international relations when might made right. Bush was even more offended by how Iraq was reported to be treating Kuwaitis and others in Kuwait. Accounts of mistreatment (some but not all of which turned out to be exaggerated) increased his determination to do what was necessary to liberate Kuwait. The same embrace of manners led the president to be forgiving of the well-mannered king of Jordan, and it had something to do with the president's relentless use of the phone to check in on his friends, a banking of goodwill that proved invaluable as the crisis wore on.

But this sense of manners and what was right was not limited to matters of policy. I remember once getting a call in my office saying to come over right away—the president wanted to meet with me to go over something I'd written for him. I rushed down the stairs to the second floor, out the door and down the outside stairs, crossed West Executive Avenue, and then ran up the stairs to the West Wing. Scowcroft and Sununu were waiting for me there, just outside the Oval. Sununu looked at me quizzically, as though I had something on my head. "What's wrong?" I asked. "Go back," he said. "Go back?" "Go back to your office and get your jacket. The president doesn't want people coming into the Oval Office during business hours without their jacket. We'll wait for you." As soon as I realized he was serious, I made the trip back over to the OEOB, put on the top half of my suit, and arrived properly attired for the meeting. Clearly, I was having trouble getting the hang of the jacket thing.

After Congress passed the resolution backing the use of force, there were several important remaining tasks. One was to determine the notifications that would precede the launching of military operations. This involved thinking about everything from military necessity when it came to coalition partners to diplomatic and political desirability when it came to the leaders of various governments or Congress. But it also required trading off the benefits of notifying others with the potential (and, in some instances, certain) lack of surprise that would result. So I produced a grid that detailed who would be told, who would deliver the news, and when and how they would deliver it. I felt something like a teacher meting out homework assignments, although in this instance the "class" consisted mostly of the president of the United States, the secretaries of state and defense, the national security advisor, and one or two others.

The other task was to draw up a formal set of war aims that the president would sign off on before we initiated the attack. National Security Directive 54 of January 15, 1991, did just that. The purposes were familiar, the most basic being to effect the immediate, complete, and unconditional withdrawal of all Iraqi forces from Kuwait. What was new were the military aims, which included precluding Iraqi missile launches, destroying any capabilities to produce weapons of mass destruction, and eliminating the Republican Guard (Iraq's most capable units) as a fighting force. Also important was the desirability of keeping both Israel and Jordan out of the fighting. The United States would not support any effort to alter Iraq's boundaries, but it would seek to replace the current leadership if Iraq used nuclear, biological, or chemical weapons, carried out or supported terrorism, or destroyed Kuwait's oil fields. The die was cast.

4. WAR OF NECESSITY

I WAS IN my office at 7 P.M. on Wednesday, January 16, 1991, the official start to Operation Desert Storm. It is important not to describe this moment as when the war began, because that was the previous August, when Saddam invaded Kuwait. Brent called to express appreciation for all the work I'd done up to that point. It was a typically decent and thoughtful thing for him to do. His call capped another frenetic day, this one spent getting the president's address to the nation ready and alerting those who needed to know in advance about the coalition hostilities. Later, over in Brent's office, we watched the speech, which made the case as to why we couldn't afford to wait any longer before acting. We also included language that set forth a narrative: "This conflict started August 2nd when the dictator of Iraq invaded a small and helpless neighbor. Kuwait—a member of the Arab League and a member of the United Nations—was crushed; its people, brutalized. Five months ago, Saddam Hussein started this cruel war against Kuwait. Tonight, the battle has been joined."

What I wrote was influenced by what Harry Truman said to the country on July 19, 1950, about why it was necessary for the United States to resist aggression in Korea. "Korea is a small country, thousands of miles away, but what is happening there is important to every American. . . . The attack upon Korea was an outright breach of the peace and a violation of the Charter of the United Nations. . . . This is a direct challenge to the efforts of the free nations to build the kind of world in which men can live in freedom and peace. . . . This challenge has been presented squarely. We must meet it squarely." The parallels between the two situations, one that marked the globalization of the Cold War and the other that marked its successor era, were striking.

The next day was eerily quiet for the most part. Once actual fighting begins, the military takes the lead, and civilians in the government properly tend to take a backseat except when significant matters of policy arise. It took some discipline not to become a CNN junkie. All the news was good about what we were accomplishing and the remarkably low losses we were suffering. Oil prices were coming down; the stock market was going up.

If it seemed too good to be true, it was. Reports flooded in of Iraqi Scud missile attacks on Israel. I first heard these reports in my office, and minutes later was over in Brent's West Wing office, which that evening became the administration's diplomatic command bunker. Bob Gates was already there with Marlin Fitzwater; soon Jim Baker and Larry Eagleburger joined us. Dick Cheney was on the phone constantly from the Pentagon, relaying what he was hearing from Israeli defense minister Moshe Arens. The Israelis were understandably angry and upset and were pushing to retaliate. Cheney's recommendation was to let them do so and requested that we authorize the U.S. military to pass the communications codes to their Israeli counterparts so that our forces could identify and therefore avoid shooting at one another if and when they operated in close proximity. I pushed back, making the case that Israeli involvement would raise a host of messy tactical issues (such as overflight of Arab countries) and would add a new dimension to the crisis and a new challenge to coalition management. I also doubted whether the Israelis could do more than we could against Iraq, given all the aircraft we had parked in the theater. The others agreed, and Eagleburger got on the phone to Israeli ambassador Zalmon Shoval to say how devastated we were by the reports but also to press him to pass the message to his government on the need to hold off acting. Shoval called back to say he had relayed our message but had no commitment. We then received word that the Scuds reaching Israel were filled with conventional high-explosive warheads and not with chemicals, as some of the initial reports had it. (Colin Powell later taught me the valuable lesson that initial reports in any crisis are almost always incomplete, incorrect, or both. It is usually best not to react quickly to what comes in and is not clearly confirmed.) This was critical; I believe there would have been no chance of persuading the Israelis to hold back if this line had been crossed. I doubt we would even have tried.

Baker then managed to get Arens on the phone to reiterate our strong preference for Israeli restraint. It was clear that only Prime Minister Shamir could decide whether to retaliate. The president (in the East wing) agreed that Baker should speak to Shamir directly. It was hard to get through; finally we made a connection, only to be asked to call back. Baker said we would, and was asked for his number. He cupped the phone, and asked those of us in the room, "What number should I give?" I responded: "You should know, Mr. Secretary. It is your favorite number: 202-456-1414." Everyone in the room had a good laugh, as only recently a frustrated Baker had controversially stated in response to a question at a congressional hearing that the Israelis should call this number, which happened to be the White House switchboard, when they were ready to discuss peace. When we stopped laughing, Eagleburger told me in a voice loud enough for everyone to hear that any chance I'd had of ever getting an embassy just evaporated. Some hours and many slices of pizza later, Baker and Shamir finally talked. I wrote a message from the president to Shamir that he sent to try to influence Israeli thinking. We all went home late that evening, having staved off Israeli military action—though for how long, we didn't know.

In the morning, we learned that the Israeli cabinet had opted for restraint. It was a remarkable set of exchanges and decisions. It was no secret that Bush and Shamir had little use for and even less trust in one another, but this was a moment in which they leveled with each other as only heads of government could. This was the closest they ever came. Shamir in particular rose to the occasion; it was anything but easy for a man who had fought his entire life to suddenly turn the other cheek. But that was exactly what he did. It was especially difficult for an Israeli leader to do given the understandable Israeli concern that inaction risked communicating weakness to the many in the Arab world who wanted to cause Israel harm. I thought it was true statesmanship and a rare example of an elected politician demonstrating courage and choosing the long term over the immediate.

Everything seemed calm, until the phone rang early the next day with reports of more Iraqi Scuds landing in Israel. Fortunately, none carried a chemical warhead and no one was killed. Bush called Shamir several times to express concern and urge restraint. The president again dispatched Larry Eagleburger and Paul Wolfowitz to visit Israel, both to demonstrate our concern and to look for ways we could cooperate short of active Israeli participation in the war effort. (Eagleburger had gone to Israel before the war started, and Patriot antimissile systems had been sent to Israel with American crews.) In order to cement the Israeli decision, we promised to devote a substantial number of assets to dealing with the Iraqi Scud problem, which in fact we did but with no discernible effect. This scenario—Iraqi Scuds landing in Israel, Israeli desire to retaliate, U.S. urging of restraint, and more U.S. military effort devoted to taking out the Scuds—would be repeated throughout the war.

Although the fighting was just beginning, I began work on how it would likely end. There were three basic scenarios for war termination: an Iraqi bid for peace once they had had enough; pressure on the protagonists coming from outside parties; and a U.S. push for peace once our goals had been realized. I doubted we would get a clean, formal "Battleship *Missouri*" outcome like the one that concluded World War II, given Saddam's likely resistance to either surrendering or complying in full with U.N. demands. Little did I know then just how complicated and ultimately significant this set of concerns would prove to be.

The possibility of an end to the fighting being brought about by outside pressure was anything but academic, as the Soviets were hard at it from the get-go. Gorbachev was pushing for bombing pauses to give diplomacy a chance. We were fending this off, fearing it would make Saddam look like a hero and give him time to improve his position. Managing the Soviets often involved the president getting on the phone to hear out his increasingly desperate-sounding friend. It seemed that the worse things got at home for Gorbachev the harder he pressed for a diplomatic breakthrough. None was possible, and even if one had occurred, it would not have altered the basic dynamics of what was going on inside the Soviet Union. But he pressed, and it was important to avoid humiliating him and to keep the Soviets in the coalition.

Within days the war settled into a rhythm. There would be daily reports from the Pentagon and CIA (often inconsistent) filled with estimates of what the bombing had accomplished. One or another newspaper or television network (in particular, CNN, which came of age during this war) would carry a story about how things were not going well. (Peter Arnett of CNN was a particular thorn in our side;

it was ironic that we spent all this effort knocking Iraqi television and Saddam off the air only to have our own media put him on.) I would spend my time thinking and writing papers for the small group and principals about how to handle messy outcomes to the fighting and more generally the war's aftermath: regional security arrangements, arms control regimes, the Middle East peace process, likely economic challenges, regional political stability. I was also writing presidential remarks for a boss who was speaking out several times a week if not more; helping to prepare for the transition from the air campaign to ground warfare; and with others doing all that could be done to buttress both coalition cohesion and domestic support for the war.

Every now and then, though, something would occur that stood out. A cabinet meeting in late January was one example. Cabinet meetings are in fact rare, in large part because the cabinet is not a body that makes decisions or even deliberates. It is too large and diverse and uneven for that. Cabinet meetings tend to be for show and, in this case, for making sure that everyone would be on the same page so that they could and would reinforce the themes of the upcoming State of the Union address. I was assigned the task of drafting the foreign policy portions of that speech, and as a result attended the meeting, sitting as usual in one of the chairs up against the wall. After a rather uninteresting few minutes devoted to the war and the speech, the president was wrapping up the shorter-than-planned session when he was interrupted by Jack Kemp, secretary of housing and urban development. Kemp didn't much care for Chief of Staff John Sununu's summary of the speech and wanted to know why there was not more time and substance devoted to the theme of empowerment. I thought he was onto something, as Bush's domestic policy lacked much in the way of themes, but a cabinet meeting is not the best place to make policy. Sununu was angry, the president appeared uncomfortable, and the speech was not altered. What popped into my mind was my previous life, when I taught at the Kennedy School of Government. This had the makings of a classic case study. "You are Jack Kemp, and it is the cabinet meeting the morning of the State of the Union speech. You were asked weeks before to make suggestions as to what should be in the speech. You sent in ideas, but you have not seen the draft text. The chief of staff briefs, and it is clear the speech does not reflect your ideas. What should you do?"

That night of January 29 could have produced material for several case studies. The focus was for obvious reasons on the State of the Union, which again tied U.S. policy in the Gulf to a broader vision of a new world order. But just before it was to be given, the U.S. and Soviet foreign ministers (Jim Baker and Aleksandr Bessmertnykh) released a statement of their own. I learned about it when an angry Brent Scowcroft phoned me asking if I knew anything about it and, if so, why hadn't I warned him before his press backgrounder? I told him I didn't know what he was talking about. I checked with Bob Kimmitt, who was similarly in the dark. I then got a copy of the text, and immediately saw the problems. The statement suggested "a cessation of hostilities would be possible if Iraq would make an unequivocal commitment to withdraw from Kuwait," something we couldn't agree to lest our military efforts be disrupted. The statement also indicated U.S. and Russian support for renewed peace efforts in the Middle East in the aftermath of the Iraq conflict, something that might appear to give Saddam credit and thereby reward him for ending his illegal occupation. There was also the matter of timing: the statement conflicted with the president's speech and made it look as if the administration was speaking with multiple voices. Clearly Baker and Dennis Ross had not anticipated the reaction; Brent and I spent the next day reassuring governments and others that nothing had changed.

It was increasingly clear that the schedule of sixteen hours a day, seven days a week was giving all of us a severe case of cabin fever. It was good to go on the road with the president on February 1. We visited Marine, Air Force, and Army bases in North Carolina and Georgia. The emotion was intense. It was also unnatural, in that one saw women, children, boys, and older men but few males between the ages of eighteen and forty-five. Trips like these recharged the president and helped deal with his restlessness and impatience. We also scheduled additional meetings that would give him war updates and sessions with outside Middle East hands. Such meetings were almost always a good use of time. The president would either hear views similar to what he was already getting from insiders, which tended to reinforce what government officials were saying, or he would hear things he had not heard, which was interesting. It was also a way to influence those who would be appearing on television or writing op-eds.

What was also going on behind the scenes was something of a struggle in the Pentagon between the Army and the Air Force. I spent a few hours in the bowels of the Pentagon one Saturday morning in early February with the senior folks at the Air Force, including Air Force secretary Don Rice and John Warden, the cerebral if at times quirky colonel who had written an influential monograph on the potential for airpower to accomplish great things thanks to modern information technology that made precision bombing a true possibility. Warden's thesis was that the classic critique of strategic bombing, one derived from the World War II experience of heavy but inaccurate attacks, no longer applied given advances in accuracy and lethality. He was confident that airpower could so disrupt the adversary's command and control that a ground campaign could be made much easier if not made unnecessary altogether. I thought we were beginning to run out of targets and that using advanced aircraft to search for and eliminate individual tanks was not a good use of our Air Force. Brent, a former airman, was also concerned that

time worked against us. Saddam would earn points for simply holding out. The Arabs opposed the destruction of Iraq, as did we. We
didn't want the expense of rebuilding it, and we didn't want Iraq so
weakened that it could no longer balance Iran. This all made me
think that time provided opportunity for developments to rock the
coalition. It was clear we would initiate the ground war soon, although the definition of *soon* was elusive.

It quickly became obvious that I was spotted in the Pentagon by
one of Dick Cheney's aides, because the next thing I knew, the secretary of defense was on the phone to Brent complaining about my
being there and getting involved in what was properly the province
of the Pentagon. I did not make a big deal out of it and agreed to
keep a low profile, but I am not sure Cheney was right. Civilians
should not be in the business of making tactical decisions, and we
were careful not to. The president was firm in his conviction that he
would not replicate LBJ and pore over proposed bombing targets.
But civilians should be involved in strategic decisions, and the question of whether and when to start a ground campaign certainly qualified as strategic. So too did the kind of targets and whether anything
should have been off-limits. Target selection became a much more
sensitive subject after a bomb hit a bunker that turned out to be
housing hundreds of Iraqi civilians. It was targeted on the assessment it was an Iraqi C3 (command, control, and communications)
site. The photographs of the wreckage were grisly. We came under a
lot of criticism and instituted a more layered process for the vetting
of targets. This was all right and proper, although I would add that
we later heard from at least one Arab ruler (King Hassan of Morocco) that a good many Iraqis, including Saddam, assuming that we
knew civilians were present and went ahead and targeted the bunker
regardless, took this as proof that we were tough and meant business. Such is the Middle East.

I spent a good deal of time thinking through postwar security arrangements. The challenge was to devise something that blended military effectiveness with political sustainability—understanding that the second of these considerations reflected what could be supported at home (given politics and all else we had to do) and in the region, where there is a long history of resistance to external presence and formal pacts. It was impossible not to refer back to ill-fated attempts during the early years of the Cold War to erect a regional security organization in the Middle East, ironically enough termed the Baghdad Pact. Arrangements premised on anticommunism and opposition to the Soviet Union fared poorly with Arab governments preoccupied with what to do about Israel. To try in 1991 to create something built around a single common threat would similarly be a nonstarter. To the contrary, there were at least three obvious threats—Iraq, Iran, and internal instability in a number of Arab countries—and dealing with the last of the three would be more a matter of internal political and economic and social reform and of advancing the peace process than anything to do with defense. If Saddam failed to survive the crisis, I was thinking of turning to a mix of international (U.N.) and regional forces (Arab League and/or Gulf Cooperation Council) to deter Iraq from further aggression. The goal was to avoid stationing U.S. forces—it made little sense to cause major political problems for the very governments we sought to assist and protect—but have a de facto presence based on regular exercising, prepositioning of equipment, and so on. This would require a good deal of air- and sea-lift and planning; the idea was to stay over the horizon but move the horizon in closer. If, however, Saddam did remain in power or if an Iraq run by someone else remained irredentist and a threat to all, we might well have to maintain a substantial presence in the region, in which case we should maintain an international coalition rather than do it unilaterally. All this argued for prolonging the war somewhat so that we could cut Saddam and the Iraqi military down to size and thereby reduce the scale of the postwar threat we would have to contend with. This became the consensus view of the small group, with the caveat that we also wanted Iraq to remain strong enough to continue to give Iran pause. We were looking for the proverbial Goldilocks outcome: an Iraq that could balance our other foe in the neighborhood without being so strong as to intimidate our friends.

As was often the case, there was the need to juggle thinking about the future with the pressures of the present. Central was the question of whether and when the ground war would start, something the Soviets in particular were going to great lengths to avoid. There were numerous attempts by the Soviets to draw up proposals with the Iraqis that would bring about a cease-fire and postpone any ground campaign on our part. Yevgeny Primakov (the former KGB official who kept turning up in one guise or another to the extent that many came to think of him as the Zelig of Soviet and later Russian foreign policy) was tireless (and, all too often, tiresome) in trying to hatch a compromise that would allow Saddam to claim some credit for what he'd done and explain why he had stopped. All of these proposals fell short from our point of view on such questions as the sequencing of what the Iraqis would have to do before they could expect us to back off; the pace of Iraqi withdrawal (we wanted days, not weeks or months); and reparations (something we and the Kuwaitis were adamant about). But it was difficult for us, because we needed to balance the appearance of openness to proposals, so as not to lose our public or the coalition, with commitment to our conditions, which were unlikely to be met by the Iraqis, so that we would not put our ground troops in the impossible position of holding off indefinitely. We tried to thread the needle with public statements that made clear what was wrong with what was being proposed by the Iraqis and/or Soviets, what we wanted and needed and why, and a deadline. It was numbingly complex, involving literally dozens of detailed matters from what the Iraqis would have to do with their equipment to what lines behind which they would have to withdraw to the basic questions of pacing and sequencing of undertakings. In the end, what decided things was not simply the refusal to give Saddam anything that smacked of a face-saver but also the need to act before there was no longer anything left in Kuwait to save. Saddam's decision to torch Kuwait's oil wells sealed his country's fate.

On February 22 we released our final statement on the matter of ending hostilities and calling off a ground effort, and gave the Iraqis twenty-four hours to agree. The deadline of noon, February 23, came and went. I drafted the short remarks the president would give later that day announcing the start of the ground campaign. "The liberation of Kuwait has now entered a final phase." Reports from Kuwait of oil fires and urban killing were awful. There was a medieval quality to it all. Meanwhile, Gorbachev not only refused to give up, but to the contrary was growing ever more frantic, shouting over the phone when he spoke with the president. Condi's view, which sounded right to me, was that he feared the domestic price of failure to head off this new phase of the war would be too much for him to withstand. My sense was that this phase of the Iraq war would be violent but brief and decisive.

The onset of the ground fighting on February 25 did not end diplomacy so much as complicate it. There were questions of whether to up the ante for what Saddam had to do to stop the war now that he failed to meet the latest deadline. A "gang of 8" meeting (the president, vice president, Baker, Cheney, Powell, Scowcroft, Sununu, and Gates) revealed deep divisions, with Baker arguing for not moving the goalposts and Cheney arguing for demanding surrender. Behind these divisions were tensions as to how long the war should continue. Baker favored an early end lest the coalition unravel, while most of the others wanted to continue to diminish what would be left of Iraq's armed forces. As was often the case, a compromise emerged: we would ask Saddam to declare publicly that he supported all the U.N. resolutions and we would require that the Iraqis lay down their arms. We would not shoot at surrendering or unarmed soldiers, but we would go for those retreating with their combat equipment. The meeting came close to failing to reach any conclusion when the president started up the fireplace in the Oval and the room filled with smoke, setting off alarms and bringing the Secret Service rushing into the room.

I continued to spend a good deal of time writing for the president. I failed to get him to include a reference to this being the "mother of all defeats" for Saddam but otherwise had most of my prose used. Things were moving fast. On one occasion I handed the president the large index cards he liked to use when he gave public remarks and he asked Brent if he'd had the chance to review them. Brent said no and asked the president if he'd had the chance. The president said no. They both looked at me as we were walking out to the Rose Garden, I shrugged, and we all laughed. By then I was over the embarrassment I had felt some six weeks before in the early days of the air campaign when I wrote some public comments for the president and got my math wrong about how long the fighting had been going on.

Things were going extraordinarily well after just a few days of the ground assault. I told the secretary of defense that he was now on the cutting edge of arms control given all the Iraqi armor that was being destroyed. (I got the now familiar slightly crooked Cheney grin in response.) Iraq announced that it accepted all the relevant U.N. Security Council resolutions and a cease-fire and would return all POWs in exchange for an end to sanctions. As always, they built in conditions that we could not and would not accept. Norm Schwarzkopf gave what was instantly dubbed the mother of all briefings, demonstrating graphically how strategy and tactics and mobility and lethality compensated for inferior numbers. It was clear that the air phase of the battle broke the backs of the Iraqis and that the ground phase cleaned up a lot of what was left. So much for all those who had predicted calamity for us.

On what turned out to be the last day of the war, I was busy drafting a potential "end of war" address for the president to deliver at some point over the next few days when Bob Gates called me. He said I should get down right away to the Oval Office. I said I was not yet done and needed about forty-five more minutes to complete a draft. Bob's voice took on an icy quality. "You don't understand. Get down here right away." I joined a meeting of the gang of 8 that had clearly been going on for some time. There was widespread concern voiced by Powell and others, which I shared, that the images of Iraqi soldiers getting shot at while they were retreating in disarray was making us and our soldiers look bad—not just in the region but in the eyes of the entire world. The president asked if anyone disagreed with ending the war that night. John Sununu volunteered that would be the hundred-hour mark. The president asked Powell to get on the phone to Schwarzkopf. Powell called him on a phone that was kept in one of the drawers in the president's desk. The president told Norm that his and the group's sense was that things had gone on long enough and that the time had come to end the fighting and asked Norm directly if he had any problems with doing that. Norm said no but that he wanted to check with his commanders in the field. He quickly got back to Powell with the word that he was fine with stopping the war as suggested and that he could accomplish what little there was left to do in just a few more hours of fighting, which the president assured him he would have. Schwarzkopf accurately recounted all this in his memoir, but for some reason claimed subsequently in an interview with David Frost that the president held him back and that a bit more time would have made a major difference.

I was surprised by both the pace of events and decision making.

The president was motivated by a desire to maintain the support of the coalition. He liked the idea of pressing for peace before it was pressed on him and staying one step ahead of calls from the coalition and Democrats that we cease operations. This would be a way to bank goodwill with the Soviets and Arabs in particular—goodwill that would come in handy if and when we turned our attention to the peace process and other regional challenges. The military seemed particularly uncomfortable with the "turkey shoot" quality of continued killing of poorly armed and trained Iraqi troops, many of whom were drafted. There was a sense the wrong people were dying, something that would not help rebuild Iraq and that would hurt America's image. (I voiced my sense that we were appearing to "pile on," an analogy drawn from football when tacklers hit an opposing player already down on the ground.) There was also the strategic rationale: we wanted an Iraq still strong enough to offset the latent desire of Iran to bid for regional primacy. And there was a desire to avoid any more American casualties.

What also colored the thinking in the room was the information (incorrect, as it turned out) that the coalition forces had essentially trapped several of the better-trained and equipped Iraqi Republican Guard divisions, who would be forced to leave their equipment behind or risk being attacked. What Clausewitz termed the "fog of war" was in effect that day. The cuteness of stopping at one hundred hours may have affected the timing by a few hours but not more. My own sense at the time (it was actually my assumption up to that morning) was that we could and should carry on for one or two more days. I believe we could have done so without endangering either the coalition or our image, and if we had done so, could have weakened Iraqi forces more than we did and further humiliated Saddam. Whether all this would have changed his ability to weather the failure to hold Kuwait and the subsequent rebellions is simply unknown. I did not argue this because there was no way to be confident of the consequences of delay and because of the decision had been essentially made by the time I arrived in the Oval Office.

The truth is there was no interest in going to Baghdad. I do not recall any dissent on this point. The consensus was that we would lose more troops in such an operation than we had lost up to that point. We had also just had the frustrating experience of going after Manuel Noriega in Panama; searching modern cities for individuals is dangerous and difficult work. We would have become an occupying force in a hostile land with no exit strategy. Such operations did not play to the advantage of American forces, which did best in open battlefields where mobility and technology and advanced arms could all be brought to bear in an integrated fashion. A march to Baghdad would have gone beyond the terms of relevant U.N. Security Council and congressional resolutions, all of which posed not so much legal considerations as political ones. Bush felt he had made a deal with the rest of the world and he didn't want to break it and in the process diminish trust in American commitments. He and we feared that the coalition would shatter if we pressed our objectives beyond what we had stated at the outset. There was also the belief that what had been accomplished would create an environment in which Saddam was unlikely to survive. The shared prediction was that the defeated Iraqi military would turn on him in retribution for this large-scale recklessness. (The previous act of grand recklessness was the decision a decade earlier to make war on Iran.) This prediction also provided a justification for not expressly requiring Saddam's removal as a precondition for ending the war even though he torched Kuwait's oil wells—an act that crossed a U.S. red line and was meant to trigger actions designed to bring about his ouster.

The president spoke to the American people from the Oval Office that same evening, February 27. The opening sentences were spare and succinct. "Kuwait is liberated. Iraq's army is defeated. Our military objectives are met. Kuwait is once more in the hands of Kuwaitis, in control of their own destiny." A week later, he spoke about postwar plans before a special joint session of Congress. There would be a larger American military presence in a part of the world deemed vital, vigilant efforts to deny Iraq weapons of mass destruction, and a new round of Middle East peacemaking. Seven months later, this last pledge would culminate in Madrid, where Israelis and Arabs came together for the first time in their history to discuss peace, face-to-face.

The results of the war were impressive and then some by any measure. Kuwait had in fact been liberated and restored to its rulers and people. Iraq's armed forces were routed. That all this was accomplished in some six weeks of combat at relatively little cost was extraordinary. It was all a testament to the skill of American servicemen and women and to their ability to take advantage of intelligence and technology.

What was avoided was Iraqi primacy over the oil- and gas-rich Middle East. An Iraq in possession of all of Kuwait's financial and mineral resources would have become not just *a* but *the* dominant local power. (Together, Iraq and Kuwait amount to some 20 percent of world reserves.) Iraq would not have needed to be in physical control of its neighbors' territory or resources in order to have been in a position to have exercised tremendous influence over them. Iraq would have been far more powerful, and the demonstration of what happened to Kuwait when it did not do what Iraq wanted would have been lost on no one. Iraq, we now know, also would have gained nuclear weapons within years.

It is important, too, to underscore what was accomplished indirectly. "International community" is a phrase commonly invoked when in reality there is little or no community of thought or action. Yet in this instance there was both. Support was near universal for the principle that military force is not to be used to change borders or, in this case, to eliminate countries. This is the fundamental rule of international order. That this rule was upheld at the end of one historical era and the dawn of another was particularly significant, since it set an important precedent. It is impossible to know what other countries would have acted aggressively had Iraq been allowed to get away with its conquest of Kuwait, but odds are appeasement of Saddam would have sent a powerful message that aggression pays. Most likely aggression would have been replicated elsewhere.

At the same time, it was and is important to take note of what was not accomplished, some longer-term costs, and the limits to the Iraq success. There is the obvious fact that Saddam managed to hang on to power as well as the reality that much of Iraq's weapons of mass destruction capacity, including three different uranium enrichment programs, survived the war. There were the direct economic and military costs of stationing troops and aircraft in the region to enforce no-fly zones over Iraq that were imposed to limit Saddam's ability to repress his own people. Forces were also kept in the region to protect Kuwait and Saudi Arabia from any new Iraqi aggression. Foreign forces in Saudi Arabia were one of the reasons Osama bin Laden gave for al-Qaida's existence, that is, to rid the country of non-Muslim people.

One should not exaggerate the degree of "international community" that emerged from the war. Agreement on one principle of international relations, in this case, the right of self-defense, should not be confused with a common definition of what constituted order. Subsequent years and developments have demonstrated that consensus on preventing genocide or stopping nuclear proliferation or thwarting terrorism or protectionism or climate change is thin. The first Iraq war constituted an important moment in world history, but not a transformation.

On balance, though, the benefits far exceeded the costs. Still, there was precious little time to reflect on the import of what we had won, much less to take satisfaction in it, given developments on the ground

within Iraq. As early as the first day of March we received word of
an uprising—an intifada, the Arabic word for "casting off"—in the
south of Iraq dominated by the Shia, a Muslim sect that had long
been repressed by Saddam but that at a minimum constituted a plu-
rality and probably a majority of all Iraqis. The question was what
if anything we would do. There was a strong disposition not to get
involved. Powell and other senior military leaders stressed that U.S.
intervention, which would have involved trying to coordinate military operations with disparate groups of Iraqis against other Iraqis,
promised to be an operational nightmare. Telling the good guys from
the bad—identifying friend from foe, in military parlance—would
be all but impossible. There was also deep concern about the political goals and orientation of Iraq's Shia. What worried me and others
was Iran's actual and potential sway.

A few days later, in early March, another intifada broke out in
the north of Iraq between the Kurds and Sunni-dominated, Iraqi
government forces. Again, there was no U.S. military response. Intervention in the north on behalf of the Kurds, who wanted nothing so
much as their own independent country, would have not just alienated Turkey but also triggered a war with it, since Kurdish independence was unacceptable to the Turks, who feared it would lead to
the breakup of their own country given the attraction an independent "Kurdistan" would hold for Turkey's sizable Kurdish minority.
We feared, too, that events could lead to Iraq's breakup, causing a
humanitarian catastrophe and fighting that would not just involve
Iraq's multiple factions but draw in its neighbors as well.

It was in between these two outbreaks that a meeting was hastily
arranged between the coalition military leadership and their Iraqi
military counterparts at the airfield near the Iraqi city of Safwan, located just north of the Kuwaiti border. Schwarzkopf was determined
to avoid the twin extremes of either humiliating the Iraqis or being

overly nice, explicitly telling Prince Khalid, the commander of Saudi Arabia's armed forces, "Please, none of this 'Arab brother' business when the Iraqis arrive. No embracing or kissing each other on both cheeks." The Safwan meeting was seen mostly as dealing with minor, technical issues, so much so that the U.S. military drafted its own instructions. Some have suggested that the United States should have insisted that Saddam represent Iraq at Safwan, something that might have weakened him further. There was a danger, though, that he could have turned the tables on us and used it to his advantage. We also thought that he was already so weakened that further humiliation was unnecessary. And it wasn't clear what we would do if he refused to come, as continuing military operations was a nonstarter.

A lot has also been said and written about why the United States did not do more to stop Saddam's crackdowns in the south and north of Iraq. Many point to Schwarzkopf's decision at Safwan to allow the Iraqis to resume helicopter flights for administrative purposes such as supplying troops—only to have the Iraqis use helicopters instead to crush the rebellions. It is true that the U.S. military representatives made this decision, but it is not fair to hold them responsible for what ensued. This was no time to be reluctant to overrule the commander in the field. Those around the president could and arguably should have argued to rescind this permission, and the president could have so ordered. But doing so would not have solved the problem. We then would have faced the need to impose the decision or to act with force if and when the Iraqis turned to other weapons to defeat those in opposition to the government. There was no reason to believe only helicopters would prove decisive. Schwarzkopf makes just this point: "[G]rounding the Iraqi helicopter gunships would have had little impact. The tanks and artillery of the twenty-four Iraqi divisions that never entered the Kuwaiti war zone were having a far more devastating effect on the insurgents." Those of us in Washington viewed reversing the helicopter decision as starting down a slippery and dangerous slope that would have risked a quagmire.

Still, it must be said that U.S. policy making during this period was ragged. There is simply no other word for it. There was a natural and perhaps understandable but no less unfortunate loss of focus and letting up after seven months of nonstop crisis. There had been a good deal of planning for the postwar period, but not for internal Iraq scenarios such as we were seeing, given the policy decision that the international coalition and the United States in particular would not become an occupying power or try to recast the internal politics of a defeated Iraq. Again, the operating assumption was that the disenchanted Iraqi military, still the most powerful force in the country, would likely oust Saddam and find someone else to lead Iraq in the "Arab way," that is, an authoritarian, Sunni-dominated state, but one without Saddam's excesses, which had led to two wars in the region in a decade and severe repression at home. Like most assumptions, this was based not on hard evidence but on a mixture of assessment and prediction—gut feelings, or "gut-int" in intelligence lingo.

It didn't help matters that by mid-March the principals and many of their deputies had scattered. Secretary Baker went off to the Middle East and Persian Gulf, largely to focus on the Arab-Israeli peace process. I tagged along with the president as he went to Ottawa, Martinique, and finally Bermuda to meet with his Canadian, French, and British counterparts to discuss postwar policy. Not much was noteworthy. What I recall was a boring dinner in Canada in which the president and Prime Minister Brian Mulroney said relatively little while the latter's foreign minister spoke at great length; Mitterrand wearing a mustard-colored suit and expressing a desire that we find a way to resume efforts toward Middle East peace and involve the PLO in the effort; and an initial meeting with John Major, who was intelligent but who in style could hardly be more unlike his forceful predecessor.

Before the rebellions took some of the glow off what had been accomplished, the president had the opportunity on March 6 to address a special joint session of Congress. I was given the task of drafting the foreign policy side of the talk. In the days running up to the speech, I spent a good deal of time with John Sununu and David Demarest working on what the president would say. Since I was in the room, I decided to go beyond my brief and suggest the president take the opportunity to build on his foreign policy accomplishments and reputation and suggest he would do the same for the country. I pushed the notion of a "new domestic order" or, better yet, "Operation Domestic Storm." Clearly on a roll, I even put forward the idea of a national security tax that would introduce one cent of gasoline tax for every two cents the price dropped below some benchmark. My goal was to reduce both U.S. consumption of oil and the deficit. Sununu's reaction was to the effect that I might know something about the Middle East, but I didn't know jack about domestic politics: everything I was suggesting could be taken as evidence that the status quo was less than sound. Proof of how persuasive I was can be found in the text of the president's March 6 speech, which included nothing along any of these lines, although just about all I'd written on the foreign policy side survived.

It was also during March that word came in early one afternoon from our embassy in Riyadh that the Saudis were asking the president to send a trusted envoy. When we said yes in principle, they came back making it clear that King Fahd very much wanted to meet with the envoy as soon as could be arranged—right away if possible—to discuss a critical, sensitive matter. Brent was the obvious person to lead a discreet mission. By 4 P.M. the president decided that Brent should go. Brent asked me to accompany him. I called Susan to tell her I would not make it home for dinner. This was hardly news, so she barely reacted. I then said I would not be home for a day or two, couldn't tell her where I was going, but asked her to pack a suitcase and bring it to the office. I was in good shape except for her forgetting to include socks. By 7 P.M., Brent, his executive assistant, Flo, and I were on our way to Andrews. We flew all night, arrived early Wednesday evening local time, showered, went to the palace, waited, and around midnight got ushered into a room. Seated there were just the king and his vice chief of protocol, who was also the translator. The king began by explaining the delay, attributing it to the need to meet with people to discuss various proposed reforms of the law. What soon became apparent, however, was his concern with reports of what the United States and others planned to do in Kuwait. He had heard calls that the Sabah monarchy in Kuwait, whom we had just restored to power, be set aside; the king was clearly worried that such developments in his neighbor could create both precedents and instability that could affect conditions within the Saudi kingdom. His basic message was that outsiders, no matter how well intentioned, should not take it upon themselves to determine the sequence and pace of political reform in traditional countries such as Kuwait and Saudi Arabia.

Brent responded by pointing out that a major goal of the war had been to restore Kuwait's legitimate government, and that it was not our intention to remake Kuwait or any other country. Once reassured, the king turned to other subjects, most notably the Palestinian issue. He noted that Israel was a fact and a permanent part of the landscape. He didn't much care how the problem was solved—Saudi sympathy for the Palestinians, many of whom had been overtly sympathetic to Saddam, was at an all-time low—just that it was taken care of. (Alas, he had no ideas about how to accomplish this feat.) On Iraq, the king made clear his hope that Saddam would not survive, a desire we made clear that we shared. That was about it. We had traveled halfway around the world for a ninety-minute meeting that to my mind had not accomplished much except to put the king's mind at rest that we were not closet revolutionaries. Other than exhaustion, the only other emotion I felt was some discomfort that Brent had been a bit too reassuring; I believed these traditional societies needed to evolve lest they become unstable and the only alternative to dreary and often corrupt authoritarianism becomes those radicalized in mosques. There would be occasion to explore and push this reform agenda down the road; debating it in front of the king before we ourselves had thought it through seemed like a particularly bad idea for all concerned. So I held back, although I voiced the view to a skeptical Scowcroft on the way back that we needed to introduce a reform element into our policy.

Much of March and April played out against the backdrop of the deteriorating situation on the ground in Iraq. We were getting hammered in the press, with comparisons drawn to both 1956 (when the Eisenhower administration was blamed for inspiring the Hungarian uprising, only to do nothing about it when it materialized) and 1961 (when the Kennedy administration organized and then halfheartedly backed the ill-fated attempt to overthrow Castro that ended up in disaster at the Bay of Pigs). The comparisons were badly overdrawn. Not all historical comparisons are apt. The rebellions in Iraq were not organized or coordinated or funded in any way by the United States. Some people may have expected that the United States would assist them, but no word had been passed or commitment given. The president's calls for the Iraqi people to overthrow Saddam were mostly made in the context of avoiding coalition military activity—in other words, if you oust Saddam, you will escape getting attacked by the international community when it moves to implement the relevant Security Council resolutions.

To me, the better parallel was Korea. More specifically, what came to mind was the decision to march north of the 38th parallel. General Douglas MacArthur pushed for and Truman signed off on expanded U.S. war objectives in the flush of tactical success following his inspired landing at Inchon. He had liberated all of the South and restored the status quo ante; not content to leave it at that, he continued north. Neither China nor the Soviet Union was prepared to allow the entire country to be in the American orbit. Hundreds of thousands of Chinese "volunteers" joined with the North Koreans to push back. Three years and thirty thousand American lives later, the United States accepted an armistice based on a division of Korea at the same 38th parallel. This was a classic case of mission creep— or, more accurately, mission leap—with an immense human, military, economic, and diplomatic cost. I had taught, with Professor Ernest May, a course at the Kennedy School based on the wonderful book May had co-authored with Richard Neustadt on the use and misuse of history for decision makers. Of course there were differences between the Korea of 1951 and the Iraq of 1991, but so too were there parallels to be seen and lessons to be drawn. Yes, it was tempting to allow U.S. objectives to change from liberating Kuwait to liberating Iraq, especially given how well the war had gone to that point. But as is often the case in life, temptation is best resisted.

This was not an argument for a hands-off stance, as the humanitarian situation in the north of Iraq was bad and getting worse by the hour. Bob Gates phoned me at home late one evening. We were both increasingly uncomfortable with the images and the reality of what was taking place. We talked about a range of possible responses, and the one that made the most sense to us both at that point was an airdrop of food. At least in principle, this held out the possibility of helping Iraqi civilians without requiring a new and major U.S. military intervention. We also discussed how we would try to keep the Iraqi military out of the area and what we would do if they in fact did interfere. The next morning we raised the idea with Brent, who was comfortable with the plan so long as it did not represent renewed military engagement. I quickly typed out a paper describing what we would do and a statement for a president who was anxious to go public with the latest demonstration that the United States was not standing helplessly by. We'd done a good deal of work in a matter of hours. In fact, we'd changed policy more that day than we had in the preceding five weeks. But I couldn't shake the sinking feeling that we were a day late and a dollar short.

The humanitarian crisis constituted but one dimension of postwar policy at this juncture. A second was to jump-start a Middle East peace process, something that had been put on hold for a year given the degree to which everyone was distracted and lest it appear we were somehow rewarding Saddam for what he had done to Kuwait. It was also important that Palestinians, many of whom were openly supportive of Saddam, realize that they had once again chosen incorrectly and that there would be no shortcuts to the process of arriving at a Palestinian state. We also had a lot of work to do with the Israeli government of Yitzhak Shamir, which was no more flexible on matters of peace after the war than it had been before. Jim Baker was anxious to get started, but slowing him down was the reality that he and Brent did not agree on the details of a new U.S. approach. Making matters more complicated was that none of us had much confidence in any approach given Palestinian and Israeli politics alike. Still, Baker persuaded all of us and the president that he should visit the region. Such a visit would be well received by the Arab governments, whose ability to associate themselves with the United States depended in part on the perception in the region that we were actively promoting a resolution of the Israeli-Palestinian conflict. Consultations would also help determine how the war might have changed prospects for negotiation. Sometimes it is better to try and come up short than not to try at all. This takes away the argument that "if only" you had done something things would have been better. It also can create new dynamics that set the stage for another initiative that might actually fare better. This was one of those times.

Yet a third aspect of the postwar policy was to determine what to do vis-à-vis Iraq and its government. On the security side, the centerpiece was U.N. Security Council Resolution 687, passed on April 3, 1991. It is an extraordinary document, the mother of all resolutions as Saddam might have put it, one that provided a basis for a long-term policy toward Iraq. It called for the elimination of all of Iraq's weapons of mass destruction and most of its missile programs, intrusive international inspections, a ban on military imports, a secure and recognized border between Iraq and Kuwait, and compensation for Kuwait and others. It seemed to take care of most of our remaining problems but one, namely, the fact that Saddam remained ensconced. There was no international support for a policy based on bringing about his removal. Leaders of most governments believe it is not the business of outsiders to decide who should rule another country and how they should rule it. Moreover, there was no desire on our part to inflict a Versailles-like vindictive peace on Iraq in an effort to persuade Iraqis to oust him. It was not just that we were unconvinced such an approach would succeed in near-totalitarian Iraq. We also needed Iraq to balance Iran and we did not want it to break apart or become a terrorist sanctuary or regional battleground. Sanctions were geared to getting Saddam to meet the terms of the resolution, not to bring about his removal or to make the people of Iraq suffer.

But it was the humanitarian crisis that captured most of our attention. Iraq was ordered not to fly any aircraft above the 36th parallel, and food was dropped from the air by coalition aircraft. It quickly became clear that this response was inadequate. I was actually away for the week following the decision to implement an airdrop, taking my long-postponed honeymoon. But I couldn't get away from the issue, as there were big protests in Paris calling for the world to do more to help Iraqi refugees. I also continued to weigh in my mind the correctness of our policy. I know that once you decide something it is important to let go and move on, but it is difficult to do so when the decision has costly consequences. Still, all the soul-searching did not change where I came out. The danger of quagmire had been real. The Kurds and Shia gambled that a weakened Saddam could not survive and they were proved wrong when he and the Iraqi army crushed what was viewed as a challenge to the state. What added to the frustration is that all this left Saddam far stronger at home than he deserved to be.

I returned to Washington more determined than ever that we do more, and found Brent and Bob in a similar place. The images on television were devastating. The so-called CNN effect is real; it does create pressures on policy makers when the cameras can record a crisis. We met that Monday morning and agreed on establishing some sort of protected encampments in the north. We had all been reluctant to take this step out of concern that we could create a permanent refugee population or long-term U.S. troop presence. We worried that one day we could find ourselves enmeshed in an Iraqi civil war. But these concerns had been not just overtaken but overwhelmed by events. Bob and I took the proposal to the small group, which quickly signed off. I wrote talking points for the president to use over the phone with British prime minister John Major, French president François Mitterrand, Turkish president Turgut Ozal, and U.N. secretary-general Javier Perez de Cuellar. Ozal was relieved to hear from the president; he had been pleading that we do more to stem the flow of refugees toward the Turkish border. It was not just the scale of the human crush, but Ozal like all Turks was nervous over anything that could reinforce a sense of Kurdish identity and nationhood, something that would appeal to Turkey's own Kurdish minority. The bottom line was that after ten days of airdrops, we essentially turned to the policy we had resisted up to that point, one of creating a safe haven for the Kurds. U.S. ground forces were sent back in—Operation Provide Comfort—but in limited number and for a limited purpose. I wrote a statement for the president to use at 6 P.M. that night. It was not his best performance—he was tired and a bit defensive—but it was better than what he had done a few days before, when he seemed overly intent on emphasizing what we would not do rather than explaining what we were doing.

The creation of the safe havens and no-fly zones in the south as well as the north of Iraq gradually turned things around. Iraqis moved back from the border. Progress in the theater allowed people in Washington to get distracted, in this instance by Bob Woodward's latest inside account of Washington decision making and by Chief of Staff John Sununu's frequent flying of U.S. government planes. It was also a time when many of the critics came out of the woodwork, rehearsing the claims that we missed warnings of war, that we stopped the war too soon, that we never should have let the Iraqis fly helicopters, that we missed the chance to oust Saddam. That some of these criticisms came from people who opposed the war only added to the enjoyment. As for those of us in the administration, there was a shift in focus to other issues. For me, it meant much more focus on the Arab-Israeli front, both to persuade people to attend a peace conference and to work out terms with the Israelis by which we would offer loan guarantees to help them provide housing and other assistance to Jews coming to Israel from Russia. Both tasks proved difficult in the extreme.

On the conference, the question increasingly came down to who would represent the Palestinians, and how we could come up with Palestinians who were not formally part of the PLO (lest Israelis refuse to meet with them) but who were acceptable to the PLO (lest Palestinians refuse to empower them). Complicating matters even more was the desire for assurances on the part of every would-be participant in a conference and peace process. The Palestinians and the Syrians wanted to know where the train was heading before they got on board. The Israelis for their part wanted to know where the train was *not* heading before they would board. The result was months of drafting and redrafting letters of invitation that were in effect letters of assurance to the potential attendees. It also required no fewer than eight trips by Jim Baker to the region to cajole the reluctant parties to accept the U.S. invitation and then to actually show up. The trick was in providing written and verbal assurances that would be enticing enough to get parties to attend but that if and when made public did not appear to be inconsistent.

On the loan guarantees, the question was how we could provide assistance without directly or indirectly subsidizing Israeli construction and expansion of settlements in the occupied territories, something that worked against the already modest prospects for peace given that it consumed Palestinian land and strengthened a lobby within Israel sure to oppose any exchange of territory for peace. Our preference was to delay the loan guarantee matter so that it did not complicate or, worse yet, undermine our already troubled attempts to bring about a peace conference.

The efforts to persuade Israel to postpone consideration of the guarantees failed. My sense is that the Israelis and their friends on Capitol Hill thought they had enough votes to create a fait accompli and essentially force the administration to back down and provide loan guarantees. We thought going ahead would encourage further Israeli settlement activity and undermine U.S. credibility, thereby all but destroying prospects for a peace conference that fall. It was hard to exaggerate how emotional it all was. For us it was not a question of Jewish emigration to Israel, which we endorsed and in many instances had helped bring about, but rather the use of public funds and subsidies to encourage their moving to the occupied territories to live in settlements. In various meetings with American Jewish leaders, we made clear that the president would go public with his and our opposition to the guarantees if there was no delay. There wasn't any, so on September 12, the president did just that, and then some, in the White House briefing room. The points I'd prepared with Brent and Larry Eagleburger were firm, and the president added to the message when, in answering a question, he described himself as "one lonely little guy" up against "some powerful political forces," that is, the Jewish lobby. I winced. On the way out of the room, I told the president and Brent that the language the president used would trigger alarm bells. They were genuinely surprised. But it did. Jewish leaders were taken aback, and the president, who did not have a prejudiced bone in his body, was hurt that they thought he was speaking in some anti-Semitic code. It helped cement the impression that the administration was unfriendly to Israel and Jewish causes, although the record—bringing about the Madrid peace conference, getting the "Zionism as Racism" resolution repealed in the U.N. General Assembly, facilitating the exodus of Jews from Russia and Ethiopia, approving large flows of aid, defeating Saddam Hussein—was very good for Israel. Tone matters at times as much as substance, and the administration paid a price for the perception that it was unsympathetic. In the end the loan guarantees were delayed, and the peace conference went forward. Interestingly, the critical breakthrough was the decision by Hafiz al-Assad, the strongman of Syria, to accept the U.S. invitation to Madrid. It was simply impossible for an Israeli leader to say no to an invitation to attend a peace conference and the chance the meet face-to-face with Arab leaders after decades of demanding just that.

I was tasked with writing the president's speech for the opening session. Both Brent and Jim Baker signed off on the draft, but then the speechwriters got ahold of what I had done and rewrote it. They did a good deal more than change "happy" to "glad," and in so doing altered some of the content and undermined much of the potential impact of the address. I lost my temper and argued that in the

Middle East the specific choice of words could matter a great deal. I persuaded Brent to make them go back to the original draft and work from it. It was worth fighting for, although it didn't do much for my relationship with the speechwriting shop. The final version sought to set a tone and lay out a vision (but not a blueprint) for what would follow, stressing that for any peace process to succeed it must provide security for Israelis and fairness for Palestinians.

The conference was otherwise both monumental and unexceptional. Like the proverbial elephant that dances, what mattered was not how well it went but that it went. Prime Minister Shamir's decision to attend, even though we had urged all governments to send their foreign ministers, added some spice, as did the angry speech by the Syrian foreign minister. Gorbachev was tired and distracted and looked like the soon-to-be-out-of-office person he in fact was. The chemistry in the various side meetings could hardly have been worse. The conference began in confusion over the entrances of Bush and Gorbachev, and ended in confusion with a debate over whether the conference was closed or adjourned. It was most significant for having ended the taboo of face-to-face meetings in a region more familiar with conflict than negotiation. There was a sense of some potential for progress between Israelis and Palestinians, who knew one another well, possibly too well. The Syrians, who tried as they might to ruin things for everyone, could not. And the Soviet era in the Middle East was over. The United States alone as an outsider was in a position to make a difference. But the real question was whether any outsider could do all that much. Both the Israelis and the Syrians had the ability to make peace but appeared to lack the will; the Palestinians, or at least those who lived in the occupied territories rather than Tunis, for their part appeared to have the will but not the ability. "Ripeness is all," wrote Shakespeare in *King Lear*, and despite the breakthrough that was Madrid, the Middle East did not appear ripe for peace.

Iraq did not fade entirely by any means. Even if the humanitarian situation had stabilized, the strategic situation had not. What was emerging was a consistent pattern of "cheat and retreat." Iraqi authorities would one way or another frustrate the work of the international inspectors supposedly empowered to discover and root out all weapons of mass destruction. The principal question for us was how to respond in a manner that would get us the cooperation we wanted and possibly shake Saddam's power base but not isolate us more than Iraq in the eyes of the world. The only tool left was military force, since there was little if anything left to sanction.

A lingering issue was what if anything could be done to weaken Saddam's hold on power. We examined any number of possibilities, from strengthening one or another opposition group to promoting coups from within the army, but nothing looked likely to succeed. Congress was pushing us to do more. On one occasion late in 1991, Brent and I went up to the Hill for an informal meeting with the members of the House Intelligence Committee. We walked them through our reason for not wanting to do more to assist exile groups lest we create a scenario in which comparisons to the Bay of Pigs would not be far-fetched. What I remember most of all from the meeting was the prediction of Steve Solarz, one of the few Democratic congressmen to actively support the decision to go to war. "I can see a year from now that it is more likely that Saddam Hussein will be in power and George Bush out of power than vice versa."

Needless to say, this was not a future we sought, and although the president's reelection was not something I could directly affect, doing something about Saddam was part of my job description. The policy had come to resemble nothing so much as classic containment in its emphasis on limiting Iraq's capability and reach and in its secondary interest in fostering regime change. The consensus was that in the wake of the postwar uprisings, the best and perhaps only way to oust Saddam was through a coup, most likely carried out by some individual or small group from within the Iraqi army. The CIA was spending time thinking about what could be done to stimulate opposition, and the JCS was thinking about what it might be able to do if we got a call in the middle of the night letting us know that something was under way and asking for our support. Gone was the notion of basing opposition to Saddam on either the Kurds or the Shia. Sanctions were part of the policy as well, the idea being that they would help create an internal environment that would encourage challenges to the regime. My own sense was that we would be extraordinarily lucky if such a challenge materialized and succeeded. It would also present us with some potentially messy scenarios and choices. I recall discussing just this over lunch in February 1992 with Richard Helms, the former CIA chief who had lost none of his patrician bearing as he'd gotten older. Most of the conversation was about Iran, which he thought was worth trying to engage diplomatically, as did I, although neither of us was sure that there were in fact authoritative Iranians willing and able to engage with us. Toward the end of the meal, though, he raised the subject of Iraq. Reports had surfaced in the press that we were trying to remove Saddam. I can still recall the warning the experienced intelligence professional gave to me. "I've spent most of my life trying to overthrow governments and I hope you guys know what you'll put in Saddam's place." It was an exchange I have played over in my mind many times since.

For all this activity and speculation, regime change remained a long shot at best. A National Intelligence Estimate was actually published in 1992 with the title "Saddam Husayn: Likely to Hang On." Much more of our focus stayed on how to ensure Iraq's compliance with Security Council Resolution 687 and with the inspections effort. It was proving difficult to come up with a consensus plan on how to deal with the never-ending pattern of "cheat and retreat." Questions that never seemed to get answered included how long we should wait before acting when the Iraqis resisted complying; what set of targets we should attack; what forces we should use; and whether we should involve others. We had similar questions about how to respond to renewed repression of Iraq's Shia population in contravention of U.N. Security Council Resolution 688, which demanded that Iraq end all internal repression and established a basis for the international community to intervene to protect Iraq's population from its government. There was also growing evidence of sanctions circumvention by the Jordanians and others.

Much of this came to a head in a strange episode in August 1992. It took place on the eve of the Republican convention in Houston. Once again there was a standoff between Iraqi officials and the weapons inspectors. Brent and I met with the president and others. There was a general disposition to act militarily, destroying targets of value to the Iraqi government so that it would think twice before again interfering with U.N. inspections. But there was also a concern that strong action on our part would lead to the accusation that the president acted simply to appear strong going into the convention. Bush was reluctant to act because of this perception even though he was inclined to act on the merits.

We were also trying to act in a manner that did not risk the welfare of the inspectors or in any way make it look as though the United Nations was a party to our decision making. We wanted to avoid doing anything that might detract from the legitimacy of the inspection effort. If we did use force, it would be pursuant to existing resolutions and authorities rather than as the result of a direct authorization to act in this circumstance. I got a call from Patrick Tyler, the Pentagon correspondent of the *New York Times*, who had learned that we were preparing to use force. I pleaded with him not to go with the story; I knew that if he printed it the U.N. would get spooked and would back off the challenge inspection. I called his boss, Washington bureau chief Howell Raines, and asked him not to go with the story. (During the course of my career in government, I had made a few such requests of journalists and usually prevailed once I explained why.) Raines refused, saying Tyler had it from a source in the Pentagon that the White House wanted to approve the attack "to help get the President re-elected." I said this was outrageous, and that anyone in a position to know the president's thinking would also know this was as far from the truth as one could get. To describe the conversation as heated would not do it justice. But no argument of mine made a difference. I thought what Tyler, Raines, and the *Times* did was wrong, both in printing the story (which destroyed the element of surprise, making it impossible to mount the military action) and in how it described what was motivating the president. Just because someone in government says something to a reporter does not make the official a credible source. This was bad journalism and bad judgment alike.

We couldn't and didn't attack after the story appeared. In some ways, this set the tone of the last six months of the administration. There were periodic uses of relatively discrete bombing raids against Iraqi targets, right up to the final days of the Bush 41 presidency in January 1993. Each time there was a drill of challenge inspections, a standoff, winding up the diplomatic and military response, talking to Congress and other governments, carrying out the limited attack, and talking to the media. It was not just exhausting, it was costly, as we were depleting our reservoir of international and Arab support for, or at least tolerance of, a demanding policy toward Saddam and getting very little for it. At the same time, other aspects of the policy appeared to be working. Indeed, the Bush presidency ended with the basic elements of a long-term policy built to contain Saddam in place: broad-based economic, political, and military sanctions designed to keep Iraq weak and to penalize Saddam for not complying fully with all international mandates; large humanitarian zones created in Iraq's north and south and patrolled by U.S. and coalition aircraft so that Iraqi citizens could lead relatively normal lives; and regular international inspections of suspected WMD sites to make it difficult if not impossible for Saddam to maintain or build proscribed weapons.

There was, however, surprising progress—surprising after all that had gone on—in the Middle East and U.S.-Israel relations. The decisive development came in July 1992 when Yitzhak Rabin replaced Yitzhak Shamir as prime minister of Israel. History is not some inexorable or impersonal flow of events. Ideas matter. People matter. Rabin made a big difference. I had known Rabin for some time in his various government posts. One image I have of him is standing alone at a reception at the home of the Israeli ambassador in Washington nursing a scotch. What was distinctive was the awkwardness for a politician and the fact that he drank hard liquor, something few Israelis in my experience did. I remember mildly chastising him for his impolitic language, referring to recent comments that he would break the bones of Palestinian protesters who threatened or hurt Israeli soldiers or civilians as part of the intifada. He looked first at his glass, then at me, and smiled. "So, Richard. What would you have preferred? That we shoot and kill them?"

Rabin flew over in August for a meeting with the president. We moved it to Kennebunkport to stress the new era in U.S.-Israeli ties and to ease any lingering tension. There were some difficult moments in the negotiation over the terms by which we would extend the loan guarantees, but the outcome was never in doubt. I actually have a stronger recollection of the tennis we played that weekend. Rabin was my doubles partner. He was just awful, hitting shot after shot into the net. After each attempt, he'd turn to me and say "Sorry" in his raspy voice. Finally I couldn't take it anymore. "Mr. Prime Minister, one of the few benefits of your job is that you don't have to apologize every time you miss a shot." Off the court, Rabin was in his element. He understood that he needed to get Israel's relationship with its most important partner back on the rails, and he would do all he could to make that happen. Bush also wanted to point to progress in this relationship and to put behind him the ill feelings of the past few years as we neared the fall election. Rabin's assassination several years later was a true turning point. He was the one Israeli leader of his time who was willing to take real risks for peace and who could persuade a majority of his fellow citizens to support such compromise.

In the end, settling the loan guarantee issue and restoring U.S.-Israeli relations to a relatively even keel were not enough. Nor were the other truly impressive foreign policy achievements of the Bush presidency, including the deft handling of the end of the Cold War and bringing a unified Germany into NATO, the liberation of Kuwait, and the Madrid peace conference. Bush found himself on the defensive, mostly on the charge that he had focused on foreign policy to the detriment of domestic policy and above all the economy. The reaction of the president and those around him was to lean away from foreign policy—avoiding getting involved in Bosnia, providing inadequate support for Boris Yeltsin's Russia—rather than to make the case for what had been accomplished at home. Making matters worse was the perception that the administration had grown tired and distracted. In twenty months, from the March 1991 end of the first Iraq war until November 1992, George Bush went from unprecedented popularity to electoral defeat. Representative Solarz's prediction, that Saddam Hussein would outlast the man who defeated him in Kuwait, proved true.

5. THE CLINTON INTERREGNUM

IRAQ POLICY DID not figure prominently in the 1992 campaign in which Bill Clinton defeated George H. W. Bush. It was difficult for Bush to exploit all that he had done to liberate Kuwait, in part because of the messy aftermath to the war, even more because emphasis on the war and foreign policy only served to highlight the perception that Bush was a one-dimensional president out of touch with domestic concerns. It was also an awkward issue for the Democratic candidate, given his own equivocal posture toward the war and the need to use force in response to the Iraqi invasion and occupation: "I guess I would have voted for the majority if it was a close vote. But I agree with the arguments the minority made." Senator Gore, the Democratic vice presidential candidate, tried to make hay out of his long-standing charges that the Reagan and Bush administrations had created the very dragon they then had to slay, but failed to gain much traction, in large part, I would like to believe, because he was flat-out wrong.

Part of the reason Iraq didn't receive all that much focus during the election campaign was that by 1992 the situation there had settled down into an increasingly familiar and unthreatening status quo. Iraq had become a country of limited sovereignty. International

inspectors enjoyed considerable access to sites suspected of involvement with chemical, biological, nuclear, or missile projects. A sanctions regime was in place that constrained what Iraqis could import.
The coalition enforced two large no-fly zones over the north and the
south of the country. To be sure, Saddam Hussein remained in power,
but it appeared his actual reach was confined mostly to greater Baghdad and the Sunni areas in the country's center and west, since the
Kurds in the north in particular enjoyed considerable autonomy.

The one time Iraq gained prominence during the transition was
when Bill Clinton, the president-elect, spoke to Tom Friedman of the
New York Times in January 1993 and suggested that the United
States would not work for Saddam's ouster and that relations could
improve even if he remained in power. "Based on the evidence that
we have, the people of Iraq would be better off if they had a different
leader. But my job is not to pick their rulers for them. I always tell
everybody I'm a Baptist. I believe in deathbed conversions. If he
wants a different relationship with the United States and with the
United Nations, all he has to do is change his behavior."

The momentary sensation caused by these remarks was the exception. Iraq was mostly on the back burner; George H. W. Bush did
not remove Saddam, but he did oust him from Kuwait and place him
in something of a box. (It would have been a very different Clinton
administration if Saddam were still occupying Kuwait or if the
United States were occupying Iraq.) This state of affairs allowed the
incoming Clinton administration to focus its attention and energies
elsewhere. A number of limited military interventions stand out: the
former Yugoslavia, in which it ultimately intervened twice with military force, on behalf of Bosnia and later Kosovo; Somalia, where
the administration inherited a humanitarian mission only to expand
it and then withdraw hurriedly when eighteen servicemen lost their
lives; and Haiti, where after a false start it intervened militarily in an
effort to stem a tide of refugees and do something about mounting

chaos. Diplomatically, the Clinton administration devoted considerable time and effort to expand the membership of NATO to include several members of the former Warsaw Pact. And in their last year, President Clinton and his senior aides were consumed by their attempts, ultimately unsuccessful, to broker a comprehensive peace between Israel and the Palestinians.

Iraq never quite disappeared, though; it is revealing that Madeleine Albright, President Clinton's first ambassador to the United Nations and second secretary of state, titled the chapter in her memoirs devoted to Iraq "Migraine Hussein" and described it as the most persistent headache inherited by the Clinton administration. The first real sign of this lingering problem came in June 1993, just five months after Clinton assumed office, when the new president ordered a cruise missile attack on the Iraqi intelligence headquarters in retaliation for the thwarted attempt by Iraqi agents to assassinate former President Bush when he visited Kuwait that April. The U.S. response, Clinton's first authorization of military force as president and a classic exercise in punitive military action, was a harbinger of things to come: an Iraqi action in contravention of an international norm or commitment followed by a limited use of military force by the United States. Such responses inflicted some cost on the Iraqis but failed to alter their basic behavior. The attack also generated criticism around the region and the world on the grounds that the United States had overreacted and at home that the administration had not done enough.

Just a month before, the Clinton administration had presented its strategic overview of Iraq and the region. The speech was written for National Security Advisor Tony Lake, but at the last minute neither Lake nor his deputy Sandy Berger could make the event. The address was delivered on May 18 by Martin Indyk, my successor on the staff of the National Security Council. The new approach was termed "dual containment" and derived from an assessment that "the current Iraqi and Iranian regimes are both hostile to American interests in the region." Rejecting the notion that U.S. policy would be predicated on each of them balancing the other, Indyk stated that the United States, working with its allies in the region and beyond, would henceforth contain (and balance) both. There was no talk of regime change; an important article the next year by National Security Advisor Lake also embraced containment as the basis of U.S. policy toward Iraq, although it did note that the United States supported the objectives of the Iraqi National Congress, the umbrella organization of Iraqi exiles established in 1992, which was committed to Saddam's ouster.

U.S. policy had come, if not full circle, then a considerable distance in a generation. The Nixon and Carter years were a time of building up both Iran and Saudi Arabia as the twin pillars of U.S. policy, with Iraq seen as little more than a Soviet friend. This was followed by balance of power, in which the United States provided limited support to Iraq to ensure that revolutionary Iran did not come to dominate the region. Now the United States was at odds with the two most powerful local states and sought to contain the influence of both. Not surprisingly, the new policy (or at least the new articulation of policy) came under some criticism, in part because it suggested Iran and Iraq constituted similar challenges when in reality they did not, and because it suggested they could be countered with similar responses, when in reality they could not.

The problem was as much one of nomenclature as anything else. The policies toward the two countries were in fact different. Containment of Iraq was "aggressive" and involved regular applications of military force, while containment of Iran was "active" and predicated on sanctions.

Viewed from a different vantage point, however, U.S. policy looked to be quite familiar. Ever since the Persian Gulf War ended in 1991, U.S. policy toward Iraq could best be described as containment. Containment, the foreign policy doctrine first articulated by George Kennan in 1946 as a guide to U.S. policy toward the Soviet Union, always had two dimensions. On one hand, it was meant to resist the outward expansion (or "encroachment," to use Kennan's term) of a threatening adversary; on the other, it was meant to take advantage of the successful frustration of the adversary and foment internal political change. One can thus view U.S. policy toward the Soviet Union as one of successful containment carried out over some forty years. Soviet reach was limited, and in the end the Soviet regime unraveled as it was unable to meet the basic needs of its population. But it was always clear that the external dimension of policy, that is, the pushing back on Soviet efforts to expand influence beyond its borders, received priority. The reasons for this bias were several. In the nuclear age, it was essential to avoid nuclear war. It was necessary to work with the Soviet regime on certain occasions and in certain situations to limit competition that could otherwise get out of hand. Also, it was impossible to design and implement a policy that could bring about regime change with any degree of certainty as to success or timing. In the end, regime change in the Soviet Union came less because of anything the United States and the West did directly than because of sustained resistance to Soviet expansion and, more importantly, internal developments within the Soviet Union itself.

This history is relevant to any understanding of U.S. policy toward Iraq because the three administrations discussed in this book each contended with the question of how to balance containment with a desire for regime change. As has been seen, the administration of George H. W. Bush clearly emphasized limiting Iraq's reach and power over fomenting regime change within Iraq. As is known and as will be discussed in subsequent chapters, the administration of George W. Bush rejected containment of Iraq and fully embraced regime change, launching a conflict to bring it about. The Clinton administration fell in between, not just chronologically but also when it came to policy, although its actions (as opposed to its rhetoric) over its eight years emphasized the external dimension of containment far more than regime change.

My own role during these eight years was one of observer. I left the White House on January 20, 1993, the last day of George H. W. Bush's presidency, the first day of Bill Clinton's. I spent the eight years of the Clinton presidency at various Washington think tanks. The bulk of the time I headed the foreign policy program at the Brookings Institution. From that perch I wrote or edited several books: on management, the use of military force, the role of economic sanctions, and U.S. foreign policy in the post–Cold War world. My involvement in Iraq and the region was mostly limited to writing the infrequent op-ed, testifying before congressional committees, or participating in one or another documentary or oral history explaining why we didn't march on Baghdad and remove Saddam "when we had the chance."

U.S. policy moved forward on multiple tracks under Bill Clinton's presidency. There was a range of efforts that sought to promote regime change, something that got the CIA and the Clinton administration enmeshed in a disastrous attempt to oust Saddam Hussein by covert means. The coup was uncovered and crushed in March 1995. There was as well a parallel overt initiative to strengthen the Iraqi opposition that lived outside Iraq, although "oppositions" would be a more accurate description given their lack of organization and unity. There was the Iraqi National Congress, the Iraqi National Accord, two major Kurdish organizations, and any number of would-be coup plotters. They were often more intent on weakening and outmaneuvering one another than they were with taking on Saddam, who often had successfully infiltrated many of the organizations and knew what they were up to. In any event, this dimension of U.S. policy was decidedly secondary.

Actual policy focused mostly on containing Saddam and on shoring up the inspections and sanctions regimes. In October 1994, two Republican Guard divisons headed south. It appeared Saddam might be contemplating another attack on Kuwait or at least testing his room for maneuver. The Clinton administration threatened a large preemptive attack, and Iraqi forces quickly pulled back. Even with this reminder of Iraq's potential for aggression, however, international support for sanctions was fading because of fatigue with a policy designed to last months not years, a desire on the part of some governments to take advantage of commercial opportunities, and the widespread belief that sanctions were hurting the Iraqi people more than weakening or influencing the regime. The administration thus favored the passage in April 1995 of what became U.N. Security Council Resolution 986, the "oil-for-food" resolution, which enabled Iraq to sell $1 billion of oil every ninety days, roughly half of which would be available to spend on medicine, food, and basic civilian needs. (The rest of the proceeds would pay for the U.N. inspections effort, relief efforts in the Kurdish-dominated north, and war reparations.) Saddam delayed accepting and implementing the resolution for some eighteen months, apparently believing he would soon get out of the sanctions box without having to accept such stringent controls. Only when it became clear that this would not happen did he change course.

Further evidence of the need to maintain the inspections/sanctions framework came soon enough. In August 1995, General Hussein Kamel Hassan Majid, Saddam's son-in-law and the Iraqi minister of industry, defected to Jordan along with his brother, who was also married to one of Saddam's daughters. Within days, the Iraqi government "discovered" literally planeloads of documents detailing Iraqi proscribed weapons programs and plans to use them. What this trove revealed more than anything was that the inspections regime was largely working. By then, Iraq possessed little in the way of nuclear or chemical or missile capability. Most of what existed was biological, which was destroyed after Hussein Kamel fled and Iraq decided the time had come to cooperate with the United Nations Special Commission (UNSCOM), the U.N. inspections agency. Kamel himself did not benefit from his decision; months later he was killed after being lured back to Iraq on promises of safekeeping that quickly proved to be empty.

What ensued were months and years of Iraqi noncooperation with the inspections effort, the threat or use of limited military force by the United States, and then at most temporary and limited improvement in Iraq's behavior. In September 1996, for example, the United States launched a modest number of cruise missiles against Iraqi military targets after Iraq moved tanks into the northern part of the country. The coalition (essentially down to the United States and Great Britain) also expanded the southern no-fly zone to further reduce Saddam's ability to control his country and harm his people.

Months later, in October 1997, frustration with the lack of full Iraqi cooperation with international inspection efforts led the U.N. Security Council under U.S. prodding to pass Resolution 1134, which essentially reiterated the call on Iraq to comply and cooperate fully with the large number of international dictates. What is noteworthy was that three of the permanent members of the Security Council—China, France, and Russia—abstained, as did Egypt, then also a member of the Security Council for a two-year period. The international coalition was gradually weakening. Saddam no doubt sensed this, as within days he evicted all Americans working for the U.N. Special Commission and demanded that the United States halt all U2 reconnaissance flights over Iraq.

Soon it was back to the by then familiar pattern of "cheat and retreat." The United Nations suspended the monitoring operation. The United States and Britain threatened a retaliatory strike and began to build up military forces in the vicinity. The U.N. further adjusted the oil-for-food program to increase the amount of oil Iraq could sell in an effort to satisfy increasingly unhappy members of the coalition who judged the sanctions to be overly harsh. U.N. secretary-general Kofi Annan negotiated an eleventh-hour agreement with then deputy prime minister Tariq Aziz that allowed for the resumption of the inspections effort, although with certain exceptions for eight so-called presidential sites. The Security Council endorsed this agreement in March 1998. Some six months later, however, Iraq announced that it was ending all cooperation with the inspections effort, only to allow the inspectors to return in early November.

Within weeks, however, it was clear that while the inspectors were back in, they were not being permitted the freedom and access necessary for them to perform their mission. This time, the Clinton administration decided to use military force. What influenced it (other than wanting to react to Saddam's defiance) was the view of the intelligence community, that while the Gulf War had damaged Iraq's WMD capabilities, "enough production components and data remain hidden and enough expertise has been retained or developed to enable Iraq to resume development and production of WMD. . . . [T]he evidence strongly suggests that Baghdad has hidden remnants of its WMD programs and is making every effort to preserve them." Operation Desert Fox lasted for some seventy hours over December 16–19, 1998, and involved cruise missile and bombing attacks against a range of Iraqi military targets and facilities suspected of being tied to missile and illicit nuclear, chemical, and biological programs. While the attack destroyed some of these targets, it in no way changed Iraqi behavior. A week later, Iraq ended (permanently it turned out) all cooperation with the existing U.N. inspections effort.

The word *dilemma* tends to be overused, but the Clinton administration clearly believed it had one on its hands. Madeleine Albright made this clear in her memoir. "We were threatening to use U.S. airpower to attack military targets, but air strikes, no matter how punishing, would not guarantee the return of inspectors to Iraq, nor permanently destroy Baghdad's capacity to produce weapons of mass destruction. No serious consideration was given to actually invading Iraq. The senior President Bush had not invaded when given the chance with hundreds of thousands of troops already in the region during the Gulf War. If President Clinton had proposed doing so in 1998, he would have been accused of being reckless and opposed by friends in the Gulf, our allies, most senior officers in our own military, and leading Republicans."

Was there another option between a limited, punitive use of force on one hand and a costly and controversial invasion on the other? There was: coercive force. Unlike punitive actions, which are designed to inflict pain and cost on an opponent, coercive force involves staging limited attacks designed to sway decision making, normally by destroying some selected targets and threatening to destroy more or other even more valuable sites unless the offending behavior is changed to the degree called for. The advantage of coercive force is its potential to accomplish important ends. Its chief liability is that it leaves the initiative with the side being attacked. At some point the contest boils down to a question of whether the attacking side is better at dishing out punishment or the side being attacked is better at taking a punch. If it is the latter, then the attacker must either admit failure or escalate. The Clinton administration was willing to take this risk in the former Yugoslavia, when it relied on nearly three months of air strikes to bring about a change of behavior by the regime in Belgrade. Although this approach was advocated by some of his aides, the president was not willing to run this risk in Iraq. He might have been right, as it is not clear Saddam would have caved. But the Clinton administration (distracted by scandal at the time—the December 1998 attacks were ended the same day the president was impeached by the House of Representatives) never worked to line up domestic and international support to use force to alter Saddam's behavior. It was well worth a diplomatic exploration, as coercive bombing might have worked. It had the advantage of possessing a rationale that could have been explained, namely, trying to bring Iraq back into compliance with what the world had already demanded of it through the resolution that ended the war. The alternative the United States chose at the time failed to restore the inspections effort and bought the United States considerable ill will even if years later it came out that Saddam was impressed by the intensity of the four days of bombing.

Not surprisingly, as the efforts to shore up the containment framework came up short, greater rhetorical emphasis was placed on the bid to bring about a change of regime in Baghdad. Secretary of State Albright explicitly acknowledged just this in her memoir: "With UNSCOM and the IAEA no longer in Iraq, we shifted our policy toward Baghdad from containment with inspections to an approach we called containment plus." Sandy Berger, who had become national security advisor in Clinton's second term, articulated this shift in emphasis in a December 1998 speech. "Through constant confrontation, our policy of containing Iraq has been successful. But that does not mean that by itself it is sustainable over the long run." Noting the many costs of containing Saddam and the concern that with time international support for the policy would decline, Berger concluded, "Our policy toward Iraq today is to contain Saddam, but also to oppose him."

The administration was in part trying to stay ahead of pressures from the outside that were calling for a policy designed to bring about regime change in Iraq. This pressure took several forms, including articles in conservative publications such as the *Weekly Standard* and open letters that garnered considerable attention. Paramount among these was the January 26, 1998, letter signed by eighteen prominent foreign policy voices (mostly neoconservative) and published under the auspices of the "Project for the New American Century." The letter argued that the policy of containment of Saddam Hussein had been "steadily eroding," and that before long it would be impossible to know with confidence whether Iraq possessed weapons of mass destruction. "The only acceptable strategy is one that eliminates the possibility that Iraq will be able to use or threaten to use weapons of mass destruction. In the near term, this means a willingness to undertake military action as diplomacy is clearly failing. In the long term, it means removing Saddam Hussein and his regime from power. That now needs to become the aim of American foreign policy."

At the time, I was vice president and director of the foreign policy program of the Brookings Institution, a Washington, D.C.–based think tank. I chose not to sign the letter, believing that it placed far too much emphasis on a policy that had little chance of succeeding and worked against containment, which wasn't faring nearly as badly as its critics maintained and that could in any event be made to work better. My description of U.S. policy at the time was "bent but not broken." I also worried about the consequences of a policy of regime change, testifying to Congress in early 1998 that "ousting regimes is one thing, restoring order and installing a better system something else again. A policy that resulted in an Iraq that was the site not only of prolonged civil war but also regional conflict involving Syria, Iran, Turkey and possibly others would hardly qualify as a success." There was also something of a contradiction in calling for Saddam to comply with international demands (something that implied a reduction of sanctions if he did so) and a policy that sought his ouster (which tended to reduce his incentive to comply with U.N. resolutions because he was unacceptable regardless of what he did). These differences were something of a dress rehearsal for the policy debates that would come to the fore during the presidency of George W. Bush.

Congress also brought pressure to bear. In October 1998, it passed the Iraq Liberation Act. Declaring, "It should be the policy of the United States to support efforts to remove the regime headed by Saddam Hussein from power in Iraq and to promote the emergence of a democratic government to replace that regime," the legislation authorized $97 million to provide military support to the Iraqi opposition. Although President Clinton signed it into law in October, the administration held little enthusiasm for it. Tony Zinni, the marine general in charge of Central Command, openly disparaged the idea that Iraq's weak and divided opposition could challenge Saddam. And speaking at the National Press Club on December 23, National Security Advisor Sandy Berger was quite open that doing what it would take to oust Saddam was a nonstarter. "The only sure way for us to effect his [Saddam's] departure now would be to commit hundreds of thousands of American troops to fight on the ground inside Iraq. I do not believe that the costs of such a campaign would be sustainable at home or abroad. And the reward of success would be an American military occupation of Iraq that could last years." Both Zinni and Berger preferred and emphasized containment.

What was apparent was that roughly a decade after the end of the first Iraq war, the U.S. position vis-à-vis Iraq was in some disarray. Inside Iraq, Saddam was firmly in control despite the two no-fly zones that constrained his ability to police his own country. Opposition to his rule from Iraqis within the country and without was weak and unorganized. Sanctions were a constraint but not a threat to the regime's survival. The international inspections effort had effectively ended despite the creation in December 1999 of the U.N. Monitoring, Verification, and Inspection Commission, or UNMOVIC, the successor to UNSCOM. It would be three years, not until November 2002, before international weapons inspectors were able to return to Iraq.

Politically and intellectually, the situation was arguably worse.

Containment was the existing policy, but within U.S. policy-making circles there was waning enthusiasm for it. International support for the policy was also fading, in large part because of empathy for the suffering of the Iraqi people, but also because of corruption (which led to sanctions evasion) and a growing desire to take advantage of the commercial possibilities believed to exist in Iraq. There was growing U.S. interest in and support for a policy of regime change— in its final days, the administration approved $12 million in humanitarian supplies to be distributed inside Iraq by the Iraqi National Congress—but regime change appeared to be more wish than strategy, since opponents of the regime lacked the means to threaten it.

Yet the reality on the ground was, to paraphrase a comment often made about Wagner's music, better than it looked. The inspections and sanctions had largely worked. Iraq was for all intents and purposes out of the weapons of mass destruction business. Saddam was in power but not in a position to do serious harm, either to his own people or his neighbors. Containment was doing better than its detractors, and even many of its advocates, realized.

The result of all this was that by the end of the Clinton administration, the Iraq situation didn't seem all that alarming, especially when judged against the rest of the international situation and the challenges facing the United States. When the forty-second president sat down with the president-elect in January 2001, Bill Clinton briefed George W. Bush on the national security challenges facing the country. He named in order of priority Osama bin Laden and al-Qaida, the absence of Middle East peace, the nuclear standoff between India and Pakistan, Pakistan's ties to both the Taliban and al-Qaida, and North Korea. Only then did Clinton mention Iraq. Time would show that the incoming president, both in what he chose to do and what he did not, either wasn't listening or simply came to disagree.

6. THE 9/11 PRESIDENCY

GEORGE W. BUSH, elected the forty-third president of the United States, could not claim a mandate. He did not run for the office promising fundamental policy shifts, something that would have likely proven difficult given that the federal budget was in the black, the country relatively prosperous, and the world largely at peace. Rather, he ran on character and a promise of change, themes that resonated with many Americans given the scandals and controversies that reverberated throughout eight years of two Clinton administrations. Still, Bush lost the popular vote, and won the electoral vote only after a contested recount in Florida. From the outset, however, Bush governed as if he had won a landslide. He and those closest to him understood that power is to be used, not hoarded, and that successful presidents generate power by using it.

Iraq, more than any other issue, reflected this central reality of the Bush presidency. Bush did not have any mandate to go to war against Iraq. The decision to attack Iraq was not part of the Republican platform or a central part of his stump speech. Iraq was not mentioned in his first inaugural delivered in January 2001. Nor was it a necessary response to 9/11 in the same sense that attacking Afghanistan and removing the Taliban from power was. Despite the suspicions and assertions of some officials, Iraq's government had no role in the attacks and no history of supporting either al-Qaida or the Taliban. No, it was a choice apparently made in the wake of 9/11, one that Bush believed would enhance his presidency and change the course of history in the critical region of the Middle East. Bush miscalculated, in that the war, rather than increasing American power, consumed it, in the process detracting from both his presidency and from American influence around the globe.

I do not recall ever running into George W. Bush during the four years I worked for his father. My first interaction was arranged by Chase Untermeyer, a friend from Texas whom I had gotten to know when we both worked in the Bush 41 White House. Chase urged me to make a visit to Austin and meet with the governor, which I did. We talked for maybe two hours at the residence. We were joined by someone I hadn't heard of before, Karl Rove. The governor told me he was thinking hard about running for president and that if he ran he was confident he would win. We spent the time talking about foreign policy. He mostly asked questions and listened. Iraq only came up when I raised it, and then only for a moment, as my point was it posed no big problem and should not garner more attention than it merited—and certainly not nearly as much attention as he was likely to hear from others.

I remember coming away from that meeting thinking that he was as good a retail politician as I'd ever met. I left behind a copy of my then most recent book, *The Reluctant Sheriff*, which argued that the Clinton administration did not accomplish nearly as much as it could or should have given the absolute and relative position of the United States in the post–Cold War world. Bush (who later told me he had read it and, as if to prove the point, assigned me the nickname of "sheriff") clearly accepted its premise. His presidency could be described with many words, but *reluctant* is not among them. Bush was comfortable with the exercise of power, and his presidency was consequential by any measure; my prediction, though, is that historians will rightly assess the consequences as mostly negative.

Our next conversation arose when the governor of Texas was considering taking a trip to Israel late in 1998 in an effort to shore up his foreign policy credentials. The two of us spoke over the phone for half an hour. I told him what to expect from Ariel Sharon, then Israel's foreign minister: a helicopter tour that would demonstrate Israel's lack of strategic depth, a stop at a settlement, lots of argument about how Israel needed to hold on to the territory it captured in the 1967 war. What I couldn't know is how much the trip would affect Bush; from all accounts, it generated great sympathy for Israel and shaped his thinking about the Middle East and what any peace process should (and should not) attempt to accomplish.

The next time I saw him was during the campaign, again down in Texas. I was one of several foreign policy hands who had been gathered by Condi Rice, who was clearly first among equals in the group of advisors. Others included Bob Blackwill, Steve Hadley, Richard Armitage, Richard Perle, Bob Zoellick, Paul Wolfowitz, and Dov Zakheim. Later on they would come to call themselves the Vulcans. I never joined the inner circle, not seeing how I could given my job at the time as the head of the foreign policy program at the Brookings Institution, a nonpartisan organization.

I came away from that meeting feeling less good than I did after my first encounter with the governor. The problem was not with the candidate so much as the advisors. The balance and mix of the group was overly hard-line for my taste. What came to mind was the first Reagan administration, when there was too much ideology, too much combativeness, and too much emphasis on modifying the nature of other countries and not enough emphasis on diplomacy, cooperation with partners, and more modest goals such as moderating the behavior of others. Prospects appeared dim for a presidency that would resemble either Reagan's second term or George W. Bush's first and only four years.

I was not surprised when I didn't get a top-level job in the new administration; I figured this was the price I paid for not being part of the campaign. In January 2001, however, I received a call from Colin Powell, already tapped to be secretary of state. We had stayed friends over the years despite the fact that we hadn't always seen eye to eye during the previous Bush presidency. Colin offered me the job of director of the Policy Planning Staff, or S/P, as it is known inside the department. I was less than enthusiastic. To be sure, it is a post that comes with an impressive pedigree—the first head of the planning staff was George Kennan, the author of the containment doctrine, and the second was Paul Nitze, the principal author of NSC 68, the document that translated containment into the actual strategy that guided U.S. foreign policy during the initial years of the Cold War. Many other talented people held the job subsequently. But the position lacks any formal interagency role, and what influence there is corresponds almost entirely to the relationship between the head of the planning staff and the secretary. There is also little in the way of operational responsibility, other than writing memos to the secretary and speeches for him. I think it was Henry Kissinger who once warned never to take a job without an inbox, and this one came perilously close. Even Kennan harbored grave doubts about the utility of the position, describing his own experience "a failure, like all previous attempts to bring order and foresight into the designing of foreign policy by special institutional arrangements within the [State] department." So I didn't say yes. However, neither did I say no, as one does not do such things lightly. What I did say is maybe, that I would think about it.

In the end and several days later, I called Colin back and made the case that I could do more for him in a more operational job. He told me that the one I suggested was already filled. After a lot of back-and-forth, I accepted the policy planning offer with more resignation than enthusiasm. What persuaded me in the end was that many of my closest friends argued that I should take it and that once I was on the inside I would figure out how to win my share of bureaucratic battles. Even more importantly, I decided it would be better to go in and learn it was a mistake to have done so than to stay out and wonder if I had made a mistake by not taking the plunge.

So I took the job, with the proviso that I would get a second hat, that of roving ambassador, something that would facilitate my undertaking more operational tasks so that there would be more to my position than simply trying to persuade others to act. Still, after accepting, I had more than one bout of buyer's remorse. This was partly because of the unpleasantness of the Senate confirmation process that was necessary for me to gain my ambassadorial status, partly because I feared that I was not well positioned to wield much influence on a range of issues I knew well and cared strongly about. In the end I was right to harbor the doubts that I did, although I was also right to have gone in. In life, it tends to be better to err by commission than omission. Most of my regrets stem from what I have failed to say or do, not from what I've actually done.

Before I could settle in I first had to endure that confirmation process. The hearing before the Senate Foreign Relations Committee was uneventful, mostly because my good friend Chuck Hagel, the moderate Republican senator from Nebraska, was in the chair. The committee approved me the next day by a voice vote, but then I learned that Senators Sam Brownback and John Kyl had put holds on me. (Holds are a delaying device that allows individual senators to prevent a vote on any nominee. They are neither constitutionally based nor legislative but rather procedural. They should be banned. Nominees should have the right to be voted up or down by the full Senate. Many senators from both parties would agree in principle, but few seem prepared to give up this power and all the leverage that comes with it in practice.) I was not pleased that the resistance was coming from two Republicans, but I was not surprised, as increasingly the fault lines defining the foreign policy debate were less between the parties than within them, that is, between moderates in both parties and either the Democratic left or the Republican (neoconservative) right. In the end, I spent more than an hour with each of the two senators, answering questions clearly prompted by some of the critical media profiles I had received. I also had to answer some forty written questions from Senator Jesse Helms, another twenty from Senator Joe Biden, and yet another twenty from Senator Chris Dodd. Helms's questions were on a range of foreign policy matters; Biden's focused on my finances; and Dodd was interested in Northern Ireland. Somehow I passed muster, and was approved by the entire Senate by unanimous consent on May 8, 2001.

Iraq surfaced early on in two distinct ways. On February 16, the new president was in Mexico, symbolic of his determination to increase the foreign policy focus on the Western Hemisphere. It was also a place and a set of issues he knew well from his time as governor in Texas. For neither the first nor the last time, Iraq upstaged other matters. U.S. aircraft hit a number of air defense sites in that country, presumably because their radars locked on coalition aircraft patrolling one of the two no-fly zones still in place a decade after the end of the 1990–91 Iraq war. The new administration was looking for a chance to signal that it was not going to be business as usual. I thought the military strikes were misguided. It distracted attention from the president's trip to Mexico—an early sign of a weak NSC process that should have made sure the administration did not step on its own story—and angered governments and people in the Middle East without accomplishing much if anything. You only get so many bites of the apple, and it made little sense to waste them by using military force for so little gain.

Even before this incident Iraq was on my personal radar. The particular dimension was sanctions, which were generally seen as being in bad shape and getting worse. Years of Arab and international criticism had taken their toll. Even though the sanctions were not to blame for the low standard of living within Iraq—Saddam and those around him were—many in the region and beyond did blame the sanctions, seeing them as a blunt instrument that was hurting the Iraqi people but sparing the regime. The other problem was that Iraq's immediate neighbors, and Jordan, Syria, and Turkey in particular, were increasingly ignoring the sanctions. To some extent this was political, as the sanctions were unpopular, but even more it was simply business, since trade with Iraq was lucrative.

The policy "answer" to this deteriorating situation was "smart" sanctions. Meghan O'Sullivan, then a young academic who would go on to influence U.S. policy in Iraq in important ways, and I had done a good deal of work on this subject at Brookings. The plan was to allow the Iraqis to import a wider range of nonmilitary goods so long as a higher share of the revenue it received from its exports (largely oil) went into the U.N.-controlled escrow account rather than directly into the pockets of the regime. The reason was simple: the U.N. would only release money for approved purchases, while the regime could use money it controlled to buy proscribed items illegally or to pay off people inside the country so as to better maintain control.

At an informal interagency meeting held at State and chaired by Powell early in the administration, there was lots of talk about whether to focus initially on shoring up sanctions or on getting the weapons inspectors back in the country. I favored the former, since that was central to keeping Saddam under control or maybe even weakening his hold. Too great a focus on returning inspectors risked ending up with "Potemkin inspections" that accomplished little but that would enable Saddam to argue for a weakening of the sanctions regime as a reward for his "improved" behavior. (I later wrote Powell that "Faux inspections or 'inspections lite,' which gave Iraq a 'Good Housekeeping Seal' absent true compliance would be the worst of all outcomes.") Powell, for his part, pushed hard for a policy of smart sanctions that would expand what Saddam could import but limit the revenues under his control. There was more than a little skepticism in the rest of the administration about both the wisdom and potential of this approach, but Powell prevailed and the president signed off on an initiative that would ease restrictions on what Iraq could import at the same time it sought to convince the so-called front-line states to send all future payments through the U.N. and to tighten controls at their border with Iraq. This initiative would not reach fruition until May 2002 and the passage of U.N. Security Council Resolution 1409. The resolution made it easier for Iraq to import a wider variety of goods. This was desirable, both for humanitarian reasons and because it would ease some of the international pressures to lift the sanctions completely. But it did nothing to make sure proscribed items did not reach Iraq. Nor did it slow much less stop the illegal exports of oil that provided a cash machine for Saddam.

For all this, Iraq did not dominate the foreign policy of the new administration. This is not to say it didn't come up early on. It did, as Ron Suskind details in his portrait of Paul O'Neill's unhappy experience as the first of George W. Bush's three treasury secretaries. Suskind describes a National Security Council meeting ten days into the administration at which Iraq received considerable and, to O'Neill, surprising emphasis. But the actual focus early on when it came to Iraq was on recasting the sanctions regime. There was a directive to look at existing military plans, but this lacked any real intensity at the time. It was more a dusting off of what was there rather than anything new.

If Iraq seemed all too familiar, U.S. policy toward the rest of the Middle East appeared markedly different. The Clinton administration made an enormous push for peace between Israelis and Palestinians in its final year. The new administration was not inclined to try, avoiding anything that resembled continuity with the Clinton administration. The widely shared view was that Yasir Arafat was largely responsible for the failure at Camp David in July 2000 and that it would be a waste of time to tee up the ball again given his continued prominence. (I thought this judgment only partially correct, as the Clinton administration erred in not building a diplomatic context in which Arafat could have confidence that his compromises would be supported and legitimized.) Mounting violence on the ground along with Ariel Sharon's victory as prime minister in Israel sealed the judgment that the situation could hardly be less ripe for diplomacy. It would be nearly seven years before this president made a concerted effort to promote peace between Israelis and Palestinians, by which point prospects had grown even more dim given the rise of Hamas and the deterioration in the day-to-day reality on the ground. Neglect is not always benign.

As for Iran, there was no inclination to engage the regime there. To the contrary, the senior level of the administration had been persuaded that Iran's government was hanging by a thread, and that any U.S. diplomatic initiative would be tantamount to throwing a rope to a drowning man. I argued to no avail that this was wishful thinking. I also argued that we should try to engage the regime there in an effort to curb some of its worst practices, including support for terror and investment in developing the means to enrich uranium. One form of engagement in particular appealed to me: dropping our opposition to Iran joining the World Trade Organization. I argued to anyone who would listen that WTO membership could actually weaken the regime by requiring greater adherence to the rule of law and international standards. No one could rebut what I said, but no one had the appetite to move on this. The result is that Iran was ignored, much as was the case with North Korea. In both instances, the countries' nuclear programs advanced considerably. By the end of George W. Bush's presidency, North Korea had tested a nuclear device and had more than tripled its stock of plutonium, accumulating enough for at least six nuclear weapons. Iran, for its part, had come close to enriching enough uranium to produce its first nuclear device. Again, neglect rarely makes a bad situation better.

Meanwhile, I got busy with policy planning. Secretary of State George Marshall's injunction to George Kennan was to "avoid trivia." I agreed, but there was a danger that too much emphasis on "big think" would leave me and us irrelevant. I saw the job as having three core elements. The most important was to be an independent voice within the building, be it to propose initiatives or to put forward alternatives to what others were recommending. A second function was to carry out broad-ranging dialogues with planning staffs and others in governments around the world. In such dialogues, I had the luxury of raising issues and agendas that those entrusted with day-to-day responsibilities could not. My third focus was the speechwriting function, traditionally an important preserve of S/P, as speeches by a secretary of state can make policy and resonate around the world. Over time, I devoted less and less time to this last function, largely because Colin Powell wasn't inclined to give policy-laden speeches. He much preferred more personal and less formal talks along the lines of those he honed during his years on the speaking circuit. I ended up giving a number of policy-filled speeches, which was a distant second-best given my lower rank and the inevitable questions that would arise about whom I was speaking for.

Early on I spent about an hour with Powell in his small back office talking about what we wanted to accomplish over the next few years. He asked for my list of priorities as we went around the world. I said that Europe was not going to play a central role, in the sense that the continent was mostly stable. This was one fundamental way in which the new century would differ from the one just ending. But Europeans would be our principal partners in tackling various regional and global challenges; the question was whether we could bring them along and what they had to contribute. In Asia the big challenge (in addition to China's rise and North Korea's nuclear program) was to devise some regional mechanisms to make sure that all the economic and increasingly military dynamism there did not spill over and lead to instability or conflict. I mentioned my sense that India was a strategic opportunity for the United States and that Pakistan was a strategic problem; I went so far as to say that Pakistan worried me more than anything else given its nuclear weapons, its weak and divided government, and the links between its security services and both the Taliban and other terrorists. I was interested in pushing free trade, an alternative to the Kyoto Protocol on climate change, and stronger ties with the major powers, including China, Russia, and Japan in addition to Europe and India.

Talk of priorities was one thing; reality proved to be another. In April, the foreign policy focus of the administration turned to China, but not in the positive way I had sought. What led to this was not any piece of policy planning on our part, but rather a Chinese fighter pilot who collided with a U.S. surveillance plane, forcing it to make an emergency landing on Hainan Island. The plane was over international water, but clearly some in China wanted us to back off. I thought it a boneheaded move by China, as it ensured that relations with the new U.S. administration would get off to a terrible start. It would also strengthen the hand of those officials in the administration who saw a rising China as a growing competitor and who wanted the United States to emphasize containment over engagement and integration.

It was difficult to know how much China's leaders were directing events as opposed to reacting to them. What was worrisome was how the authoritarian Chinese government began to lose control over its policy to more strident voices, often heard in Internet chat rooms. In China, communism and socialism are slogans, religion is repressed, and democracy is not allowed. So what flourishes is mostly materialism. But man cannot live on bread (or rice) alone, and something must fill the political vacuum. Nationalism is thus dangerous. China will have to manage its domestic debate just as we will have to manage ours if this relationship, one more likely than any other to define the character of the twenty-first century, is to be more cooperative than competitive.

After a false start, in which the president was overly assertive in what he said and overly involved in what was going on, "crisis management" was transferred to the State Department, where Powell and his deputy Rich Armitage quickly defused matters. The only problem were comments that surfaced in the media suggesting that State had saved the administration's bacon, which worked to fuel the perception in the White House that the State Department was hostile or at least disloyal real estate and that Powell was not a team player.

Differences were by no means limited to China policy. Iraq was both a cause and a reflection of administration tensions. Beyond the State Department, there was little interest in shoring up the existing sanctions regime. This bias would prove to have enormous adverse consequences, for although it would not have been easy, the United States could have done a good deal to make sanctions more effective. For example, we could have subsidized the Turkish and Jordanian economies for the approximately $500 million a year they would have forfeited had they curtailed most of their illicit trade with Iraq. Conventional military force or even covert action could have been used to shut down the Iraq–Syria oil pipeline that was a major source of revenue (nearly $3 billion over twelve years) to Saddam. It is possible, too, that Syria could have been persuaded to simply shut down the pipeline as part of a broader normalization of its ties with the United States. Unfortunately, a diplomatic approach along these lines with Syria was unacceptable to the Bush administration. We know now that 84 percent of the hard currency that reached Saddam during the years sanctions were in effect (1991–2003) did so via trade arrangements with Jordan, Turkey, Syria, and Egypt or because of smuggling. Only 16 percent of the money that reached Saddam was the result of kickbacks and other abuses of the U.N.-run oil-for-food program under which Iraq could legally sell oil and import a wide range of goods. Most of the attention has been on the scandals associated with the U.N. program, but the real scandal was that the United States and other governments looked the other way rather than work to shut down trade that was known to be illegal and known to be taking place.

Tightening sanctions simply didn't excite most people within the Bush administration because sanctions did not hold out the hope of regime change. What did excite these people was finding ways to bolster the Iraqi opposition to Saddam Hussein. This was part of a larger preference for escalating the importance of Iraq and bringing about new leadership there. My problem with this bias was twofold. First, I didn't think it worth it. I saw Saddam as a midlevel problem but not more. I could live with containment and thought it could be made more effective. Turning Iraq into a central focus of U.S. foreign policy would not only be an uncalled-for distraction but would make us appear to be the side that had provoked a crisis. I also doubted the feasibility of any policy that was based on supporting the Iraqi opposition to effect a change in regime. The opposition was weak, divided, and compromised, and all we would manage to do is get a lot of people killed and ourselves embarrassed if we took Saddam on through them. I thought former CentCom commander retired general Tony Zinni had it about right in describing various proposals for arming the Iraqi opposition (many of whom had stronger ties to London than Baghdad) as a likely "Bay of Goats," that is, a fiasco reminiscent of nothing so much as the misguided and unsuccessful attempt to support a rebel force to overthrow Fidel Castro some forty years ago.

To the extent regime change was sought, there were only two possibilities. The "cheaper" path was through a coup, most likely led by a senior military figure. I spent hours at the CIA meeting with Director George Tenet and others discussing just this. Recent history was filled with reports of failed coups that demonstrated all too well just how unlikely this was. The problem was that we had no way of knowing if a coup was likely to be attempted and, if so, if it was likely to succeed. We figured, though, that by the time we knew about a possible coup (say, if we were asked to assist in some way) Saddam was almost certain to know about it, too, given his informants within the Iraqi army. In short, we could not count on Saddam being replaced from within by some alternative Sunni strongman who was prepared for Iraq to meet its international obligations. More broadly, it is wise not to expect too much of covert action. History suggests that on occasion it can be a useful complement to policy, but rarely can it constitute the bulk of policy.

"The only sure way to oust the regime and put something better in its place," I wrote in a memo to Powell in the spring of 2001, "is through prolonged military occupation and nation-building. This would be costly by any and every measure and impossible to sustain politically either at home or in the region in the absence of a clear cause, such as Iraqi use of WMD or a new invasion of Kuwait." But I did not see any of this as cause for despair. The United States had viable policy options, including continued sanctions, more intense military strikes when Saddam's behavior warranted a military response, and prosecution of Saddam for war crimes. Just as importantly, the current and projected situation was not intolerable. Saddam Hussein was a nuisance, not a mortal threat. Trying to oust him, however desirable, did not need to become such a preoccupation that it would come to dominate the administration's foreign policy absent a major new provocation. The United States had more important goals to promote around both the region and the world that would be put in jeopardy were it to get bogged down in Iraq.

What also made me uneasy was the pattern of interagency discussions and decisions that was emerging on this and other topics. On almost every issue, from the Anti-Ballistic Missile Treaty, the International Criminal Court, and global climate change to what to do about Iran and North Korea, the State Department was isolated and outnumbered. To some extent this was a matter of foreign policy outlook. The State Department and those who work there are by temperament and training inclined toward diplomacy and working with others. In this administration, those elsewhere were not. I tried to put this in the most favorable light one day in July when, speaking at an event sponsored by the Nixon Center, a centrist, Washington-based think tank, I took issue with those who described the administration as unilateralist, describing its philosophy instead as "à la carte multilateralism." I did not intend it as more than a way of finessing a question, but my unscripted, on-the-record comment caught on in a big way, ending up as a front-page story in the *New York Times*. My own view is that it is right to be selective about the form of multilateralism—it need not be some formal, universal membership organization such as the U.N. but instead could be a regional or functional grouping or even some informal coalition of the willing. But it is also true that this administration was too quick to dismiss the benefits of multilateralism and legal frameworks and too quick to go it alone. Multilateralism is more and more essential, not simply as a way to get others to share burdens, but also as a way to forge global arrangements that are essential to address global challenges such as the spread of nuclear weapons, terrorism, protectionism, disease, and climate change—challenges that have emerged as the hallmark of this era of international relations.

Accounting for the unilateral bias to the administration's foreign policy were bureaucratic factors as well as ideological leanings. One was the Office of Vice President, the OVP. When I was in the previous Bush administration just a decade before, the vice president's cast of foreign policy advisors was two. I thought this was about right, since the vice president should be something of a minister without portfolio, a counselor, and a sounding board. The staff grew by several people under Vice President Gore, and now there were a dozen national security aides. Essentially a personal staff had been transformed into what was tantamount to a small, independent agency. This gave the vice president a voice at every meeting at every level—in addition to his own voice at principals' meetings and what he said to the president in their regular private sessions. On top of all this he was also handed responsibility for specific issues, such as energy policy. This all accorded Dick Cheney an extraordinary opportunity to press his point of view—which, in the case of energy policy, meant that the administration embraced a woefully imbalanced and inadequate policy that placed unrealistic emphasis on increasing domestic production and all but ignored reducing demand, something the vice president saw as "a personal virtue" but not a matter of public policy.

A second factor was the effective silencing of the Joint Chiefs of Staff by Secretary of Defense Donald Rumsfeld. If the Pentagon building has five sides, the Defense Department has three. There is the civilian side (the office of the secretary of defense) as well as the uniformed side, the Joint Chiefs of Staff. (The third side, that of the departments overseeing the individual armed services, has not traditionally been involved in interagency policy making.) In previous administrations in which I had served, the Defense Department would send two representatives to each meeting and each would effectively say his own piece. More often than not, the JCS representative would come out closer to the more moderate point of view, be it put forward by State, the Office of the Secretary of Defense (OSD), the intelligence community representative, or the National Security Council person. I often thought this was because the military professionals understood all too well that they would be the ones fighting and dying in the name of some policy abstraction. They also tended to hold realistic views on the limits to what military force could accomplish. In any event, in this administration, the Joint Chiefs essentially lost their independent voice. Secretary of Defense Rumsfeld preferred to deal directly with his field commanders—the so-called CINCs, or combatant commanders—who lacked a Washington voice, while more independent military voices in Washington often found themselves sidelined.

The third factor was the orientation of the National Security Council. In principle and design, the NSC ought to be neutral on policy or at least determined to make sure that its honest broker role enjoys pride of place before it assumes the stance of counselor. It was also my hope (and Powell's) that in that latter capacity Condoleezza Rice would come out closer to the position of State. On most issues, however, the NSC staff and leadership alike leaned toward the stances put forward by OSD and OVP. Partially this was a function of some of the individuals chosen to serve on the NSC staff; partly this was simply the result of what Condi wanted. Over the years, she and I had been mostly in the same place, more pragmatic and moderate than anything else. In this incarnation, however, Condi emerged as someone more intellectually and politically conservative than the person I was familiar with. Why this happened I do not know. It is possible she changed, be it as a result of 9/11 or other experiences, or it is possible she found herself in political circumstances that required or at least encouraged such change. It didn't really matter, as the result was the same. Her pronounced conservative leaning made it at least two and a half to one against State on almost every issue just by the time we sat down with our interagency peers. This was what the president sought; he told one journalist friend of mine that he didn't want to have a lot of split decisions that left his administration divided and gridlocked. Presidents tend to get the NSC they want, and this was no exception. What this president didn't get was the NSC he needed.

It didn't help that the president held the State Department in low regard, with White House chief of staff Andy Card telling Powell at one point that he (Powell) was the only person at the State Department the president trusted. Actually, I am not sure the president and those around him trusted Powell all that much. Powell was too popular, too moderate, and too independent for their taste. More than once the White House let it be known that Powell had strayed off the reservation and was not speaking for the administration. Powell, for his part, never felt comfortable with what he viewed as the macho, towel-snapping atmosphere of the informal "meetings after the meeting" at this White House. Rumsfeld, Cheney, and Rice would hang around with the president and engage in West Wing bull sessions; Powell tended not to. The president, who didn't have close ties to either Cheney or Rumsfeld at the outset, over time developed them, but not with Powell, who the president felt did not respond to his overtures. Whatever the reason or reasons, the bottom line is that George W. Bush and Colin Powell never forged the sort of close relationship that is essential if a secretary of state is to succeed.

Making matters worse from my perspective was the relative weakness of many of the senior State Department officials. They were career foreign service officers, knowledgeable professionals one and all, but ill-equipped in most instances to compete with their more ideological, politically appointed counterparts elsewhere in the government. Political appointees tend to arrive with a shorter time frame and a developed policy agenda whereas careerists tend to take the longer view and are more reactive and deferential. I suggested early on to Powell that he bring in more outsiders to strengthen the team at the top of the State Department, but he demurred. He regularly told me to relax, that with time the early excesses of the administration would wear off. My sense at the time was that he misread the situation. Powell was the best processor and integrator of information I have ever worked with. He was thus ideally suited for his previous stints as national security advisor and chairman of the Joint Chiefs of Staff. But he was less well suited for a position where he would have to advocate, especially when the playing field was tilted against him as it often was. Too much of the time this left him and us playing defense, reacting to the agenda of others. Powell to his credit often succeeded in sandpapering away the roughest edges of their positions, but at the end of the day it was more often than not still the positions of those at the Defense Department, the Vice President's office, and the NSC that mostly shaped U.S. policy during George W. Bush's first term.

The terrorist attacks of September 11, 2001, were a turning point for the administration, for the American people, and for the United States in the world in ways still not fully understood. It was a powerful and costly lesson that globalization is a reality, not a choice. To turn on the cliché, the world is not Las Vegas; what happens there will not stay there. Another metaphor may be more apt. The United States cannot be a giant gated community.

A good deal of the investigation of the 9/11 Commission properly focused on why the attack succeeded. There were many reasons, including the lack of information sharing and coordination between the CIA and FBI. But I thought then and think now that a big part of the reason was that policy makers did not take the subject of terrorism nearly as seriously as they should have. Until 9/11, most experts thought of terrorism as not much more than a nuisance—a tragedy for those directly affected, to be sure, but not a major national security concern. People in the national security field gravitated toward relations between and among the major powers and the regions where they were present or clashed, such as Europe, Asia, and the Middle East. Terrorism was something of a sideshow, the province of a few specialists. Two terrorist bombings in East Africa and the regular intelligence about al-Qaida changed the outlook of many senior officials in the Clinton administration, but the Bush administration, populated at high levels by people who had been outside government for eight years, was not sensitive to this altered reality. Again, it took 9/11 to change this.

I was in Dublin on 9/11 as part of one of my regular swings to London, Dublin, and Belfast required by my position as U.S. envoy to the Northern Ireland peace process. I was just completing lunch at the Irish foreign ministry when word arrived that a plane had flown into one of the towers of the World Trade Center. I called my office, where people confirmed the report. Not thinking it more than an accident, I rode over to keep my scheduled meeting with Irish prime minister Bertie Ahern. In his office we watched additional news footage of the second plane flying into the second tower; by then it was all too clear this was no accident but premeditated terrorism. Ahern and I had a desultory conversation about Northern Ireland; during the meeting he received a call from his foreign minister, Brian Cowen, who was in the West Bank about to meet with Yasir Arafat. Ahern cupped the phone, asking me if I thought we would be unhappy if the meeting went ahead. I said no, that it would be okay, especially if Arafat could be persuaded to come out against the attack and terrorism of any sort. (It turns out he did.) We then went out and did a press conference, little of which was about local issues. Surreal doesn't begin to capture how it felt.

Following the press conference I went ahead with my schedule, which meant going on to Belfast. (I wanted to return home, but there was no way to do it given that most planes had been grounded. I also figured I could accomplish more where I was.) In Belfast I saw the leaders of the local parties as well as the British secretary of state for Northern Ireland, John Reid. The irony was inescapable: there I was in a city that had come to be a symbol for terrorism, and I was in many ways safer than if I had stayed in Washington. What had happened also gave me a powerful talking point. I told Gerry Adams and Martin McGuinness, the leaders of Sinn Fein (the political wing of the Provisional Irish Republican Army or IRA, which for years had carried out terrorist attacks against the British government and its security services) that there would no longer be any tolerance whatsoever in the United States for acts of political violence against anyone. The time had come for the leadership of the Irish Republican movement to turn the corner, once and for all, and put terrorism behind them. I said I was confident that I was talking not just for the U.S. government but for all Americans, including those who had historically been sympathetic to their cause. I was bluffing to some extent, but time would prove me correct. This was one reason that years later the IRA gave up not just terrorism but its arms, paving the way for a political breakthrough in Northern Ireland that made it possible to establish a local government in which Protestants and Catholics share power.

I hitched a ride back to London with Reid, returned to my quarters at the residence of U.S. ambassador Will Farish, and worked out of the U.S. embassy in London, since there was still no way to fly home with all planes grounded. I was frustrated, being away from my family and colleagues at this time, but there was nothing I could do about it. I felt somewhat more connected after attending a memorial service several days later at St. Paul's Cathedral. The good news is that my staff, led by Don Steinberg, a former U.S. ambassador to Angola, didn't miss a beat, providing Powell much of what he needed in the days after 9/11 in the way of a foreign policy response.

I wrote a long personal email from my makeshift office to Powell that captured what I had been thinking. The essence was that we always knew that a large attack against the United States would occur, given who we were, what we did, the open nature of American society, and the recognition by our adversaries that they would fare better against American cities or embassies or military bases than against U.S. armies in the field. What distinguished the September 11 events, though, were their audacity, scale, and success. For years the academic debate about terrorism had drawn a distinction between traditional terrorism (car bombs, hijackings, etc.) and so-called grand terrorism, which was assumed to involve weapons of mass destruction and a potential for thousands or tens of thousands of casualties. What we had just experienced made the distinction meaningless. What made a terrorist attack grand was its design and execution more than the selection of explosive.

There was and is no solution to terrorism, I wrote to Powell. No amount of American strength or primacy would ever be translated into invulnerability. Terrorism was thus similar to other transnational challenges such as drugs and proliferation. What was needed was a range of responses, from prevention to passive and active protection (defense) to consequence management. In the process, we needed to be careful in our use of military metaphors. A "war on terrorism" could mislead. Wars were largely fought on battlefields by soldiers using military instruments. But the military might not be the principal tool in the antiterrorism arsenal. Skyscrapers and subways and malls had become the new battlefields, and no one wore uniforms. Intelligence, I predicted, would prove to be the most valuable tool against terrorists. Wars tended to have ends, but there was no end in sight to the terrorist challenge. It was thus better to think of terrorism as akin to disease, an all but inevitable facet of modern life that one must constantly struggle against with a range of measures. The numbers were not reassuring. Terrorists succeed even if they fail most of the time. Or to look at it from our perspective, we would pay a large price even if we were to succeed 99 percent of the time.

Moreover, many of the so-called answers to terrorism were not answers at all. Some called for isolating ourselves, suggesting that if the United States did not involve itself in the world's disputes it would be less of a target. But this ignored that we had interests that required U.S. involvement. It also ignored that in many instances what animated the terrorists was not so much what we did but who and what we were.

I predicted that U.S. Middle East policy was also likely to be singled out as a likely cause of what had transpired. This, too, was to be rejected, if only because nothing short of Israel's elimination (and possibly not even that) would be likely to meet the demands of those fanatics behind much modern-day terror. There was no normal or traditional political agenda here in which reasonable or imaginable compromise could be expected to deliver results. We wanted to embrace the twenty-first century; Osama bin Laden wanted to return to the seventh century. Compromising on the fourteenth century was not an attractive outcome. And speaking of Bin Laden, we needed to be wary of overpersonalizing the enemy. The problem went way beyond any one individual or organization. We would be in this for the long haul even if we scored a success against a particular individual or group.

I thought we should explore the prospect of encouraging the introduction of a stronger international norm against terrorism, to include not only states but nonstate actors and both those who carry it out and those who aid and abet terrorism in any way. But there were likely to be two major problems in gaining global support. One would be definitional. We could well get mired in a counterproductive debate over whether someone was a freedom fighter rather than a terrorist. Second, we were unlikely to get people to sign on to anything resembling an open-ended grant of authority to act. Given the U.N. Charter's provision in Article 51 of a universal right to act in one's self-defense without further legal or diplomatic backing, it could be argued, however, that we did not need any more authority than we already had.

I also urged that we use what had happened as a justification to approach Pakistan, possibly dispatching a presidential envoy who would essentially argue that Pakistan must cut off the Taliban if it did not want to become a rogue state in our eyes. This was unnecessary, since it turned out that the Pakistani intelligence director was in Washington, which gave Powell's deputy Rich Armitage the opportunity to deliver that warning. Armitage was the perfect choice to deliver such a blunt message. He was Powell's closest confidant, physically imposing (he looked like the football lineman he once was and could bench-press enough weight to prove it), a Vietnam veteran with considerable combat experience, and a politically savvy straight shooter. The message got through, as the Pakistanis improved their performance markedly. Where the Bush administration dropped the ball was in not following up over the years and in failing to tie the large flows of U.S. military and economic assistance to specific measures of Pakistan's continued performance in fighting terrorism.

As for military responses against terrorists, these tended to be difficult in the case of nonstate actors, who often presented little in the way of a physical target. The sort of "shoot cruise missiles from a distance" approach that had become the norm in recent years accomplished little. This required that we think more about small teams that go after small groups. State sponsors offered much more of a target, although here we would still have to proceed carefully given such considerations as their ability to retaliate. Other tools, such as diplomacy, sanctions, greater intelligence cooperation, and the like, may be less dramatic or satisfying but should not be overlooked or undervalued. In the end, what was most important was that we put ourselves in a better position to lessen the likelihood of successful future terrorist attacks. Military retaliation would be an element of such a response, but it was unlikely to be the most important.

I was clearly in sync with the administration on some of the issues—presenting Pakistani leaders with a fundamental choice between ties with the Taliban and ties with us, reorienting our military approach for dealing with terrorists away from cruise missile attacks and toward the use of ground forces, targeting not just terrorists but the states harboring them—but out of sync on others, above all the degree to which foreign policy became militarized. I also didn't mention Iraq, not consciously but simply because it seemed far-fetched to me that Iraq was involved in this operation given Saddam's mistrust of independent terrorist organizations and his desire to see sanctions and international scrutiny of what he might be up to inside Iraq fade, something much less likely to happen if he could be connected to this action.

We now know that Saddam and Iraq had no involvement in 9/11 and little involvement with terrorism. The few contacts between Iraq and al-Qaida appear to have been inconsequential. But it is worth noting that the first instinct of the president was to push the bureaucracy to find a connection between Saddam and the attacks. Paul Wolfowitz, then deputy secretary of defense, argued at the Camp David meeting convened on September 14 that the attack was too grand for al-Qaida to have accomplished on its own and that the United States should go after Iraq. And a number of influential voices from outside the administration echoed the calls that in the wake of 9/11 the United States needed to attack Iraq and oust Saddam Hussein. But they were wrong; Saddam had little time for either terrorists (whom he worried he could not control) or Islamists (who in the end could pose a threat to his secular leadership).

I finally flew back from London a few days later on the first United flight to the United States. I arrived back in a different Washington:

9/11 had changed the pace and focus of the government; the only thing that was quite like it in my experience was the aftermath to the Iraqi invasion of Kuwait a decade before. But some things were the same. Powell had tasked the Policy Planning Staff with putting together a white paper on 9/11. The idea was to explain what had happened and why, in an effort to establish a foundation and support for whatever set of responses would follow. We finished a solid draft and were then told it was going nowhere. The official reason was to protect intelligence sources and methods, but the actual reason may have had more to do with a White House effort to cut the secretary of state down to size and ensure that he did not become the face of the administration on this issue. Many around the president never grew comfortable with Powell's enormous public popularity.

I was also busy with a host of follow-up actions. Every crisis brings opportunity along with it, and this was no exception. There was an opening to establish an international norm against terrorism, one that would outlaw intentional attacks on civilians to advance political aims. States that directly supported terrorism or that allowed (be it out of choice or weakness) their territory to be used by terrorists would forfeit the normal rights and protections of sovereignty. Other states and the international community more broadly would gain the right to intervene. This was consistent with the notion that global challenges could be met best with collective responses. We needed to integrate other countries into such efforts—and in the process bring about a more integrated world that would be better able to defeat or at least contend with various threats. The administration never pushed hard to establish an international norm against terrorism, but it did end up with far more international cooperation in the realms of counterterrorism and homeland security than had existed previously. It was entirely correct to argue there should be no distinction between terrorists and those who harbored or in any way abetted them. This provided the basis for removing the Taliban from power and it sent a message to others who might consider doing something similar to what the Taliban had done.

In mid-October I was named the secretary's "personal representative" for the future of Afghanistan, and then days later the U.S. government's coordinator for the future of that country. My task was to pull together the disparate elements within the administration and work with the U.N., other governments, and the Afghans in preparing for what would come after the Taliban were removed from power. Overall U.S. policy had five dimensions, what were dubbed the five (Olympic) rings: military, humanitarian, diplomatic, reconstruction, and security. I had concerns about our military strategy versus the Taliban, but this was not my responsibility. Getting humanitarian help inside Afghanistan was complicated by the Taliban, the competing Afghan factions, and some of the neighbors. But again this was not my principal role. My purview was the latter three rings, and included such matters as organizing the notoriously difficult to organize Afghan opposition; working to get Afghanistan's neighbors to cooperate rather than back competing factions; and establishing a postliberation force to ensure internal security until such a time as the Afghans themselves could do this for themselves.

Within days of getting the new assignment I flew up to New York to meet with U.N. secretary-general Kofi Annan and his experienced advisor and frequent envoy Lakhdar Brahimi. We sat at Kofi's conference table. I laid out our political goals (a broad-based, representative government), plans for humanitarian aid, and our initial thinking about long-term security arrangements. Although we all knew one another well, they were clearly surprised, but pleasantly so, with what I had to say. It had been some time since a Bush administration representative had told anyone at the U.N. anything remotely resembling the theme that "we will back you."

The one area on which it was difficult for me to engage was the question of what sort of security arrangements the United States was prepared to support. I had no instructions on this last matter, which liberated and constrained me at one and the same time. Just before going up to New York I was one-half of the "plus two" accompanying Secretary Powell at an early November NSC meeting in the White House Situation Room, located in the basement of the West Wing. (The other half was Andrew Natsios, who was orchestrating the humanitarian response.) The entire senior team—the president, Powell, Condi Rice, Chief of Staff Andy Card, Don Rumsfeld, the JCS representative, John McLaughlin (George Tenet's deputy at the CIA)—was arrayed around the table. Vice President Cheney was at one of his secure locations and participated by a secure video link. There was lots of talk about the humanitarian situation. Frustration was high with logistical difficulties and the lack of political credit being garnered for what we were doing. My turn came about halfway through the meeting. I had prepared a short briefing but never got through it as the president peppered me with question after question. He and we had a come a long way since that first meeting years before in Austin.

In the end, I managed to make most of the points I'd prepared, but in a rather disjointed way. Condi was silent, but Don Rumsfeld commented on just about everything, as was his style. Rumsfeld was forever the confident college wrestler, one who specialized at probes designed to keep others off balance. He did it by asking questions and more often than not by introducing issues that pushed the conversation in unintended directions. This was consistent with his proclivity to circulate "snowflakes," short memos that raised provocative, fundamental questions that were difficult to mesh with day-to-day policy considerations. A perfect example was his October 16, 2003, memo on terrorism. "Are we capturing, killing or deterring and dissuading more terrorists every day than the madrassas and the radical clerics are recruiting, training and deploying against us?" The honest answer was no, but there was no connection that I could discern between the memo and policy making.

On this day, as was often the case, Rumsfeld entered the meeting carrying a huge pile of papers, dropped them down with a thud on the table, and announced that he hadn't had the time to read what his staff had prepared. I took this as a signal that he would not be bound by what had been decided by the deputies. Colin sat tight-lipped lest he blow a fuse. I came away with only part of what I wanted. I got a green light, but a reluctant one, to continue working with the U.N. on putting together a process that could lead to a broad-based, post-Taliban Afghan government. I emphasized that diplomacy was likely to be far more successful (and the pace of political progress would pick up) once there was a significant military win.

Several things were apparent. Confidence in the United Nations was low. So too was desire to work with allies, since offers of help in Afghanistan in the aftermath of 9/11 were met with little more than a shortsighted and arrogant "thanks but no thanks." This was consistent with a tendency to view multilateralism as a constraint rather than a force multiplier. Also low was enthusiasm for making a meaningful U.S. military contribution to Afghanistan once the Taliban were defeated. Indeed, administration enthusiasm for heavy involvement of any sort in Afghanistan was muted. There was a pervasive sense that it was an all but hopeless investment given the country's unruly history, the legacy of a weak central government, and the tradition of resistance to outsiders. At one point early on I traveled to Rome to visit with Zahir Shah, the former Afghan king who lived in a villa just outside the city center. It was an obvious thing to do, as many Afghans and others were suggesting he could be a rallying point for anti-Taliban Afghans. At the last minute, though, Washington got cold feet, and Steve Hadley told Rich Armitage I could not go ahead and meet with the aging king. There was a concern that the

United States should not be seen to be taking sides. I thought this was crazy; the former king was a symbol of the country. Also, our meeting had received considerable public attention, and canceling it now would raise a rash of questions about U.S. intentions. I had to phone Armitage and get him to persuade Hadley to drop the objections to the meeting. After several calls and conversations, I got a green light but was told to avoid cameras. By then, though, I had done something to my back, and could barely stand. So not having cameras in the room was fine with me, if only because the eighty-something king was moving better and standing straighter than I was. In the end, Zahir Shah finessed every question I asked. After an hour that seemed much longer, the only thing that was clear was that we could not depend on the former monarch for anything. We would have to work with the U.N. and build an Afghan opposition that would work together from the ground up.

It was difficult to gain traction on this until it became clear that Afghanistan would in fact be free of the Taliban yoke. Much to my frustration, this did not happen until early November. We needed a significant military victory that would establish the momentum in our favor, but it was proving slower going than anticipated, because our military efforts were too small and spread too thin, and because of the limits of our Afghan partners. It was hard to coordinate a first-world air force and a collection of third- or fourth-world militias. Gradually, however, the tide turned; the victory at the city of Mazar-e-Sharif proved decisive, creating a snowball effect, much as we predicted.

Ironically, the military victories made my job both easier and more difficult. Military victory was a necessary prerequisite for all else, but it also made our Afghan partners (the collection of warlords known as the Northern Alliance) less inclined to work with other Afghans who had a lesser role on the battlefield. I hit a brick wall when I tried to get some of the opposition elements to meet in either

Istanbul or Ankara. This failure may have been a good thing, because a meeting consisting just of the Northern Alliance and those around the former king was too narrow a basis for proceeding. (The Northern Alliance was the group that came to power several years after the Soviet-backed regime collapsed in the mid-1990s. They then failed to rule effectively, paving the way for the Taliban.) I and we switched gears and threw our support behind the U.N. secretary-general's representative, Lakhdar Brahimi, and his plan for a pan-Afghan gathering convened under U.N. auspices. But the Northern Alliance was hanging tough; I got through to their "foreign minister" on the phone, and he parried every suggestion I made for a time and place for a broadly based meeting given what he repeatedly described as "the new political and military realities." In the end, though, after weeks of politicking, a pan-Afghan leadership was created at a meeting in Bonn, Germany, ably guided by Brahimi and my State Department colleague Jim Dobbins.

I write about Afghanistan for several reasons that have to do with Iraq. Many critics of U.S. Iraq policy assert that one of the costs of the U.S. commitment there was that it drew attention and resources from Afghanistan. Gary Schroen, in the CIA at the time, alleges in his book *First In* that "aid and assistance [to Afghanistan] were significantly cut" and that "as early as March 2002 the U.S. military began to withdraw many of the key units involved in this [counter-terrorism] effort, in order to allow them to regroup and train in preparation for the coming war with Iraq." It is certainly true, as Schroen and others charge, that Iraq increasingly garnered extraordinary high-level attention, but it is not clear any of this came at the expense of Afghanistan. Also not clear is that Iraq in fact drew economic or military resources that otherwise would have gone to Afghanistan. (Even Schroen admits that withdrawn units were replaced by other units of high quality.) I say this because I never once heard anyone say, "We should not or cannot do this in Afghanistan because of the need to set aside dollars or troops for Iraq." The failure to capture or kill retreating al-Qaida and Taliban elements at the battle of Tora Bora was a failure born of tactics and overreliance on Afghan units and above all the ill-advised decision to limit the number and role of U.S. forces. But again, I know of no evidence that U.S. troop numbers were kept down to preserve them for a possible war to come. My own reading is that troop numbers were kept as low as they were because the secretary of defense and others wanted to demonstrate that traditional American approaches to warfare were overly conservative and that new technology and tactics at the heart of defense transformation had rendered using large numbers of troops obsolete. Also, many of the critical decisions taken vis-à-vis Afghanistan were made some eighteen months before the start of the Iraq war and maybe six months before the decision was all but made to go to war.

None of this should be read as defending what the United States did and did not do in Afghanistan. The focus on going after terrorists was understandable and necessary but insufficient. The United States could and should have done more to assist the post-Taliban government, particularly in the way of providing security and extending the reach of the central government. There was a clear reluctance to do so, however. Some of this stemmed from an innate skepticism about Afghanistan and some from a near allergy to nation building. There was a widespread view that ambitious nation building would be resisted by the tribes and would in the end fail. I could not argue with absolute certainty that this view was wrong; all I could and did say was that it would certainly be self-fulfilling: if we did little we would have little to show for it. Some of this same skepticism about nation building limited what the United States was initially prepared to commit to Iraq. Again, though, I have no evidence that the administration was "holding back" in Afghanistan in order to reserve resources for Iraq. This view gets further support from the fact that most of those involved in the decision making affecting Afghanistan did not believe that an Iraq war would require great amounts of military resources on our part. This should not be taken as an argument that Iraq had no impact on the attention and resources policy makers could devote to Afghanistan. It most surely did, but not for several years, until U.S. casualties in Iraq skyrocketed and U.S. force levels there increased.

My Afghanistan role was more operational than most of what I got to do in government during this stint. During this same time, I was also working on the draft national security strategy. Under the law, the administration is obligated to provide on an annual or at least regular basis to the Congress and the public a comprehensive statement of overall national security strategy and foreign policy. Condi and I discussed this at one of our first meetings, and she asked me in my position as head of policy planning to do the first draft. We also discussed what it might say, and for the most part we agreed that it should reflect many of the same themes that had informed her article in the January–February 2000 issue of *Foreign Affairs,* many of which were consistent with my own thinking, including the need for the United States to focus on building constructive relations with the other major powers in order to tackle the global challenges of the day.

I then discussed this assignment with both Colin Powell (who was fine with having Policy Planning undertake the drafting) and with my staff, and I entrusted much of the actual drafting to Drew Erdmann, a young, Harvard-trained Ph.D. in history whom I had hired. Much of the draft was built around the concept of integration, my idea that the goal of U.S. foreign policy ought to be to build cooperation and partnerships with other powers so that regional and global arrangements could be put in place that would be better able to contend with the challenges central to today's world, from the spread of weapons of mass destruction and genocide to climate change, protectionism, and regional conflicts. In the process, we made clear our rejection of both isolationism, a dangerous folly in a global world, and unilateralism, something that we couldn't sustain and that in any event would not work given the nature of global challenges. There was also discussion of the need to promote democracy, human rights, and the rule of law, but this was secondary to the emphasis on building effective multilateralism.

We were just about done with a draft when 9/11 happened. It was apparent that what we had written had been somewhat overtaken by events. It was not just that we had underestimated the importance of terrorism and counterterrorism, but also that 9/11 created new urgencies and opportunities. So we produced a new draft that reached Powell in early December, one that devoted more space to terrorism, but placed it within the same context, that is, the need to integrate other countries in efforts to develop regional and global arrangements to deal with existing terrorists and to discourage young men and women from choosing to become terrorists in the first place. He signed it out and sent it over to Condi without changing a word. It would be months before we heard back, and not until the summer of 2002 that we saw a new and much-changed document.

7. PRELUDE TO WAR

THE WORLD ECONOMIC Forum gathers several thousand of the global good and great each winter for several days of panels and parties or, less formally, schmooze and booze. Normally held in the ski village of Davos in the Swiss Alps, the conference was moved to New York in January 2002, partially in solidarity with the Americans, partially in recognition that 9/11 would be the text or subtext of nearly all that transpired and so escaping to Davos just didn't make sense or feel right.

I normally attended the annual forum, since it provided an efficient way to see a great many people in my field within a few days. Most of the time tended to be spent talking and drinking coffee during the day and something stronger at night. I would also speak at several sessions. This year's "Davos in New York" was no exception, and I was one of several speakers at a luncheon session on Afghanistan. The dominant questions in the air involved the size, capacity, and role of the international force that would be built and inserted into the country, since there was no Afghan police force or army to depend on. A closely related question was what if any role the United States and its forces would assume. I was an advocate for U.S. participation in any international force, but I knew all too well from interagency meetings I'd participated in that I was in the minority in this. Still, I was confident that in the end we would agree to participate, although probably at levels lower than I would prefer. At the forum, then, I stressed that security was the top priority for Afghans, that training an Afghan military and police force was an essential but long-term proposition, and that it was incumbent on the international community to provide the bulk of the country's security in the interim. We could not afford to fail a second time in Afghanistan along the lines of what had transpired in the aftermath of the Soviet era when disarray among the locals paved the way for the Taliban and, indirectly, 9/11. It was rare in life to get second chances, but this was one. I argued for a force (what became known as the International Security Assistance Force, or ISAF) of two or so divisions that would extend over the country. There were important questions as to participation, cost, and mandate, but given the growing disarray on the ground and the fact that the Afghans wanted such a force, I was convinced it would not just happen but happen with U.S. participation. I was so confident of this outcome that I said all this and more at an on-the-record meeting, leading to a front-page story in the *New York Times* the next day that quoted me by name saying we might need an international security force of twenty-five thousand troops deployed across the entire country for several years.

I was not reprimanded so much as I was ignored. Within two months, it was obvious that I had lost the policy battle over what the United States would elect to do in Afghanistan, since we chose not to contribute troops to ISAF and would only agree to the establishment of a small (five-thousand-man) international force that was confined to the Afghan capital of Kabul and approved for six-month intervals. U.S. troops sent to Afghanistan would act independently and have as their sole mission the pursuit of terrorists. Any nation building would not involve U.S. military personnel in a central role. Over time, this became a self-fulfilling policy that increased the odds the government of Afghan president Hamid Karzai would hold little sway beyond the capital. What we have seen since is a revival of warlords, a resurgence of poppy production, and a return of the Taliban. Although U.S. and international involvement has subsequently increased substantially—combined American and NATO troop levels reached sixty thousand at the end of 2008—the United States forfeited the best moment to change the historical momentum and to impose order. Efforts to do so in the future will encounter increased armed resistance and the impatience that inevitably results from renewed nationalism.

An undercurrent throughout the forum was the president's State of the Union speech, delivered just days before. As was the pattern, White House speechwriters would produce draft after draft, and one or two of them would be sent over by the national security advisor's office to the secretary of state for comment. On the Saturday morning before the speech, Powell asked me to read a draft just sent to him. Early on in the text the president declared a goal of preventing regimes that sponsor terrorism from threatening the United States and its friends and allies with weapons of mass destruction. Following that there were perhaps two paragraphs of material devoted to criticism of North Korea, Iran, and Iraq, one after the other. Then there was a pause, followed by a line to the effect that terror states and their allies constitute an axis of evil. I told Powell that the speech was too narrowly focused and too dark; in the months since 9/11, we had seen the world come together in important ways. Powell called Condi with that and a few more specific comments. We never saw a draft or the final version in which Iran, North Korea, and Iraq were directly connected to the axis of evil. (The actual text was "States like these, and their terrorist allies, constitute an axis of evil, arming to threaten the peace of the world.") When I heard the speech, I thought this description and explicit linkage to the three states both wrong and wrongheaded, in that each of the three posed a different sort of problem and that clustering them in a dramatic phrase would likely make it more difficult to build necessary international support for dealing with them. Even so, we all underestimated the impact those words would have.

This was not the only area where policy was going off the rails. Whatever discipline 9/11 had introduced was fast receding. I had particular problems with evolving Middle East policy. Various peace plans named for former U.S. senator George Mitchell and George Tenet were tabled, but all suffered from their emphasis on tests that had to be met before there could be forward movement and from their lack of content or vision as to where the process was headed. Such sequentialism coupled with a lack of direction all but guaranteed a lack of support for the United States among Palestinians and Arabs more broadly. What was needed was a clear articulation of what the United States envisioned in the way of peace; absent that, there was little for those in the Arab world who advocated diplomacy over armed struggle to point to. They needed an argument, but the United States was failing to given them one.

With little confidence my views would prevail in an administration that had difficulty in getting beyond Arafat's flaws, it made more sense to devote time and energy to a related issue that was getting little attention and was less of a political minefield, namely, how to promote political and economic reform in the Arab and Muslim world and how to reduce support for and promote greater intolerance of terrorism. Months later (in December 2002) these themes would come together in a speech I gave at the Council on Foreign Relations in Washington, D.C. I argued that there are many models of democracy; that elections do not a democracy make; that democracy takes time to build and requires an educated populace, independent media, and the full participation of women; that economic and political reform tend to be mutually reinforcing; and that while democracy can be assisted from the outside, it is best built from within.

I did not have Iraq in mind; nor did I think for a moment that democracy was something that could be imposed by military force. What was surprising at the time is that I was favorably quoted by the neocons (Bill Kristol later told me he actually took some heat for this) who more normally attacked me for my lack of enthusiasm for going after Saddam.

This was a long-term effort in every sense. In the meantime, with Powell off to India, Pakistan, Afghanistan, and Japan (for an Afghan donor's conference), I went off on one of my periodic swings to London, Dublin, and Belfast in order to push the Northern Ireland process. Soon after returning I left again, this time for Egypt, Jordan, and Israel. In Egypt and Jordan, what I heard was consistent and strong: You need to do more about the mounting violence between Israelis and Palestinians and the associated suffering of the Palestinians. If you do not address this, and you go ahead and attack Iraq (as many inferred from the State of the Union address that the United States was about to do) you will overload the circuits and undermine the position of your moderate friends in the region. I heard this from ministers in the Egyptian government and from the king in Jordan. In the process, they made clear they held no brief for either Arafat or Saddam. It was just that anti-Americanism had reached a new high in the aftermath of what was widely viewed as an American green light to Israeli prime minister Ariel Sharon (then widely viewed in the Arab world as the personification of Israeli aggression) to crack down on Palestinians. One senior Egyptian official put it this way to me: "If you attack Iraq, I'll be happy to go in on the first tank. But first you must do something to improve the situation of the Palestinians." On Iraq, the general message was that any attack must succeed in ousting Saddam, be done quickly, and not result in the country's breakup lest Iran become the strongest country in the area. In Israel, meanwhile, there was deep and broad unhappiness with the violence and with a Sharon government that was clearly unable to deliver either peace or security. The Israelis did not share the administration's preoccupation with Iraq. Actually, it was just the opposite. The Israelis I met with feared that Iraq would serve to distract the United States from what they viewed as the true threat, which was Iran. I asked one of Sharon's closest advisors why they didn't voice this point of view. Following a shrug and a wistful smile, he said, "We know how important this is to some of our friends, and we don't want to upset our friends." It was thus with more than a little bemusement when, years later, I read the book by Stephen Walt and John Mearsheimer that criticized what the authors saw as the exaggerated impact of the so-called Jewish lobby, suggesting that Israel was partially responsible for pushing us into the second Iraq war.

My travels only reinforced my view that we were not doing enough in the region to promote peace. Why the administration was so reluctant to do more had little to do with the often heard argument that it feared alienating American "friends of Israel." It also went beyond the "let's not do what Clinton did" bias. Most relevant was the reality that many people in the administration simply agreed with the Sharon government and others in Israel who wanted to have nothing to do with either Arafat or the Palestinian Authority. They were right that Arafat and those around him were not doing nearly as much as they could or should to rein in the violence, but waiting for a perfect partner who would embrace democracy and reject violence before there could be meaningful steps toward peace was a prescription for going nowhere. The fact that the vice president's office and the secretary of defense had a seat at the table equal to the secretary of state's also increased the odds that diplomacy would be hobbled.

Powell returned from his own trip to the Middle East even more frustrated than before. I made the case that we had a great deal at stake, including the stability and orientation of Arab regimes, terrorism, and an increase in oil prices, and noted, too, that we would never get Arab governments to address internal reform if they were preoccupied with the Palestinian issue. I also rejected the notion that war with Iraq would transform the region for the better; it was more likely in my view to make things worse. More to the point, it would be difficult to wage such a war successfully without the support of local states. We needed to do more than address the region through the lens of security and counterterrorism; what was also needed was a political dimension. In particular, the president needed to spell out a vision that would make the case to Palestinians as to why they should reject violence and embrace diplomacy.

Powell raised many of these points with the president, but more persuasive was the visit in late April to Crawford, Texas, of Saudi crown prince Abdullah. He had been angry with U.S. policy toward his region for some time, and had refused even to visit the United States to see the current president despite private requests that he come. The Saudis were unhappy and then some; in a meeting held just days before the president was due to meet with the crown prince, Abdullah told Cheney that all he and other Saudis cared about was the willingness of the United States and the president to rein in Sharon, and that if Bush was not willing to do this, then there would be serious consequences for U.S.-Saudi relations and for the region. The "business as usual" joint statement proposed by the U.S. side was rejected out of hand. The president's description of Ariel Sharon as "a man of peace" clearly pushed the Saudis close to the edge. Bush had made matters worse in late March when, dressed in work clothes and leaning back in a chair on his porch in Crawford, he spoke casually about the mounting violence in the occupied territories. At several points the crown prince's entourage appeared prepared to leave town. (I say "appeared" because it was difficult to know what was real and what was theater.) The crown prince said he was sorry he came. Powell had to talk the crown prince into not leaving in a huff. At the end, things came together, but it was a close-run thing.

Afterward, Powell and I concluded that nothing less than a major presidential speech laying out U.S. views on what constituted a fair peace would do. The president had a major credibility problem in the region, and Powell could not operate effectively absent greater clarity on whether the president in fact backed him on this issue. So Powell and I pressed for a presidential speech every chance we got, even handing over building blocks for such a speech to Condi at one point in early May. Finally a decision was made at the White House to go forward; the bad news was that the initial drafts bore little resemblance to what we'd suggested. In the "be careful what you wish for" department, I was beginning to regret that we had argued so hard for a speech, fearing that a letdown would be worse than nothing. I thought the phased "road map" approach the White House was leaning toward was far too sequential: first the Palestinians would need to reform, then they could expect a serious diplomatic process. Requiring that they first be democratic all but assured there would never be a real peace process, something that may have been the real motive of some who advocated this precondition. It also ignored history in that Israel had entered into enduring and productive peace agreements with decidedly nondemocratic Egypt and Jordan. Moreover, I disagreed with the near absence of any indication of what the United States believed peace should actually look like; phase three of the road map, which was to deal with so-called final status issues, was intentionally left blank. Powell tried with Condi and got nowhere, so he suggested I take a turn. I got her on the phone from Paris. I remember pacing up and down on the rue de Seine for half an hour one rainy Saturday, arguing over my cell phone against the hard sequential approach in the draft and in favor of a more forthcoming bottom line. I did no better than my boss; Condi was not prepared to recommend that the president discuss what might be in a peace agreement. In the end, the president did break some useful ground in his June 24, 2002, address, but there was precious little that would give the Palestinians hope in either the near or long term or provide their leaders with a rationale for turning away from violence and those who advocated it.

My frustrations over Middle East policy were part of something larger. I was clearly on a different page than my colleagues on a large number of issues besides the Middle East: the decision on steel, giving domestic producers unwarranted protection against imports, an action that made no economic sense and that was inconsistent with the U.S. commitment to free trade; the handling of the Venezuelan coup, in which the United States appeared to set aside its commitment to democracy and due process in order to see Venezuela's anti-American president ousted; policy toward Afghanistan, where my push for a large U.S. peacekeeping presence went nowhere; the abrogation of the Anti-Ballistic Missile Treaty, for decades a pillar of strategic stability; the unwillingness to negotiate with North Korea or Iran; the growing militancy toward Iraq. The president had locked into 9/11 as a foreign policy template. The problem was that 9/11 could not provide such a construct for the United States at that moment in history. It was too narrow in what it involved, too black-and-white for a world that often required a foreign policy that was gray and nuanced. Demanding that others are either with us or against us, as the president did in his November 6, 2001, address, was counterproductive: it increased anti-Americanism, and it ignored that it is preferable to have limited partners than either passive bystanders or active opponents. To have had as much domestic and international support as the United States had after 9/11 was unique or at least rare. But we came away with little to show for it beyond the ouster of the Taliban and some buttressing of international efforts against terrorism. I also thought it an error to place military force so close to the center of so much of what we were doing. I tried to advance some of this thinking in a speech to the Foreign Policy Association in New York in April 2002. Arguing that we should "move from a balance of power to a pooling of power," I advocated a doctrine of "integration" in which the United States would work to bring other countries (including former Cold War foes) into arrangements consistent with American interests and values and that would promote peace and prosperity in an era defined by global challenges. William Safire built his column around it a few days later, suggesting I was speaking for the secretary of state and representing one of two competing schools in an ongoing debate within the administration over the course of American foreign policy. It is true that what I was advocating represented an approach to the world that emphasized diplomacy and multilateralism, but I am not sure I was speaking for anyone but myself and a few others in the State Department. If there was a debate inside the Bush administration, it was one-sided and muted.

Early that spring I sat down and did one of my periodic "what next" pieces on Iraq for the secretary. It was the first memo I had done for Powell on Iraq for some five months. In December 2001, I had argued in favor of containment and against going to war. I was concerned that a war would meet with little regional support and distract us from higher priorities given the inevitable costs. "Should Saddam be removed and Iraq occupied by American forces, the country's future will become primarily our responsibility.... This would likely require a prolonged American presence in Iraq." My recommended emphasis was on constraining Iraqi WMD capabilities and shoring up regional and international support for containment and effective sanctions. "A renewed effort to reintroduce UN inspectors, absent from Iraq for almost three years, will shift the burden of proof back onto Saddam and his continued failure to comply with existing UN resolutions requiring him to demonstrate that Iraq is WMD-free."

By late April 2002, I had grown increasingly concerned that the president was putting himself and the U.S. government in a box given his bellicose public statements. I urged that we develop and push for the reintroduction of international weapons inspectors with demanding—essentially unconditional—terms we could live with if Iraq in fact accepted them. (As a rule of thumb, it is wise to avoid advancing a position or demanding something of another party unless you are prepared to take yes for an answer. This applies to governments as well as persons.) This might mean that Saddam would remain in power. We would then need to promote regime change with other tools, an objective that would likely require years of overt and covert effort and even then might not succeed. In this light, I also advocated the United States consider pushing for the prosecution of Saddam for war crimes given what he had done to the Kuwaitis as well as his own people. I suggested as well that we should be building up the Iraqi opposition, but that we emphasize the political rather than the military dimension, since the former might lead to something useful and the latter would lead at best to nothing and at worst to a debacle. The United States should begin consulting with regional states (including Israel) about how best to deal with Iraq. We could reassure the Arabs somewhat by making clear our commitment to an intact Iraq and by doing more to improve the plight of the Palestinians. We should assume two things: that any war would require that the United States bear the lion's share of the burden of the fighting, and that any war with Iraq would be followed by years of arduous nation building, with the United States again in the position of having to provide a good deal of what was needed.

It was around this time that a small interagency group was created to start planning for an Iraq war. Chaired by Steve Hadley, the deputy national security advisor at the time, its purpose was less to assess the desirability or necessity of going to war with Iraq than to prepare for one. Marc Grossman, the undersecretary of state for political affairs, often represented the department, although Rich

Armitage (Powell's deputy) also would go on occasion. But neither Powell nor Armitage took the process all that seriously or as evidence that a decision to go to war had in effect been made.

By late spring and summer 2002, however, it was Iraq that was increasingly dominating interagency deliberations and the attention of senior officials. The first strong public indication came with the president's June address at the U.S. Military Academy graduation at West Point. The thrust of the speech, that deterrence could not be relied upon in an age in which rogue states and terrorist groups could acquire weapons of mass destruction, was a harbinger of the delayed National Security Strategy and, more important, a rationale for launching a preventive strike against Iraq. My sense that something was up was reinforced when those who worked with me on the Policy Planning Staff began to come back from meetings around the government and report that those of their counterparts known for advocating going to war with Iraq appeared too cocky for comfort.

I got the chance in early July to question Condi directly during one of our regular sessions in her West Wing office. These meetings and for that matter all our interactions were not without some awkwardness. Condi had been a close friend, someone I had worked with and with whom I would go to or watch football games, as she liked doing such things as much as my wife loathed them. Now she had gone from being a peer in the previous Bush administration to being decidedly senior to me in this one. It is never easy for relationships to adjust to changes in status, especially when there are two persons who disagreed as much and as often as we now did on issues we each believed we understood as well as if not better than the other. On this occasion, I told her I was worried Iraq would come to dominate the administration's foreign policy and that it would prove far more difficult to do and yield far less in the way of dividends than its advocates advertised. She brushed away my concerns, saying the president had made up his mind. I pushed back, but then moved on to other issues scribbled on my yellow legal pad when it was clear there was nothing to be gained by revisiting things with her. Any war was still necessarily some time off given the far-from-complete state of preparations, and despite what Condi said, I figured there would be opportunities down the road to raise my questions and press my position. There was also the fact that while I was against going to war, I was not hard over. I assumed that Iraq did possess biological and chemical weapons and might act with greater aggressiveness because of them, actually use them, or conceivably transfer them to some other state or group. My secondary concern was that if we were to go to war we do it right. This meant setting it up in the best possible way, including with new U.N. Security Council resolutions, improving the Israeli-Palestinian situation, and coordinating with Iraq's neighbors and others. It also meant a quick war fought with an abundance of ground forces. And it meant a readiness to nation-build in the aftermath. I was less than confident that any—much less all—of these conditions would be met.

Still, I emerged from the meeting quite taken aback by the way Condi had shut down conversation on Iraq. I rushed back to the State Department and raised what I'd learned with my boss, who, as was his wont, remained quite calm and, in this case, confident that matters had not advanced as much as I had inferred from my conversation with Condi. He soon realized I was closer to the reality than he had thought and asked to see the president. On August 5, Powell was invited to dinner upstairs at the White House with the president and Condi. Colin advocated strongly that the United States consider attacking Iraq only after gaining international and congressional backing. This approach, he argued, would not only be best if the country went to war, but obtaining such backing would also be the best way to render war unnecessary. Powell told the president that there was a chance that a new U.N. resolution and increased U.S. and international pressure could lead Saddam to back down and finally meet all the demands that had been put to him, in which case the United States would have to accept Saddam's remaining in office and content itself with a "regime that had changed" rather than "regime change." The president said that he understood. Powell also warned the president that a war would not be easy and that the United States would "own" Iraq in the sense that we would inevitably be an occupier for a time and not just a liberator. Powell predicted it would "take the oxygen out of the room" of American foreign policy, leaving little in the way of time and resources and political capital to deal with other challenges. The president held firm on the essential policy, although he agreed to go along with Powell's approach. My sense is that Bush thought Powell was exaggerating the costs and consequences of attacking, although it is possible he thought Powell's predictions accurate but still a price worth paying given the expected benefits.

Others soon caught on as well to the fact that a decision to go to war with Iraq had been all but made. Just days after my meeting with Condi, Sir Richard Dearlove, or "C," the head of Britain's Foreign Intelligence Service (MI6), went to Washington to meet with senior U.S. officials. We now know from the so-called Downing Street Memo of July 23, 2002 (written for David Manning, then Prime Minister Tony Blair's diplomatic advisor and later his ambassador to the United States) that Dearlove found "a perceptible shift in attitude. Military action was now seen as inevitable. Bush wanted to remove Saddam, through military action, justified by the conjunction of terrorism and WMD." What the memo went on to say was even more damning in light of subsequent events. "The intelligence and the facts were being fixed around the policy. The NSC had no patience with the UN route, and no enthusiasm for publishing material on the Iraqi regime's record. There was little discussion in Washington of the aftermath after military action."

It is important to be clear about the significance of my conversation with Condoleezza Rice and the Dearlove consultations. The suggestion is not that a formal decision to go to war had been made in the summer of 2002 and was kept secret. Rather, by July the president had reached the conclusion that it was both necessary and desirable that Saddam should be ousted, and that he was prepared to do what was necessary to bring it about. That this would almost certainly require the use of military force by the United States was not an obstacle. Getting Congress and the U.N. on board was judged to be desirable but not essential. Although the formal decision to go to war would not be made for six more months, by mid-2002 the president and his inner circle had crossed the political and psychological Rubicon.

Interestingly, it was around that same time—in August 2002, exactly a dozen years since the first Iraq war broke out—that a war of a different sort erupted in Washington. It was the start of a war over the war. This was totally in keeping with history. In my experience, all wars are fought three times. There is the political struggle over whether to go to war. There is the physical war itself. And then there is the struggle over differing interpretations of what was accomplished and the lessons of it all. August 2002 saw the joining of this first phase of what would become the second Iraq war. The opening salvo was launched by Brent Scowcroft, first in an appearance on the CBS Sunday morning show *Face the Nation*, then in an op-ed that appeared in the *Wall Street Journal* on August 15. Brent's article was nothing less than a "throw yourself in front of the train" effort to derail the momentum toward a war that Brent judged to be both unnecessary and ill-advised. The thrust of his argument was that taking on Saddam would be a costly distraction that would result "in a serious degradation in international cooperation with us against terrorism. . . . An attack on Iraq at this time would seriously jeopardize, if not destroy, the global counterterrorist campaign we have undertaken." In the parlance of this book, his argument could be summed up as "unnecessary war, bad choice."

I had not read the article prior to its publication. But I was not at all surprised with what it said, since Brent (who was and is a close friend) and I continued to speak and see one another often, and whenever we did, Iraq naturally came up. I was well aware of his stance and for the most part agreed with it. Still, I thought Brent's decision to publish the piece was a true act of conscience and courage given his close relationship with the president's father and the fact that Brent was at the time heading up the president's Foreign Intelligence Advisory Board. Like most everyone else who read it, I was impressed with how explicit he was. I learned afterward that Brent had not shown it in advance to the president's father, although he did send him a courtesy copy after he sent off the text to the *Wall Street Journal*. Brent actually thought through the sequencing, and decided not to discuss the article with the former president beforehand or send him a draft lest he put the forty-first president in an awkward position, especially as he sensed that the elder Bush largely agreed with what he had written. Brent sent the piece at the same time to Condi, not to solicit reaction, but in the spirit of "don't surprise your friends," even or especially when you knew you and they disagreed. He finally heard back from her, but not until the morning the piece appeared in the paper. No one on Condi's staff had seen fit to pass the faxed piece from Scowcroft on to her. To say that the current national security advisor was unhappy with the published views of the former national security advisor fails to capture the intensity of the criticism Brent absorbed over the phone that morning.

Her unhappiness was shared by others in the administration who feared Brent might just succeed in stopping or at least slowing the momentum toward war. They had some reason to be worried, as the public reaction to the article demonstrated that Scowcroft was not alone in his concerns. The administration's response came both swiftly and without warning in the form of a speech on August 26 by Vice President Cheney to the VFW in Nashville. "Simply stated, there is no doubt that Saddam Hussein now has weapons of mass destruction. There is no doubt he is amassing them to use against our friends, against our allies, and against us." Cheney was quite specific on the extent of the nuclear threat. "We now know that Saddam has resumed his efforts to acquire nuclear weapons.... Many of us are convinced that Saddam will acquire nuclear weapons fairly soon." What Cheney went on to do was construct the case for a strategy of military prevention (which he termed preemption) and the need to apply it to Iraq.

I thought the vice president's speech badly overstated the Iraqi threat. It is true that U.S. intelligence had underestimated how far various Iraqi programs had advanced at the time of the first Iraq war, but that did not constitute evidence that Iraq's progress was being underestimated again. The case that Iraq possessed biological and chemical weapons appeared robust to me (even though we now know the truth was otherwise); the case that it was close to possessing nuclear weapons did not bear cursory scrutiny even then. As a rule of thumb, it is time to reconsider your position if you have to cook the books to make your argument. This was one of those times.

Much has been written about the vice president's tendency to adopt the "one percent solution," that is, what needs to be done if there is only a one percent chance that something might be true. This is essentially what social scientists term "worst possible case" analysis. To be sure, there is utility in considering high-consequence, low-probability scenarios, and it is always useful to ask the "What if we are wrong?" question. But raising such questions is one thing; allowing them to dictate policy is quite another. It is almost always possible to construct a pessimistic scenario about another party's capabilities, intentions, or both. But to have such possibilities drive policy would lead the United States into an unending series of negative actions that would over time become self-fulfilling and bankrupting.

The examples are unlimited, but it is useful to consider one that is actually being debated. It is true that China might one day emerge as a geopolitical rival. There are those who advocate taking steps now to try to prevent that from happening or steps based on the assumption that it will happen. The problem with such actions on our part is that they would alienate China and create a self-fulfilling prophecy, bringing about a costly, dangerous, and distracting rivalry that would not be in this country's interest. It would be far smarter to put in place policies that increase the chance that China will end up integrated into the international system and act as an occasional partner. These steps can be complemented by some policies (often described as "hedging") that put us in a position to protect our interests if China does become a threat. But the dominant thrust of U.S. policy should be to invest in positive outcomes so long as they are judged to be more likely than the alternatives. As a result, "most likely case" analysis is far better than "worst possible case" when it comes to providing the intellectual foundation for policy making, although again some allowance can be made for the latter where the consequences are judged to be especially great.

I disagreed, too, with other aspects of what the vice president said. It was wrong simply to dismiss out of hand the utility of international inspections. Obviously, they had to be designed and carried out in a manner that would provide real confidence. This in turn required that Iraq provide the necessary information and cooperation so that inspectors would not face the impossible task of looking under every roof and inside every vehicle. But given adequate information and cooperation, inspections could be useful. Above all, though, my reaction was one of disbelief that a speech of this sort could have been given without getting cleared by the CIA and without vetting by the National Security Council. What happened is that the vice president told the president that he would be giving a speech on Iraq but did not go into detail. When I served on the NSC staff, it was inconceivable that the vice president could simply go off and give a substantive speech on such an important topic without first having it checked out by the intelligence and policy community. That Vice President Cheney was able to do this and apparently suffer no adverse consequence confirmed my impression that the national security process was deeply flawed. Perhaps not surprisingly, the speech also accomplished what the vice president and most others in the administration sought, which was to reestablish the march to war.

So much has been speculated about Dick Cheney and his role in the administration of George W. Bush. One reason there is so much speculation is that Cheney himself is as tight-lipped as they come. Like most committed fly fishermen, he is comfortable with silence. (He once refused to take his friend Ken Adelman fly-fishing on grounds Adelman talked too much.) I should add that Dick Cheney and I always got on well, or at least I thought so until I learned that his staff was reading accounts of my conversations abroad supplied by U.S. intelligence agencies. Either Cheney or someone on his staff thought I was having unauthorized contacts with Iranian officials. Although I strongly believed the United States was misguided in its refusal to deal directly with Iranian representatives, this charge was absolutely untrue.

Cheney is more conservative in the pessimistic sense than many realized, possibly because of his moderate demeanor, which people often confuse with political orientation. One does not need to act radical to be radical. Brent Scowcroft is quoted as saying that Dick Cheney had changed and was no longer the Cheney he knew from the previous Bush administration. This is, of course, plausible, possibly caused by health, possibly by events (9/11 in particular) and

Cheney's reaction to them. In addition, people tend to become a "purer" form of themselves as they age, much as a sauce left on the stove becomes stronger as it is reduced. Context also plays a part in how people act. A decade earlier, Cheney was operating in a very different context, namely, an administration dominated by pragmatic internationalists in which he was the outlier. Now he was in a context in which his views were shared to a large extent by the president and other senior aides except Powell, a situation that allowed Cheney to be himself. That helped explain why he could oppose going to Baghdad to remove Saddam Hussein in 1991 and favor it a decade later.

Yet another signal of where policy was heading was the arrival of the revised National Security Strategy. Although important aspects of what we had drafted regarding relations between the major powers survived, "revised" doesn't quite capture what happened to what we had provided. The new text was maybe one-quarter the length and, more important, included several paragraphs building on the president's June 2002 West Point speech and that made the case for prevention. "We must adapt the concept of imminent threat to the capabilities and objectives of today's adversaries . . . the greater the threat, the greater is the risk of inaction—and the more compelling the case for taking anticipatory action to defend ourselves, even if uncertainty remains as to the time and place of the enemy's attack." I argued at length with Philip Zelikow, a former colleague from the NSC staff of Bush 41 whom Condi had brought in to write the new draft and who would go on to be the executive director of the 9/11 Commission. I predicted that the revised strategy document would be read as little more than a justification for launching a preventive (what the paper incorrectly termed "preemptive") war against Iraq. I feared that by doing this the United States would make itself the political target of great criticism and draw attention away from Iraq's failure to meet its international obligations. My entreaties had no effect, and the document was released in September 2002 pretty much as it was and with the predicted result.

The substance of the strategy paper was not wrong on the face of it. It is true that international law has long recognized the legitimacy of preemptive action, that is, action against an adversary preparing to attack imminently. But the operative word here is *imminent*. Iraq did not constitute an imminent threat; it was at most a slowly gathering one. What was being foreshadowed then was a preventive attack, something with far less acceptance and legal basis. A world in which preventive attacks became commonplace would be a world of constant conflict, as governments could justify early military action against rising powers (to nip them in the bud before they got too strong) or simply neighbors with whom there was a history of war (in order to catch them at an unsuspecting moment). It is not at all clear that Iraq warranted such action even if widely held suspicions about Iraqi WMD capabilities had been correct, which we now know they were not.

By August the participants in the debate over whether to go to war with Iraq had divided into three camps. There were the advocates, led by the vice president (and his staff), the civilians in the Defense Department, the national security advisor and her staff, and the so-called neocons on the inside and the outside of the administration, who believed it was urgent that the United States attack, that the operation would easily succeed, and that all sorts of good things in the region would flow from it. The advocates also believed that we could do most of what would be required by ourselves and that we should involve the Congress, the U.N., and allies as little as possible. A second camp housed the skeptics, including Brent Scowcroft, Republican congressman Dick Armey, and most Europeans I encountered. They saw little or no urgency in the United States acting against Iraq, believed it would prove difficult, and predicted that it would trigger all sorts of bad things in the region and the world, including

instability in neighboring Arab states, terrorism, and economic problems brought about by more costly oil. There was as well a third
camp, which included people who leaned toward either of the other
two, but who for one reason or another (usually because they were
torn, thought the war inevitable, or both) were focusing on the "how"
more than the "whether." They were interested in calming the Israeli-
Palestinian situation, in gaining U.N. authority, in building international support, and in getting Congress on board. Here I would place
two former secretaries of state—Henry Kissinger and James Baker—
and the secretary of state at the time, Colin Powell.

I was a cross between the second and third groups. I was skeptical
of the need to go to war given all else we had on our plate, all the
likely problems a war would trigger, and the absence of a compelling
answer to the question "Why now?" I also felt strongly that if we
were to go to war it was essential we do it right lest the undertaking
prove as costly and as counterproductive as I feared it otherwise
would.

My own impact on Iraq policy was extremely limited, and certainly far less significant than it had been a decade before. Given my
position as head of the Policy Planning Staff, I had little interagency
role. Other than making my case to Condi and others whom I could
get to listen, my principal function was to support the secretary of
state. By early 2002, I had already sent Powell a number of overview
memos about Iraq strategy. But now that it was clear a war was
more likely than not, I switched gears and reoriented the work coming out of the Policy Planning Staff.

Policy making has something in common with football. Activity
at any time during a game is concentrated on the part of the field
near the line of scrimmage. It makes little sense to position oneself in
the end zone at the far end of the field if one wants to be a factor.
Much the same holds for policy. If all the interest and attention is
focused on one set of questions, it is usually of little or no value to

place yourself totally outside the debate and raise concerns that are judged to be irrelevant. Where one can influence policy is by trying to stretch or push the debate. Returning to a football analogy, if the ball is on the thirty-yard line, one is more likely to influence policy if one argues for changes that would move the ball a few yards down the field than if one suggests a total change in game plan. To have argued against the war after a decision was all but made to go ahead with it may have made me and other skeptics feel better but would have reduced any influence we might have on planning for the war and its aftermath. As a result, the Policy Planning Staff focused on producing two sets of papers: one on all that needed to be done in any run-up to a war, the other on what would have to be done in the aftermath. I also did a good deal of work with people in the intelligence community on how we might stimulate a coup from within the Iraqi military and what we would do if one were to materialize.

I sat down late that August and wrote out a memo for Powell on Iraq, essentially trying to capture where the policy debate stood. On the side of going to war, I listed several arguments: dealing with the WMD threat, the "positive domino" effect that could follow success in Iraq, the world-order case that U.N. Security Council resolutions not be ignored, ensuring that Iraq could not threaten world access to oil, and U.S. credibility, that is, that many would conclude we had blinked and lost our nerve if we didn't follow through after all the warnings we had issued and all the threats we had made. On the "against" side of the ledger there were also numerous arguments: it was not at all certain Saddam would use or transfer any WMD that he did possess; the scenario in which he was most likely to use any WMD would be one in which we sought his ouster and he figured he had nothing to lose; war could well stimulate terrorism, regional instability, and a spike in anti-American sentiments; it would be expensive; it would take time, attention, and resources that would otherwise be available for other foreign policy priorities; it was quite possible the "positive domino effect" might not materialize; and the credibility argument was overstated, that is, not going to war could be readily explained if, say, the Iraqis actually accepted a robust inspections regime. It did not occur to me to include the argument that the stated rationale for war, Saddam's possession of weapons of mass destruction, might not exist.

It was not hard to discern where I leaned, which was toward the negative. If we did proceed, I pointed out it would be the first significant discretionary war undertaken by this country since Vietnam. It would be a war of choice, not one of necessity. As a result, the margin for error was reduced; we had to get it right. This argued for policies that resembled those that had worked so well the last time, including pushing for a U.N. Security Council resolution along the lines of 678 that provided international authority for using military force, building a broad-based international coalition, initiating contingency dialogues with Israel and other neighbors of Iraq, getting Congress on board, making sure there was an active public diplomacy campaign, and preparing for adverse energy contingencies. I also thought we needed to do something on the Israeli-Palestinian front. Here there was no parallel to the earlier crisis, since in that one we could not appear to be rewarding Saddam for his aggression. In this case we were free to act, and needed to do so both on the merits and to reduce Arab resistance to a U.S.-initiated conflict. I also argued we needed to make a good-faith effort to get weapons inspectors back inside Iraq on terms we could live with. Regime change could not and should not be the reason for going to war. It would set a dangerous and destabilizing precedent: a world in which stronger countries routinely intervened in the affairs of weaker countries to bring about changes in regime would be far messier and more violent. Rather, the reason for war needed to be Iraqi noncompliance with the Security Council and its call for Iraq to satisfy the world community that it did not possess weapons of mass destruction. If Saddam refused to do this, regime change might be required, but it needed to be portrayed as a means and not as an end in itself. Last, I argued that we should only go to war if we were prepared to see it through, something that would require a large-scale, long-term occupation that would have to be much more intrusive and demanding than what we had mounted in Afghanistan.

The memo on discerning the lessons of a half century of nation building turned out to be the largest single project we undertook during my tenure at Policy Planning. I asked Drew Erdmann to take the lead, although virtually the entire Policy Planning Staff was involved. We carried out an in-depth examination of the lessons of U.S. experiences with nation building throughout the twentieth century. Among the nearly two dozen cases were Cuba, the Dominican Republic, and Haiti early in the twentieth century, Germany and Japan at the end of World War II, and more recent cases such as Korea, Panama, Haiti, Afghanistan, Kosovo, and Somalia. A number of themes emerged. The U.S. government needed to understand just what it was inheriting and then determine the scope of its ambitions. "The larger the gap between our ambitions and the situation we inherit, the larger must be our commitment in time and resources." History suggested you tended to get what you paid for when it came to nation building.

It was essential that everything possible be done to prevent the emergence of a security vacuum once the battle was won and the regime removed. "Every past reconstruction success was built upon a bedrock of basic security. Without order and security at the local level, all else is jeopardized. . . . Warlords and organized crime syndicates swiftly fill any vacuum created by the absence of security, police, and judicial authority. Once in place, these forces prove difficult to dislodge and constitute spoilers that challenge the entire reconstruction effort. Delay in bringing order to everyday life during the initial phases of reconstruction can be costly." This called for the rapid deployment of large numbers of military and police forces from the outside, the demobilization of existing forces of the occupied country, and the simultaneous rebuilding of police and military forces making use of many of those who had been serving in existing forces.

Beyond matters of security, the memorandum suggested the United States should not take ownership of those economic activities most critical to the country lest it appear as though the war had been fought for narrow or selfish purposes. This argued for not asserting control over the oil sector but rather letting the Iraqis run it. It also meant recasting the oil-for-food arrangement so that Iraqis could gain access to the resources that were rightfully theirs. Only the most senior echelon of the former political leadership should be barred from holding office. "We should preclude only a small number of members of the old regime—the upper echelons of the Ba'ath (Renaissance) Party, the military, and the security services, as well as any indicted war criminals—from participating in the post-Saddam political order. We will most likely need the assistance of many associated in some way with the old regime to maintain order and establish a new viable state." To do more would be unreasonable in that many people joined the party simply because it was a necessary step to get access to jobs and education. It would also be counterproductive in that we would need many of these people to run the country. We should resist trying to impose an individual leader on the country. He would lack any legitimacy. Instead, following a period of direct control, we should support a political process that would produce a new indigenous leadership. It was essential to keep the neighbors out and to limit any meddling on their part. (This was motivated by a desire to get the country up and running on its own steam and to avoid having the defeated country become a battleground for the neighbors.) Some sort of a political process akin to the Afghan "six plus two," which regularly brought together Afghanistan's immediate neighbors along with the United States and

Russia, was needed for Iraq. Last, we recommended that the United States take the lead on the security side but allow the international community and the U.N. in particular to assume oversight of political and economic matters.

We sent the product—a fifteen-page, single-spaced memorandum with case studies attached—to Powell in late September.* He read it carefully and agreed with most of it. He also sent it around to his counterparts, including the secretary of defense, the national security advisor (for herself and the president), and the vice president. Others, including many individuals testifying before the Senate Foreign Relations Committee and those in the State Department involved in the so-called Future of Iraq project, were making similar points and stressing the difficulty of what was sure to confront the United States after it defeated and removed Saddam and his regime. No one could argue that these perspectives had not been raised, although it was true that the lack of any meaningful interagency process or oversight of the aftermath made it all too easy for the Defense Department (which was essentially left by the NSC to oversee itself) to ignore advice from the outside.

By September, policy direction was clear. Thanks to his own advocacy and support from British prime minister Tony Blair, Secretary Powell had a green light to try to build international support around a resolution that would make far-reaching demands of Iraq and authorize the use of force if the demands were not met. On September 12, the president took advantage of his annual address to the U.N. General Assembly to challenge the world body to pass such a resolution. To do this was a last-minute decision, and, consistent with Murphy's Law, the final version of the speech on the teleprompter did not include the agreed-upon language. The president ad-libbed, stating, "We will work with the UN Security Council for the necessary

* The full text of this memorandum appears in the Appendix beginning on page 279.

resolutions." I sat up in my chair, as the president and others wanted all this accomplished in a single resolution. They did not want to return to the Security Council any more than was absolutely necessary, which in their view meant getting all they needed in one go. No one seemed to notice the plural "resolutions," which several months later became a major issue when the British government determined it desirable to have a second resolution, one that explicitly authorized armed intervention, before it could go to war against Iraq.

The president's U.N. address was but one of his public statements. He and other senior officials regularly referred to the fact that Iraq possessed weapons of mass destruction and the reality that the world did not have the luxury of waiting until all questions were resolved lest the proof be a mushroom cloud. Also expressed with frequency and conviction were allegations of ties between Iraq and al-Qaida. Much was made of Saddam's offer of twenty-five thousand dollars to widows of Palestinian suicide bombers although there is no evidence to suggest it in fact happened. The rhetoric increasingly outpaced the evidence; all uncertainties and doubts were ignored. This is not to say doubts about the extent of Iraqi activity were nonexistent; indeed, it was in reaction to an expression of presidential displeasure over the strength of the intelligence about Iraqi WMD that George Tenet tried to reassure the president by declaring emphatically that the case was a slam dunk—extremely strong.

In the meantime, the momentum toward war was further strengthened by votes in the House and Senate on October 10 and 11 respectively that authorized the use of force. The votes were one-sided: 296-133 in the House, 77-23 in the Senate. I was struck by the contrast between these votes and the much narrower margins by which Congress went on record a decade before in the run-up to the previous Iraq war. What made this disparity in support so striking was that the case a decade before was so much stronger legally, strategically, and diplomatically. The 1991 conflict was a war of necessity if there ever was one, whereas what was being contemplated here was a classic war of choice. Yet the war of choice was approved by Congress with far larger majorities. The only explanation was the triumph of politics. Many of those voting this time around simply did not want to be on record in the wake of 9/11 opposing a war that was then popular, expected to cost little, and predicted to accomplish a great deal.

The publication in October 2002 of an intelligence community assessment of Iraq's weapons of mass destruction had a large effect on thinking and politics alike. "We judge that Iraq has continued its WMD programs in defiance of UN resolutions and restrictions," it began. "Baghdad has chemical and biological weapons as well as missiles with ranges in excess of UN restrictions; if left unchecked, it probably will have a nuclear weapon during this decade." The NIE judged that Iraq was "reconstituting its nuclear weapons program," that Saddam "probably has stocked at least 100 metric tons [MT] and possibly as much as 500 MT of CW [chemical warfare] agents," that Iraq "has some lethal and incapacitating BW [biological warfare] agents and is capable of quickly producing and weaponizing a variety of such agents," and has "established a large-scale, redundant, and concealed BW agent production capability." The overall effect was to reinforce the certainty that Iraq possessed weapons of mass destruction, which at least made the war a reasonable option even to those of us who would have preferred that we not go down that path. Not once in all my meetings in my years in government did an intelligence analyst or anyone else for that matter argue openly or take me aside and say privately that Iraq possessed nothing in the way of weapons of mass destruction. If the emperor had no clothes, no one thought so or was prepared to say so.

Why was the intelligence on Iraqi WMD so wrong? One senior intelligence official at the time described it as the proverbial perfect storm. Not having inspectors on the ground after 1998 resulted in a loss of "ground truth." Years of judgments layered one on top of the other made it difficult for anyone to question basic assumptions; mind-set was a major problem. There may also have been some overcompensation for past underestimation of Iraqi WMD. All this helped to create an environment in which sources that should never have been judged trustworthy were judged to be credible. I know of no attempt to falsify intelligence by anyone in the U.S. government. It was more a case of people selecting ("cherry-picking") reports that supported a certain position and going with them despite questions about their accuracy. Policy makers tend not to question judgments that fit their preconceptions or preferences. (Some also fight hard against those that do not, which can lead some analysts to hold back lest they incur wrath and jeopardize access.) And tradecraft was flawed since sources were not properly vetted in several instances, in part because analysts did not always have access to information about the sources themselves. It should also be pointed out that much of the Iraq-related intelligence was right. The intelligence community was right in judging that there was no operational tie between Saddam and al-Qaida and in predicting the nature of the aftermath. Still, the profound overestimation of Iraqi WMD programs was an intelligence failure of the first magnitude.

Diplomacy came to a head long before any of this was known or even suspected in most quarters. On November 8, the U.N. Security Council passed Resolution 1441, an extraordinary document that declared Iraq was in "material breach" of its obligations under a host of previous U.N. resolutions, provided Iraq a "final opportunity" to comply with calls for its disarmament, detailed what was required in the way of cooperation with U.N. inspectors (UN-MOVIC), and warned Iraq that "it will face serious consequences as a result of its continued violations of its obligations." The resolution was ambitious in what it required, but vague on what would follow if these demands were not met. In particular the resolution did not

settle the question of whether it authorized the use of force or if another resolution was required. For the moment, this uncertainty
didn't matter. What was obvious was that there was enormous international pressure on Iraq to reverse its policy of resisting international inspection of its alleged weapons programs. The Iraqi
government quickly caved. Inspections were resumed that same
month, and in early December the government released a trove of
documents relating to its programs. It was clear that what it had
provided was still inadequate, but it was also clear that the years of
Iraq thumbing its nose at the United States and the world had come
to an end. What was less certain but increasingly predictable was
what would follow.

8. WAR OF CHOICE

IRAQ WAS THE dominant issue as 2003 began. I decided to make a last-ditch effort at slowing things down. I closed the door to my office and typed out a memo to Powell that argued that despite all the buildup it was not too late for the United States to back off using force. To be sure, there would be real costs, both actual and perceived, if we did stand down. Saddam would remain in place; calling things off would raise questions among friend and foe alike as to what we were made of. There would even be some people in the Middle East, always a cauldron of conspiracy theories, who would conclude that the United States actually wanted Saddam to remain in power. And it might well prove even more difficult to gain international support for using force down the line if we balked now. But like all policy options, the costs of this one had to be weighed against the costs of continuing down the path we were on, which I believed were far larger. If we did not attack, there were steps that could and should be taken that would give us a rationale for not attacking and leave us better off in the absolute. These steps included an open-ended series of robust inspections; tightening the sanctions by compensating Syria, Jordan, and Turkey for shutting down all smuggling and trade outside U.N. control; maintaining a higher than usual tempo of military deployments and exercises in the region; initiating war crimes proceedings against Saddam; and mounting an active public diplomacy program that called for regime change and re-minded Saddam and others that we were prepared to use military force if his cooperation with U.N. weapons inspectors was anything less than full and unconditional.

I knew what I argued here was explosive—if it leaked, it would be a major story and then some—so I handed the memo to Powell rather than send it to him through the formal secretariat. I told him to give it to the president on the off chance Bush was having second thoughts and was feeling trapped. I wanted Bush to know he re-tained a way out. Powell read it and put it in his pocket—literally. I didn't expect him to give it to the president, but to use the arguments if an opening presented itself. Apparently, none did. And even if it had, there was no real chance that the memo would have changed anything. I wrote it as much as anything for my own peace of mind. The president was too committed to turn back.

How did George W. Bush reach this point? I will go to my grave not fully understanding why, although I believe I have a good if not complete understanding of how this second Iraq war came about. There is no certainty, as there was no meeting or set of meetings at which the pros and cons were debated and a formal decision taken. No, this decision happened. It was cumulative. The issue was on the table from the outset of the administration, but it was not going anywhere in particular. As I once wrote Powell, "September 11 changed the debate on Iraq. It sharpened the focus on the threats posed by Saddam's continued rule, highlighted the possibility of an Iraqi version of September 11, and underscored concerns that con-tainment and deterrence will be unable to prevent such an attack." Before 9/11, Iraq was simply one of many concerns on an evolving foreign policy agenda. After 9/11, the president and those closest to him wanted to send a message to the world that the United States was willing and able to act decisively. Liberating Afghanistan was a start, but in the end it didn't scratch the itch. Americans had no long-standing history or feud with Afghanistan. Also, there was a pervasive pessimism when it came to Afghanistan, in the sense that most of the advisors around the president held out little hope that Afghanistan could ever be made into something much better.

Iraq was fundamentally different. The president wanted to destroy an established nemesis of the United States. And he wanted to change the course of history, transforming not just a country but the region of the world that had produced the lion's share of the world's terrorists and had resisted much of modernity. He may have sought to accomplish what his father did not. The arguments put forward for going to war—noncompliance with U.N. resolutions, possession of weapons of mass destruction—turned out to be essentially window dressing, trotted out to build domestic and international support for a policy that had been forged mostly for other reasons. The fact that Iraq was not involved in 9/11 or tied to al-Qaida (despite repeated intimations and claims by the president and others to the contrary) mattered not. Indeed, the president's instruction to counterterrorism coordinator Richard Clarke to look for a connection between Iraq and 9/11 when there was no reason to suspect one seemed more than anything to reflect a desire to justify a course of action Bush was already inclined to take. The fact that Secretary of Defense Donald Rumsfeld instructed Central Command in November 2001 to begin planning for a war with Iraq reinforces this point.

Paul Wolfowitz was clearly of the view that Iraq constituted a major strategic opportunity. That he would think this came as little surprise to me. I had first met Paul in 1979, when both of us were working in the Pentagon on, among other things, what to do about the Soviet threat to the Persian Gulf. His strength was an ability to think outside the box and to raise first-order questions. This was also a weakness, since in policy making the moment for first-order questions inevitably passes and it is time to tackle detailed questions of implementation. This was not his forte. Paul was also something of an intellectual romantic, believing in the possibility of revolutionary change for the better. All of this contributed to his judgment that Iraq (and, through Iraq, the Middle East region) could be transformed at little cost. As it turned out, the transformation was in important ways for the worse and anything but cheap.

Why was this president so attracted to taking on Iraq? From what I saw and heard, his decisions were not, as some of his detractors claim, the result of any shortage of intelligence or because he was manipulated by his vice president and others. Bush is smarter, much smarter, than people generally understand. He also had a good fix on the attributes and weaknesses of those around him; Bush read people as well as you would expect from someone who succeeded in getting elected president. His fault was that he was quick to reach conclusions (be it about policy or people) and often viewed changing course as a sign of weakness, something a strong leader (to his way of thinking) would resist. My reading of him is that he was attracted to do what was bold. Such big actions appealed to his competitive side—what better way to confound one's critics?—and served the desire to distance himself from his father, who favored prudence and tended to eschew the dramatic.

I would see this president only intermittently: at some relatively large interagency meeting, when Powell would take me in tow for one of his regular Oval Office sessions, or when high-level visitors would come from the U.K., Ireland, Northern Ireland, or some other country I was heavily involved with. The longest conversation we had during the time he was president and I was working in the State Department was in the conference room on board Air Force One flying back from the Northern Ireland summit held at Hillsborough Castle just south of Belfast in April 2003. For more than an hour it was just the three of us—Bush, Powell, and me. We were all dressed casually.

Bush was generous toward me despite the fact the summit did not achieve the breakthrough we had anticipated; if he was disappointed he didn't show it. He asked a good many questions about the Council on Foreign Relations, as it was already known that I would be leaving government shortly to go there. What struck me more than anything, though, was how comfortable he was with his decision to attack Iraq. Here we were, three weeks into the war, and he appeared totally at peace with what he had decided and how it was unfolding. It was real confidence, not bluster. But I was struck, too, by how unconcerned the president seemed to be with all the complications that I and others had predicted would come his and our way. Again, he had a penchant for the big and dramatic and was not about to allow the doubts of others or the details to sidetrack him.

Would there have been a second Iraq war had there been no 9/11? Counterhistorical questions are impossible to answer confidently. Before 9/11 there had been some activity in the bureaucracy about Iraq, but there is little evidence that it amounted to more than background noise. Sept. 11 transformed the administration into the proverbial hammer looking for a nail. Iraq became that nail. Absent 9/11, I do not believe there would have been the felt need to attack Iraq or the domestic political context to support such a strike. Matters likely would have drifted until Saddam attempted to break out of what remained of his box, either stimulating the world to respond with military force or accepting (as had been the case with the Clinton administration in 1998) the new status quo.

But 9/11 did happen, and the president and the administration were motivated to attack Iraq and oust Saddam. There were several indicators in 2002. In January 2003, the State of the Union address constituted another attempt by the president to reinforce the case for war, in particular the infamous citing of the "evidence" that Iraq had sought to import uranium from Niger when it was widely known within the government that no such effort had in fact taken place.

Days before, he had ordered the establishment of the Office of Reconstruction and Humanitarian Assistance (ORHA), the Defense Department–run agency that would oversee post-Saddam Iraq and help avert the humanitarian crisis expected to follow battlefield success.

The question of what to do about Iraq came to a head in late January 2003 at a special session of the U.N. Security Council chaired by the French, that month sitting in the chair of Security Council president. The nominal subject of the special session was to review the war on terrorism. Powell was unenthusiastic about attending, it being Martin Luther King Day. He was also skeptical, fearing the meeting (which the French insisted be at the ministerial level) would be a waste of time at best or, at worst, spin out of control, which it quickly did. Powell, with more than a little justification, felt ambushed by his French and German counterparts. Both European governments were playing to public opposition to war and animosity toward the Bush administration. More than once I thought back to a meeting some months before in Paris. I was there for policy planning talks, and it turned out to be just after the French had changed foreign ministers. Hubert Vedrine, the man who called the United States a "hyperpower" and tried without much success to explain he meant nothing critical by it, was out; Dominique de Villepin, the elegant protégé of French president Jacques Chirac, was in. Hearing I was in Paris, de Villepin asked to see me, and the two of us had an hour-long one-on-one in his small office at the Quai d'Orsay. The meeting could not have been friendlier, and was transacted in English, something that would never have been done years earlier when every French diplomat was under instruction to use his native language. It was just as well, given that his English was not only better than my French but at least as good as if not better than my English. The new foreign minister went out of his way to promise me, and through me Powell, that he would never do anything to embarrass Powell, and that if he disagreed with U.S. policy, he would make his disagreements known privately.

It was also in January that I was invited for breakfast at the residence of Jean-David Levitte, the new French ambassador to the United States. The guest of honor was Maurice Gourdault-Montaigne, the diplomatic advisor to President Chirac. What stuck in my mind was an exchange over what would happen if the inspectors actually found WMD in Iraq. Gourdault-Montaigne and the ambassador said this would demonstrate that the inspections were working and deserved more time. I said this was untenable. French policy could not have it both ways: to argue for continuing inspections if nothing were found—and for continuing the inspections if something were found. I predicted that if some weapons of mass destruction or materials were found, the view in the United States would be that war was justified, since it would prove the Iraqi declaration was dishonest. Both seemed taken aback by my stance, although a few days later, when the ambassador came to see me at my office at the State Department, he said he had since heard exactly the same thing from other Americans, Democrats and Republicans alike.

My experience in Davos late that same January was revealing. I showed up on a Friday, and for a day was the target of intense, sustained anti-Americanism, almost all of it the result of differences over Iraq. I did my best to defend the administration's policy, making the case that Iraq was not in compliance with Security Council Resolution 1441 and that allowing more time to pass would not on its own improve matters. I was both comfortable and uncomfortable doing this: the former because I continued to act on the assumption that Iraq possessed weapons of mass destruction, because of which my opposition to the war was muted; the latter because I questioned the need for the war and believed that one of its champions inside the administration should have been there rather than me to face the music.

Powell showed up the next day. I had phoned to warn him what he was about to walk into. I also told him that the speech we had prepared for him to give was inadequate given the strained atmosphere at Davos. So I sketched out some ideas, and when he arrived the two of us sat in his hotel room and produced a new text that included more language about the U.S. role in the world and bolstered the section on Iraq, adding a line that "Multilateralism cannot become an excuse for inaction." In the end, it turned out to be what many thought was Powell's best foreign policy speech and came closest to articulating an approach to American foreign policy that he agreed with (emphasizing diplomacy and multilateralism) while still managing to be a reflection of administration policy. For two years I'd been trying to persuade him to give such a speech; afterward, he teased me that I'd snuck it in on him. But it was well received, and it did manage to calm the waters, if only partially and temporarily.

The march to war gained additional momentum in early February, when Powell accepted the assignment of making the case for attacking Iraq to a skeptical U.N. Security Council and world. It had all the makings of this generation's Adlai Stevenson moment, an echo of the dramatic "J'accuse" delivered by the former Supreme Court justice (who was then U.S. ambassador or permanent representative to the United Nations) during the Cuban Missile Crisis. Stevenson dramatically displayed satellite photographs of preparations in Cuba for Soviet missiles. Instead, Colin Powell's presentation to the U.N. Security Council is widely held to be a stain on his otherwise extraordinary career. Some have called it a tragedy. I saw it more as irony. To understand why, it is necessary to go back to where he and we began. Powell was given the assignment for one reason: he was by far the most credible spokesman of and for the administration, far more than the president or anyone else. People around the country and the world trusted him, in part because of his record, in part because he was viewed as practical and reasonable rather than ideological. Many outsiders were clearly taking their lead from him. Powell understood all this perfectly well. The fact the administration came to him gave him more leverage than was customary; the fact that he understood his reputation was on the line made this naturally cautious and rigorous person even more so.

I was not involved in the minute-to-minute preparations of Powell's presentation, but two of my staff members were—Lynne Davidson, formerly George Tenet's speechwriter at the CIA and now Powell's, and Barry Lowenkron, a long-term CIA hand who was now one of my deputies. Also heavily involved was Larry Wilkerson, a former deputy of mine who was close to Powell in the Army and was now his chief of staff, and John McLaughlin, George Tenet's number two in the intelligence community. The entire drill was compressed into several days. The NSC never delivered on its promise to provide a draft presentation contributed to and approved by the intelligence and policy communities. Instead, the project was farmed out to the vice president's office, which provided a forty-eight-page script that no one else had seen or vetted. It was a deeply flawed document, filled with all sorts of selective and unsubstantiated accusations about Iraqi support for terror and possession of weapons of mass destruction. Powell, believing that much of the "intelligence" supporting the draft was suspect, made the early decision to throw it out and start over. He made it clear he only wanted to include material that came from multiple sources with a respectable track record. The recent NIE on weapons of mass destruction replaced the script from the vice president's office as the basis for the presentation. I would get involved when drafts emerged; I would read them, mark them up, and get my comments inserted into the process. By the end, all involved felt confident of what was in the text. Those from my staff as well as Powell and Wilkerson also felt good about how much the product had changed from what the vice president's office offered up. In government, sometimes you measure progress by what you prevent as well as by what you accomplish, and this was one of those times. People were exhausted, but the exhaustion was mixed with satisfaction, as the individuals I knew best believed they had prevailed in insisting on intellectual honesty, with the result that what Powell would say to the Security Council and the world would be accurate.

I myself harbored no doubts. The intelligence about biological weapons vans seemed strong; the idea of mobile vans housing production facilities seemed totally plausible. I was aware of the debate over "artillery tubes" and whether they were in fact artillery tubes or components for centrifuges intended to enrich uranium. People I respected were confident that what we were looking at were not simple artillery tubes. For his part, Powell noted the debate. He left out any reference to yellowcake coming from Niger, the claim made by the president in his State of the Union speech that would later come back to haunt the administration. Satellite photos depicting recently doctored sites suspected of housing illegal weapons were viewed as furnishing yet more evidence that Saddam was playing a shell game, moving illegal weapons and smoothing out the sand just before inspectors arrived. This is why I describe Powell's performance as ironic. All involved at the time thought they had done an excellent few days' work and included only what was certain. The sense was that we had held the line against those who were prepared for him to stretch the facts. We had held the line, but even so some of what Powell stated was wrong, not because he went beyond his brief, but because the brief as approved by the CIA was wrong.

At the time, Powell's performance in the Security Council was widely viewed as a home run. The British, though, while mostly pleased with the presentation, were not satisfied, as Prime Minister Tony Blair needed a second resolution that went beyond 1441 and explicitly authorized states to use all necessary means, that is, military force, to bring about full Iraqi compliance with all relevant U.N.

resolutions. Blair's need was tied to the revolt by fellow Labor Party members in the parliament, many of whom opposed a war absent such a second U.N. resolution authorizing it. In effect, what the British wanted was this war's equivalent of Security Council Resolution 678, which preceded the previous Iraq war. It was not in the cards, though, in that the Iraqis had done nothing this time around that was perceived to be as egregious as invading and dismantling an independent country.

But the debate surrounding a second resolution went beyond Blair's political needs. There was also the legal matter of whether the Iraqis had moved into compliance with international demands that it cooperate with weapons inspectors. By November 2002, the Iraqis had changed their behavior quite a bit, agreeing to the return of the inspectors, who were permitted considerable leeway to perform their mission. But the Iraqis never provided the detailed information requested by the inspectors. The purpose of the U.N. effort was never designed to uncover Iraqi noncompliance. This was too high a bar given the unlimited number of places available to hide proscribed weapons. Instead, the U.N. effort was designed to confirm Iraqi compliance, something that required cooperation and the provision of relevant data. But this was a distinction mostly lost on others. The bottom line is that Iraqi actions did not constitute a casus belli for France or Russia or China, which left the British and the United States isolated and frustrated within the Security Council.

Actually, the United States was frustrated twice over, as it only reluctantly agreed to seek a second U.N. resolution at Blair's behest. Most in the administration believed they had all the authority and grounds they needed and opposed returning to the U.N., a body they tended to view with suspicion or downright hostility. To be fair, the U.S. position that it didn't require a second resolution was not without merit in that the first resolution passed months before by the Security Council (1441) could be construed as providing authority to act. Again, Iraq was not providing the needed information for inspectors to verify that it was in compliance with its obligations. It was therefore in violation of the cease-fire. But this is legalism; the political reality is that most of the rest of the world believed a second resolution was essential if any use of force was to be legitimate.

There was actually a mini-debate within the administration about whether to press for a second resolution regardless of its poor prospects. Some in the administration favored doing so as a means of pressuring others to stand up and declare themselves against going to war even if it did not appear that we had the votes to win. I never understood this logic and thought this approach misguided, and instead argued that the worst of all outcomes would be to lose a vote and then go to war. This would be widely viewed as an arrogant slap at others and raise even more fundamental questions concerning the legitimacy and legality of what the United States was contemplating. I also thought it would do real and lasting damage to the United Nations. Far better would be to explore getting a second resolution and then pull back if it consultations demonstrated it was likely that we could not prevail in the Security Council. I argued all this out in a memorandum that Powell distributed to the principals. Fortunately, this position carried the day, and the administration decided to pull back if and when it became obvious that no international consensus favoring war would emerge.

By early March, the attempt to build consensus behind a second Security Council resolution came to an end. The gap within the Security Council was simply too large to bridge. Iraq's "declaration" of the history of its weapons of mass destruction programs and activities was the final straw for the administration. The material provided by Iraq was widely seen as inadequate and therefore another sign that Iraq had no intention of complying fully with what the United Nations and the international community had required. This is consistent with the February 14 report of Hans Blix, the chief weapons inspector, who noted that he had found no weapons of mass destruction, but that many proscribed weapons and items remained unaccounted for.

It is impossible to write about this history without addressing Saddam's behavior. More than anyone else except President George W. Bush, he was in a position to prevent the war. Why did he not simply give the international community all it wanted? He of all people knew that he was not hiding any weapons of mass destruction. Saddam apparently believed this would be a sign of weakness that would be exploited by his internal opponents, the Iranians, or both. He clearly calculated that it would be less risky and costly to absorb what he assumed would be a limited American attack than it would be to admit to the world that he had complied with its will and no longer possessed weapons of mass destruction. It is also possible that he felt that the Russians and/or French would prevent a war so long as he met the Americans halfway. I would like to be able to report here that I put forth such explanations or at least considered these possibilities and dismissed them. But I cannot. It simply did not occur to me that Saddam's resistance to full compliance, both as regarded disclosure and cooperation with weapons inspectors, may have been a considered decision on his part. Nor do I have any recollection whatsoever that this explanation occurred to anyone else in either the intelligence or policy communities. Again, assumptions can prove dangerous, and any analytical or decision-making process must require that someone be tasked with putting forward alternative interpretations of what has taken place or what could.

One other alternative scenario merits mention. What if Saddam had complied fully and unconditionally with the relevant Security Council resolutions? There is the question of whether he would have survived, which we now know was the question that most concerned him and that led him to resist international pressures that he comply. But there is also the question of how the United States would have reacted. Was President Bush prepared to take yes (or "uncle") for an answer? Again, it is hard to avoid the irony: Saddam resisted policy change for fear it would lead to regime change; Bush resisted accepting policy change for fear it would rule out regime change. My sense is that most around Bush would have advised him to reject whatever Saddam offered. This view is reinforced by the historical reality, in that Saddam came close to full compliance in the days just preceding the war. What would likely have proven critical was the reaction of Tony Blair and Colin Powell. If either was prepared to publicly declare that what Saddam was doing was acceptable and that war had as a result become unnecessary, it would have been extremely difficult if not impossible for Bush to argue that attacking Iraq was in fact justified.

The war began on March 19, somewhat earlier than anticipated because of intelligence (incorrect as it turned out) as to where Saddam was. The president opted to attack in an effort to decapitate (literally and figuratively) the Iraqi leadership. The attack went ahead and failed to have the desired effect. It was interesting to contemplate what might have transpired had the intelligence proved correct and had Saddam in fact been killed. It is at least possible that history might have unfolded quite differently—especially if he had been replaced quickly by another Sunni "strongman" from within the army who agreed to abide by relevant U.N. resolutions.

In the event, the war began in earnest soon after the unsuccessful attempt to take out Saddam. I was surprised, not in the immediate sense, but in the larger sense that some twelve years after the end of the previous war with Iraq the two countries were back at it. It was just over two years since George W. Bush had become president, a year and a half since 9/11. It was not just a war of choice, but the first preventive war launched by the United States in its history. It was begun not just to disarm a regime but to oust it, in the process transforming a country and the region.

People have often asked me why I didn't resign over Iraq. They also asked me (and continue to for that matter) why Powell didn't resign. I have thought a good deal about this and had even written years before about the question of when it is right and appropriate to resign. Putting aside personal reasons (health, finances, family, etc.) I believe there are two policy-related grounds for resigning. (I do not subscribe to the peculiarly British tradition of resigning when something goes wrong on your watch. It may not be your fault, and even if it was, you may still be able to do more good by staying than by leaving.) The first instance when resignation is warranted is when a person fundamentally disagrees with a major issue. In my lifetime, several people resigned from the National Security Council staff over the Nixon administration's May 1970 decision to extend the war to Cambodia. Secretary of State Cyrus Vance resigned over President Carter's decision to use force to try to free the American hostages from Iran. Several relatively junior foreign service officers resigned over the lack of a robust American response to Serbian brutality in Bosnia in the 1990s. In the case of Iraq, although it obviously constituted a major issue, and although I disagreed with U.S. policy, my disagreement was not fundamental. Earlier, I described my position as being 60/40 against going to war. No organization could function if people left every time they lost out on a 60/40 decision. Had I known then what I know now, that Iraq no longer possessed weapons of mass destruction, then it would have become a 90/10 decision against the war, and in that circumstance I would have left had the president gone ahead all the same. Whether he would have gone to war knowing then what we do now about Iraq's lack of WMD is another one of those "What if?" questions, arguably better left to historians and novelists. Asked precisely this by ABC's Charles Gibson on December 1, 2008, Bush refused to answer. "You know, that's an interesting question. That is a do-over that I can't do. It's hard for me to speculate." My hunch, though, is that he would not have done so. A proven absence of WMD would have removed the principal argument for going to war—even if it would not have removed the principal motive. International and, more important, domestic opposition would have been too great absent some new action by Saddam Hussein that could have been portrayed as a new casus belli.

As for Colin Powell, it would have taken a great deal for him to resign in protest over a single policy decision, given his military background. Powell possessed a powerful sense of loyalty and duty and patriotism, all of which meant he was willing to put up with a lot that made him uncomfortable. It was no accident that Powell chose to keep a portrait of George Marshall, another general who became secretary of state, prominently displayed in his office. Powell would cite the anecdote in which Marshall, returning to the department after having lost an intense argument with Truman over the decision to recognize the state of Israel, was asked by aides if he was going to resign. "No, gentlemen. You don't take a post of this sort and then resign when the man who has the constitutional responsibility to make decisions makes one you don't like." Powell also possessed great confidence in his own considerable skills, which in turn gave him the belief that if he remained on the inside he would be able to help ensure that policy came out better than it would have had he left. Whether a decision to go to war against Iraq absent a belief that Iraq possessed weapons of mass destruction would have met that criterion for him is unclear. But again, that was not the context in which any of us was operating. If I had resigned, it would have been a one-day story and would not have affected the course of history. Had Powell resigned, it would have been a major story, but my sense is that Bush would have pushed ahead.

The one exception to the above might have been if, again, either Powell or Tony Blair dissented publicly at the eleventh hour on grounds that there was no WMD or that Saddam had complied fully with Security Council resolutions, rendering war unnecessary. I distinguish that here from a scenario in which Blair's government fell over the policy. If this had happened, my view is that Bush would have seen it as a loss but not a fatal blow, the result of British politics. But if either Powell or Blair had taken the initiative to dissent from the policy and called on Bush to alter course, the president would have been hard-pressed not to give the inspectors more time. Of course, neither man was so disposed given what both thought were the facts about WMD and Iraq's noncompliance. But I cannot think of anyone else (excepting Saddam) who was in the position to have altered Bush's trajectory once it was set.

The other situation in which resignation is warranted is when there is a pattern of policy decisions that makes clear that there is not a good fit between the individual and, in this context, the administration. In baseball, the batter who fails two out of three times is considered a star and, if he can sustain that pace over a career, is likely to end up in the Hall of Fame. In government, failing "only" two out of three times is a prescription for frustration. My rate in this administration was worse that that: besides Iraq, I lost the argument on increasing troop commitments to Afghanistan, offering a conditional package of incentives linked to behavior changes to both North Korea and Iran, putting forward a more ambitious approach to the Israeli-Palestinian conflict, and suggesting alternatives to and not just rejecting those international accords (such as the Kyoto Protocol on climate change or the International Criminal Court) that we found fault with. Adding to the frustration was the fact that I was often called upon to defend in public and in meetings with officials from other governments policies I had argued against. Cordell Hull, FDR's secretary of state, described himself to a friend as "tired of being relied upon in public and ignored in private." I empathized all too well. On many occasions I had to rebut in public or in meetings with foreign counterparts precisely the arguments I myself had put forward inside the U.S. government. That this occurs on occasion is inevitable and part of what any professional must expect and deal with. But when it becomes the norm it is time to consider whether what you are doing makes sense.

It is very difficult for someone like me to walk away from government. It is what I trained to do. I worked hard to get where I was. Government service at its best can be interesting, it can be heady, and it can matter. There are few things in life more exciting and fulfilling that participating in and even contributing to history. When it works well, government also entails a collaborative dimension that is uniquely satisfying. And even when government proves to be frustrating, as it often does, there is the hope that you can somehow overcome the adversity and have a positive impact on policy. All this helps to explain why the outs struggle so hard to become ins every four years.

Nevertheless, my thoughts about leaving crystallized in the wake of three incidents. There was the time I walked into a room with the French foreign minister, only to hear a stage whisper, "Ah, here comes the reasonable face of American foreign policy." Then there was the call from a friend who had just been talking at a university in China. The first question from a student: "I just read a speech on U.S.-China relations by Richard Haass. Does he speak for U.S. foreign policy?" The third simply involved my wife calling me an "enabler." It stuck with me in part because there was more than a little truth in it. I didn't feel any need to leave (the administration, not my wife) in a huff, but I was clearly increasingly open to doing something else. A number of interesting possibilities opened up in early 2003. I decided to allow my name to go forward for one of them, the position of president of the Council on Foreign Relations, and when it was offered to me, I decided to accept.

This was all some time off. In January 2003, the decision was made by the president to put the Defense Department in charge of what would come after the battlefield phase of the war. There was some logic in this, in that almost all of the Americans on the ground were soldiers and this was an occupation. Still, I questioned the wisdom of this approach. It was akin to playing tennis and having one player make all the line calls. It was also odd given the clear lack of interest in nation building expressed by the civilian side of the Defense Department. The Pentagon should have been in charge of security issues, but the NSC ought to have been placed or placed itself in the position of overseer, with Treasury in charge of financial matters, State in charge of political and diplomatic, and so on. But Defense had the advantage of having the most people on the ground and the most experience. It also was at the zenith of its prestige in the aftermath of the battlefield phase of the war. No one in the U.S. government was disposed to take it on. I also detected throughout the State Department a sense that Defense, having advocated for the war, should now sleep in the bed of its own making.

There was also more than a little hubris in play. As noted, Defense Department officials were riding high in the wake of what seemed to be an impressive and inexpensive military victory. Proposals from the State Department that the United Nations, which had a great deal of experience in dealing with postconflict situations, be given a lead role in liberated Iraq were roundly rebuffed. I advocated the U.N. playing a role in Iraq akin to what it had done in Afghanistan. But there was no appetite for this, because there was little trust in the U.N. and because many U.S. government officials had their own preferences in the Iraqi exile community (most notably Ahmad Chalabi) regarding who should come to power in post-Saddam Iraq and feared they would not get their way if the U.N. oversaw the political process. In the end, the U.N. was left with a minimal role.

There was also the matter of international economic involvement in post-Saddam Iraq. There was little interest in bringing in governments and companies from countries that had not supported the war. What motivated this view was a sense that to the victor should go the spoils, and that French and Russian firms should not benefit in any way given their opposition. I was surprised and dismayed: I thought that Iraq needed all the help it could get, that the United States needed more, not fewer partners, and that we could rebuild Iraq and rebuild some torn relationships at one and the same time. It is extraordinary that many people throughout the U.S. government thought Iraq was a jewel to hoard and not a burden to share. But they did.

Yet another unpleasant development in the aftermath was Pentagon vetting of which American officials would get to serve in Iraq. Two members of my staff, both in their thirties, wanted to serve there. One was Meghan O'Sullivan, an Oxford-educated specialist whom I had brought with me from Brookings. There we worked together on a series of books dealing with economic sanctions and incentives, and at State, Meghan had become my principal aide for the work I was doing in Northern Ireland. She had a limitless capacity to work hard and was one of the few people I have ever encountered who could master the most intricate detail without losing sight of the big picture. The other was Drew Erdmann, the Harvard-trained historian who was central to our drafting of the National Security Strategy and then later the long study of lessons learned from U.S. nation-building experiences throughout the last century. Both remarked to me that this was likely to be the defining experience for their generation and they wanted to be part of it.

Jay Garner, the retired general placed in charge of ORHA, the organization set up to oversee U.S. efforts to deal with the humanitarian challenge expected to dominate post-Saddam Iraq, was happy to accept Drew, but reported back that he did not want Meghan. When pressed, he said that he was acting under instructions from the secretary of defense, who in turn had hinted strongly that he was taking his orders from the vice president. Meghan's sin was associa-

tion with me—both in general and in the work we had done suggesting that a policy predicated on sanctions toward Iraq might be in the
best interests of the United States. I spoke with Powell, and he threatened Rumsfeld that he would deny Garner the services of anyone
from the State Department if Meghan were rejected. Rumsfeld re-
lented. It is yet one more curiosity that over the next four years
Meghan became one of L. Paul Bremer's main aides in Baghdad,
perhaps the American most trusted by Iraq's political leaders, and
ultimately a deputy national security advisor overseeing policy toward Iraq who shepherded the change in policy known as the surge
through the government. Powell could not, however, persuade Rumsfeld that Garner should accept Tom Warrick, a somewhat eccentric
but knowledgeable State Department officer who held strong but
not always welcome views about how the United States should go
about the task of rebuilding Iraq and which Iraqis they should work
with.

The battlefield phase of the war lasted only some six weeks. On
May 1, 2003, President Bush landed a fighter plane on the deck of
the USS *Abraham Lincoln* and emerged from the aircraft against the
backdrop of a banner saying "Mission Accomplished." As was the
case twelve years before, the fighting had gone more quickly and more
easily and had proved less costly than many anticipated. Few expected
that this would prove to be the high-water mark of the second Iraq
war; nothing else would prove quick or easy or inexpensive.

Donald Rumsfeld infamously stated that a country goes to war
with the army it has. In the case of the second Iraq war, this was only
partially true. The United States went to war with much less than the
army it had. The second Iraq war was a war of choice twice over:
that it was fought and how it was fought. More than anything else
the relatively low number of troops brought to the theater (approximately 150,000, roughly one-third the number of American troops
in the previous Iraq war) all but guaranteed the United States and its

few coalition partners would not be in a position to assert and maintain order once the formal battles were concluded. The 150,000 number was about one-third the level of forces called for in war plans developed at Central Command in the late 1990s. There were good reasons for lowering this number in light of the deterioration of Iraq's armed forces and advances in U.S. technology—but this calculation did not take into account the much greater requirements of Phase IV, post-warfighting scenarios.

Why did the United States go about its war planning in this way? Again, assumptions played a part. The administration uncritically accepted what a small number of academics and exiles told them, namely, that the Iraqi people would welcome Americans as liberators and there would be no need for a heavy occupation. There may also have been arrogance at work, as civilians in the Defense Department seemed determined to demonstrate that they could improve upon the previous Iraq war and in so doing render obsolete the Powell Doctrine and its call for large numbers of troops. Making matters worse is that planning for Phase IV began late (Garner was only appointed in January 2003, just months before the war) and planning for combat operations was never integrated with planning for the war's aftermath. Tactical and strategic decisions that made sense in one context (for example, having U.S. units move with great speed and largely avoid cities) had large and adverse consequences for the other as security vacuums emerged in urban areas that were quickly filled by hostile irregular forces.

No one can legitimately argue that those who made the decision to go in relatively light were not warned. Powell and I both thought this was dangerous, and after talking with Paul Pillar, the national intelligence officer for the Middle East, I commissioned studies from the National Intelligence Council about what the United States could expect to encounter in a liberated Iraq. Two National Intelligence Council reports emerged in January 2003: *Regional Consequences* of *Regime Change in Iraq* and *Principal Challenges in Post-Saddam Iraq*. Both were later declassified. The latter in particular was troubling, as it predicted that "The building of an Iraqi democracy would be a long, difficult, and probably turbulent process. . . . [A] post-Saddam authority would face a deeply divided society with a significant chance that domestic groups would engage in violent conflict with each other unless an occupying force prevented them from doing so." Army chief of staff Eric Shinseki was upbraided by his civilian bosses for stating before a congressional committee that several hundred thousand U.S. ground troops were needed to do this right. He ought to have been heeded rather than criticized.

The only good news is that the president rejected an approach to ousting Saddam Hussein and building a successor government that never passed the laugh test, namely, the idea (most popular in the civilian side of the Defense Department) to build a force of Iraqi exiles into military units that would spearhead a popular uprising to overthrow the regime. What was imagined was a liberation rather than an occupation. Significant sums were spent on building an exile force in Hungary of all places, but in the end it amounted to little and even lost the support of its original proponent, Ahmad Chalabi, when he saw it would not be his instrument to use as he saw fit. Indeed, much of this option reflected the agenda and appeal of Chalabi, a prominent Iraqi exile with a controversial past (one that included charges of financial impropriety) who for reasons I never understood (and to this day do not) mesmerized a number of Americans, persuading them that he was the man to lead post-Saddam Iraq. Interestingly, one of the few proponents of going to war inside the administration who didn't fully buy into Chalabi was the president, who rejected plans to install him at the head of a new government.

My own experience with Chalabi was anything but positive. I met him in the early 1990s when I was still at the White House, and formed the impression that he was mostly out for himself. He came to see me and pressed me for U.S. backing; I said we would not extend any support to him, but would support an umbrella organization of Iraqi opponents to Saddam if it was truly representative, that is, nonsectarian. The Iraqi National Congress was the result, although it never met the standard of being truly representative and gained negligible traction within Iraq. Nothing over the years altered my view that Chalabi was a clever, manipulative self-promoter who lacked military experience and much in the way of a political following inside the country—unless the country in question was the United States. Any doubt about this latter contention was erased by the picture of Chalabi sitting behind first lady Laura Bush at the 2004 State of the Union address.

It didn't take long for it to become painfully clear that postwar events were not unfolding as anticipated by the war's optimists and enthusiasts. To paraphrase the then secretary of defense, stuff was happening. Widespread looting was the first strong indication that the United States had not prepared for what was emerging. Everything that was not nailed down, and a good deal that was, disappeared. Garner estimates that as many as seventeen of Iraq's twenty-one government ministries were rendered useless. This made the task of reconstituting Iraqi government capacity all but impossible. The looting was a terrible development, one that encouraged further contempt for authority and disorder. U.S. authorities compounded matters by being slow to appreciate the true nature and scale of the insurgency they faced and then making a series of ill-advised decisions, including the official disbanding of an Iraqi army that had mostly disintegrated and not doing more early on to re-create a new one. Denial of employment opportunity to many former members of the Ba'ath Party made matters worse. The net result of dismantling the existing instruments of authority and not doing more to establish replacements was to create a security situation exploited by released criminals and radicals of every stripe. What was worse, a good many Iraqis were let loose on the streets with guns in their possession and anger at an occupation that was not what they bargained for.

This story of a botched aftermath has been told many times by many others and needs little recounting. Suffice it to say that the United States got it wrong for several years in many ways, from assumptions about how Iraqis would react, to the number of troops required to do it right, to forging an acceptable strategy for building a new political order.

All this said, it is best not to treat the war's aftermath as a single period, since U.S. policy evolved significantly in both the political and military domains. The initial phase of planning for the aftermath took place just before and during the war itself. Much of this was done independently by the various departments, notably Defense and State. There was some but not much interagency consideration or coordination. It would be years before the aftermath was made the priority it should have been from the first moment war was envisioned.

Planning is never better than the assumptions fed into it (and sometimes not even that good). This was no exception. Much of the political preparations were near useless as they were predicated on a short-duration, low-cost effort, as well as the notion that Iraqis would greet U.S. personnel "with sweets," as welcome liberators. Much has been written about the Future of Iraq project run out of the State Department. The reality was considerably less than the hype. These reports were long in detail but for the most part lacked practicality or relevance in the field. They were not taken seriously (for good reason I thought) by planners in the Defense Department. At the same time, U.S. military requirements were underestimated as predictions of widespread resistance and disorder were largely rejected. The human tendency to pay attention to those predictions that buttress preferences and discount those that do not was on full display. And largely missing was any rigorous mechanism to scrutinize and challenge preferences held by those in policy-making positions of responsibility.

Making things worse was the shortage of local knowledge. This was driven home to me several years later when, in September 2007, Iraqi prime minister Nuri al-Maliki visited the Council on Foreign Relations in New York. We sat down for half an hour before his speech, and given his lack of English, I did my best to make him comfortable using my rudimentary Arabic. I welcomed him and asked him how he was feeling. Saying he was good, he then asked me how I was doing. "*Ana mabsut*"—I am fine—I replied. He looked at me quizzically and repeated his question. "*Keef halek?*" (How are you?) "*Ana mabsut*" I repeated. He tilted his head, squinted his eyes, and then turned to his ambassador for assistance. After a pause, the ambassador burst out laughing. "What you said, Richard, means something very different in Iraqi Arabic than in the Egyptian. Rather than fine, it means you are lying flat on the floor being beaten." Given what was going on in Iraq at the time, it seemed all too apt.

There were two contending U.S. approaches to the aftermath. One was a traditional occupation, in which the United States would assume a dominant political role and military presence in the country until Iraqis were deemed ready to take over. A second placed a much greater emphasis on building up the Iraqis so that they could look after themselves sooner rather than later. In the end, U.S. policy would reflect both of these, but not in the intended ways, since the United States was never able to synchronize the political and military dimensions of its policy.

My own preference was for a large U.N. role on the political side complementing a large American role in the security realm. The problem was that there was simply no support for bringing the United Nations in. The fear was that the U.N. would shape a political process in ways that would not help those exiles and Kurds that many in the administration wanted to see in positions of power. So the U.N. never got asked—which may have been just as well, because there was little support inside it for taking on a large role in a war that most who worked there opposed. (What little support there was inside the U.N. for getting involved in Iraq essentially disappeared in the wake of the August 2003 bombing of the U.N. headquarters in Baghdad. The attack killed Sergio Vieira de Mello, the U.N. secretary general's talented special representative in Iraq. It also killed Arthur Helton, a senior fellow at the Council on Foreign Relations, who was meeting with Vieira de Mello at the time of the bombing.) The irony is hard to escape: many around the administration opposed U.N. involvement because they wanted the United States to control events, while many in and around the U.N. wanted no part in reconstructing Iraq because they wanted the United States to reap what it had sown.

The inadequacy of preparations for the aftermath became quickly apparent once Garner and his small team arrived in Iraq in April 2003. The situation on the ground was unraveling fast. U.S. forces lacked the numbers, orders, training, and organization to deal with the widespread looting. Actually, a principal reason Garner (a retired Army general) was selected for the job was his past role in organizing large-scale relief operations in northern Iraq in the wake of the previous conflict. But this time around the crisis was political and military, not humanitarian, and pervasive, not limited to one region within the country.

The political side was turning out just as bad. Efforts led by Zalmay Khalilzad (who would later become the U.S. ambassador to Iraq and later still the U.S. representative to the United Nations) to construct a representative and legitimate political process along the lines of what had been done in Afghanistan came to naught. The split between exiles and those Iraqis who had endured Saddam's tyranny proved too great. Those who had remained on the outside often turned out to be even more inflexible, that is, sectarian, than those who had stayed behind and had some experience with living and working with one another. Within weeks, it was clear to all on the ground and in Washington, in uniform and suits alike, that the Garner mission was not succeeding and would not.

With illusions of stability and a rapid assumption of political authority by Iraqis shattered, the United States embarked on a very different approach to Iraq later that same spring. One way to describe this new phase was occupation. This is accurate but incomplete, since occupation rarely is and was not then an end in itself. Another way to view the period from May 2003 through the end of June 2004 (when Iraq regained sovereignty) was the beginning of the U.S. effort to build political institutions and military capacities in Iraq. This was the period that coincided with the appointment of L. Paul "Jerry" Bremer as the head of the Coalition Provisional Authority.

Bremer and those around him did themselves no favor with the draconian de-Ba'athification they set in motion. Under Saddam, Ba'ath Party membership was a necessary prerequisite for entry into many schools and careers and many Iraqis joined for practical rather than ideological reasons. Some de-Ba'athification was required, but it should have been confined to the most senior officials and officers. The disqualification of so many Iraqis denied the country the experience and skills it desperately needed at the same time as it alienated many of the Sunnis who, without access to the new Iraq, supported or at least tolerated the most violent elements in their own community, some of whom came from outside the country and were associated with al-Qaida. Exacerbating matters was the lack of careful implementation. Appeals could rarely be heard in a timely manner. Things got even worse when Bremer decided to put Iraqis in charge of the process. Selected for this sensitive task was none other than Ahmad Chalabi, who unsurprisingly proceeded to use his newfound power to advance his own agenda.

Prospects for stability were also undermined by the decision to disband the Iraqi army and not act with dispatch to reconstitute it. An Iraqi army could have been built on the foundations of Saddam's, if, as it has been argued, it was impossible to keep Saddam's army intact. But the result was not simply the loss of a potentially useful partner to help maintain public order, but also the loss of control over weaponry and individuals with military experience. The army was along with the Ba'ath Party one of the cornerstones of the old Iraq; it was inevitable that the society would dissolve and order would deteriorate if both institutions were allowed to disintegrate and those who were part of them alienated from the occupational authority and those Iraqis who chose to work with it.

The fact that Bremer and others in the field claim these decisions were directed by officials in Washington, and many officials in Washington said these decisions were taken in the field, is both illuminating and depressing. Nothing captured this so well as a meeting in the fall of 2003 among Condi Rice, in her capacity as national security advisor, Powell, and Secretary of Defense Don Rumsfeld. Rice asked Rumsfeld to instruct Bremer on some policy matter and Rumsfeld replied that he could not, given that Bremer worked for the White House!

Where the critics go too far, however, is in suggesting that the whole notion of an occupation was both misguided and unnecessary and that events would have turned out markedly better if only the United States had empowered Iraqis from the outset. The exiles, and Chalabi in particular, lacked the necessary domestic base. He was widely held to be corrupt, lacking in any military experience, and sectarian, more interested in punishing Sunnis than in forging a broad-based successor regime. Iraq needed a period of occupation in order to bring about a new political order and in effect a new society; what it didn't need is the occupation it got.

Although Iraq regained its sovereignty in July 2004, this sovereignty was more in name than in fact. U.S. political and military authorities were "in control" but events were out of control. Over the next two and a half years the situation in Iraq steadily deteriorated. The politics-first approach to the occupation was clearly misguided as sectarian violence came to dominate the country. It was a time of some progress, including two elections and a constitutional referendum. But what political progress there was did not translate into improved security. Indeed, the decision to hold elections so early in the aftermath, a decision that reflected American ideology as well as an attempt to placate the powerful Shia clergy that wanted to establish majority—Shia—rule, was deeply flawed. It served mainly to reinforce sectarian identities that contributed to the civil war that would come to envelop much of the country. It is hard to exaggerate the importance of getting the sequencing and pace of state building right; alas, it is equally hard to exaggerate the difficulty.

There was something of a theological flavor to debates in Washington over whether what was going on inside Iraq constituted a civil war. What is undeniable, though, is that the war on the ground in Iraq provoked a political war within the United States. Just as clear was that by the end of 2005 and early 2006 the Bush administration was fast losing control of both theaters. It didn't help itself with the publication in November 2005 of a National Security Council–authored document entitled "National Strategy for Victory in Iraq." It was impossible to read the text and not conclude it was wildly divorced from Iraqi reality. It was so bad that after receiving an advance copy from a friend at the NSC I wrote him back asking if someone had stolen his email account and was circulating bogus material. The creation of the bipartisan Iraq Study Group in March 2006, however, calmed the domestic debate and bought precious time for the administration, even though the president (showing considerable political courage) rejected many of the study group's recommendations (made when it reported in December 2006), including sharply reducing U.S. military presence and activity in Iraq. Unfortunately, he also rejected the proposal to convene a regional forum that would involve Iraq's neighbors in the search for stability, something that likely would have proven useful.

By the summer and early fall of 2006 it was increasingly clear even to the war's most ardent advocates within the administration that U.S. policy was failing and that Iraq was on the verge of descending into a state that would meet anyone's definition of civil war. Even worse, a civil war in Iraq could all too easily morph into a regional war, much as Lebanon's internecine conflicts had drawn in many of its neighbors. The National Security Council reclaimed authority over the conflict and embarked on what proved to be the most systematic and careful review of Iraq policy options it had undertaken at any time during this administration. This provided the backdrop to changes in U.S. policy announced in early 2007. This may be an instance when even hindsight is less than 20/20, but the surge—the increase in U.S. forces by some thirty thousand troops— was only one factor influencing subsequent developments. More important was the adoption of a strategy that came to resemble classic counterinsurgency. Rather than position large numbers of U.S. forces on large bases and have them focus on attacking terrorists and militias, the new strategy emphasized protection of populations, something that got American troops out of their bases and patrolling in smaller numbers in a manner more associated with a muscular form of peacekeeping. This change, which predated the surge, increased trust between Sunnis and coalition forces, which contributed to the realization by many of Iraq's Sunnis that Sunni extremists who had come to Iraq were a threat to their future. They increasingly began working with the United States (which was prepared to arm and train local Sunni tribesmen) to defeat extremists. Iraq's Shia militias, most likely with the prodding of Iran, made a bid for power in the streets, but in the process alienated large numbers of Iraqis and dramatically reduced their challenge to the American presence.

The question is whether these improvements will endure given the lack of strong national institutions and a lack of meaningful political reconciliation among Iraq's Sunnis, Kurds, and Shia. Moreover, even if improvement does come to Iraq, the result will almost certainly be something markedly less than a normal or model state. At best, Iraq is likely to remain a divided and sometimes violent and dysfunctional country. Iran, by virtue of geography, ethnic and religious ties, and its own efforts, will remain the strongest external influence for years to come.

This projection may prove to be overly pessimistic. By mid-2008 something of a virtuous cycle appeared to be developing, in which improved security was leading to improved economic conditions, which in turn was reinforcing more stable politics and security. Again, though, important questions persist about the durability of the improvements and the likelihood that more "national" politics (including the sharing of oil revenues, the disposition of the contested city of Kirkuk, and the resettlement of the four million Iraqis who fled or were forced from their homes) will emerge. Still, the improvements that we have seen make it possible to discuss the war's benefits, which more then anything stem from the removal of Saddam Hussein. Eliminated with him was the scenario of his having remained in power buoyed by higher energy prices and constrained less by eroding sanctions. And, at least in principle, there is the possibility that Iraq could still have features that others in the region would want to emulate.

But even if the positive cycle continues, it will not reduce the direct and indirect costs to the United States or many of the consequences of the war. There are the obvious costs: in American lives (more than four thousand), American casualties (more than twenty thousand),

and dollars ($1 trillion plus or minus depending upon the accounting; it is impossible to speak of financial costs with precision given among other things the long-term costs of medical and other veterans programs). There is the human cost in Iraq, a cost that includes not only the tens of thousands of lost lives but the four to five million Iraqis who fled from their villages and homes and ended up as refugees in neighboring countries or as displaced persons within their own country. The war in Iraq certainly stimulated terrorism there in the short run; what we do not know is what the long-term consequence of the war will be when it comes to thousands of young men who have been radicalized and trained on Iraq's streets. Afghanistan had its "blowback" and Iraq might as well. U.S. military forces that have been tied up in Iraq have not been available for use or threatened use elsewhere. It will take a generation to replace the equipment and maybe longer to recover from the personnel costs, which include those who have not reenlisted and those who chose alternative careers. Iraq absorbed the most precious of resources: the time and attention of senior policy makers. On the political side, the Iraq war may have actually set back the cause of promoting democracy in the region, since democracy came to be widely associated with disorder. Iran has gained strategically and is now along with Israel one of the two most influential local states. Not only has Iran emerged as the principal external influence inside Iraq, but the Iraq that served as a balancer and foil to Iran no longer exists. U.S. credibility has taken a hit, in that U.S. claims, say about the nuclear programs of others such as Iran's, are viewed with greater suspicion. As a result of the decision to go to war, perceptions of incompetence, and such abuses as Guantánamo and Abu Ghraib, U.S. prestige has suffered throughout the world and anti-Americanism has increased. In the short run this will work to reduce U.S. influence; in the future, it could well bring to positions of power individuals whose worldviews were formed on the premise that the United States is a threat. Adding to the diplomatic cost of the war was the refusal of the administration to exploit initial battlefield gains in Iraq to negotiate a firm limit to Iran's nuclear ambitions. Instead, all too many policy makers, heady with apparent success, rejected diplomatic opportunities in the belief that regime change in Tehran and Damascus would be all but certain to follow and, when it did, would solve U.S. problems with those governments. By the time senior policy makers realized this was unlikely to occur, the moment of opportunity had come and gone, and the United States was left to deal with challenges, including Iran's nuclear program, from a much-weakened position.

I have used the word *irony* on several occasions, and it is difficult to escape it. An administration that came into office belittling nation building ended up doing just that and then some. It was an administration that began in the camp of the realists and ended up outdoing Woodrow Wilson in its muscular embrace of the need to promote democracy. And more than anything else, a war launched to transform the region did so in ways never intended. The second Iraq war, a classic war of choice, served to narrow American choices.

9. TAKEAWAYS FROM TWO WARS

FEW IF ANY would have predicted that U.S. foreign policy in the initial decades following the end of the Cold War would be defined to a considerable degree by two armed conflicts with Iraq. But it was. That the two conflicts were undertaken by a father and his son for such different reasons, in such different ways, and with such different results, constitutes one of the great curiosities of this or any era, as those who write about American history are sure to conclude.

My judgment is that the first Iraq war was not only a war of necessity but a largely successful one at that. It was necessary for reasons both symbolic and strategic. A failure to have responded to Iraqi aggression against Kuwait would have set a terrible and likely destabilizing precedent at the outset of the post–Cold War era, something that would have made this era far more disorderly and dangerous than it has turned out to be. Inaction also would have established Iraqi control over Kuwait's substantial energy reserves, leading to great influence and possibly effective domination of the region's energy supplies, and provided Iraq both time and opportunity to develop nuclear weapons.

This reference to energy and its relationship to the first Iraq war should not be read to mean that energy was the motive in the sense that the United States was seeking either commercial advantage or physical control of Iraqi resources. This applies to the second Iraq war as well. Energy mattered, but only in the strategic sense of enhancing Iraq's and the region's importance. But even without it, Iraq would have significance given its regional role and concerns about proliferation and terrorism. It is also worth noting that the United States went to war after 9/11 against Afghanistan—what I would term a war of necessity—even though energy concerns were absent. The same holds for the decisions to intervene in Somalia, Bosnia, and Kosovo, three wars of choice.

The judgment that the first war with Iraq qualified as a success derived from the fact that the principal war aims—the reversal of Iraqi aggression and the restoration to power of the Kuwaiti government—were accomplished. That both aims were realized at only modest human, economic, and military cost to the United States and to great domestic and international applause only reinforces the judgment that what the United States did constituted a success. It is also worth noting that the first Iraq war is consistent with the precepts of the just war: it was fought for a worthy cause, it was likely to succeed, it was undertaken with legitimate authority, and it was waged only as a last resort.

This is not to suggest that the first Iraq war should be viewed as a textbook case of how to conduct foreign policy. The administration of George H. W. Bush misread Iraqi intentions; more could have been done (although it is impossible to know with what effect) to deter an invasion. U.S. intelligence badly underestimated just how much work Iraq had done on weapons of mass destruction. The end of the war also could have been better handled. More of the Iraqi army should have been bottled up and either disarmed or destroyed. Signals to the Iraqi population about what the United States was and was not prepared to do should have been made more clear. More could have been done sooner to lessen the humanitarian tragedy. But the critics go too far, since it remains uncertain and even unlikely that U.S. policy could have brought about Saddam Hussein's ouster and replacement by someone and something markedly better at a reasonable cost.

The second Iraq war was not necessary. To paraphrase what a French statesman of the eighteenth century said about an ill-advised and unwarranted execution, it was a blunder. There were other viable policy options available to the United States, in particular reforming the sanctions regime in a manner that would have allowed Iraq more leeway in what it could import but also would have limited the resources coming under the regime's direct control. Inspections could have been designed to provide considerable if not total confidence that Iraq was not developing weapons of mass destruction. Odds are that Saddam Hussein would have remained in power, but his ability to have threatened his neighbors and his own citizens would likely have been circumscribed. The United States could well have accomplished a change in regime behavior and a change in regime threat without regime change.

A comparison with just-war thinking is again useful. Here, the second Iraq conflict comes up short. The worthiness of the cause, the likelihood of success, the legitimacy of the authority to undertake it—all were questionable. Not even its advocates could argue it was a last resort. Looking at the war and the decision to wage it through this lens is useful, not just for moral reasons, but for practical ones, because the criteria for determining the justness of a war offer a good guide to predicting domestic and international reaction to a policy. The fact that the policy fell short of the standard was not a reason not to undertake it, but it did constitute grounds for being far more careful before so doing.

Some would grant that this second war was not necessary but

would hasten to add that it was justifiable or even desirable. The best argument for this perspective is the ouster of Saddam Hussein and the avoidance of a possible (but by no means inevitable) future in which Saddam broke out of constraints imposed on him in the wake of the first Iraq war and dedicated enormous resources to military might and adventures. Avoiding this certainly belongs in the plus column; the problem is the associated costs that were detailed in the previous chapter and include the American, coalition, and Iraqi lives lost and diminished, the huge financial expense, the lasting impact on the U.S. military, the relative enhancement of Iran's position in the region, the rise in terrorism and anti-Americanism, and the hard to measure but all too real cost in the time and attention available to senior officials to devote to other pressing concerns. George W. Bush inherited a robust economy, a budgetary surplus, a rested military, and, even after 9/11, a world largely at peace and well-disposed toward the United States. He handed off to his successor a recession, a massive deficit and debt, a stretched and exhausted military, two wars, and a world marked by pronounced anti-Americanism. I am hard-pressed to find another set of back-to-back presidential transitions in which so many of the basic features of the domestic and international landscapes changed so dramatically for the worse. The Iraq war of course cannot be blamed for all of this, but it absorbed a great deal of this country's resources and, as a consequence, contributed significantly to the deterioration of the absolute and relative position of the United States in the world. It is quite possible history will judge the war's greatest cost to be opportunity cost, the squandering by the United States of a rare and in many ways unprecedented opportunity to shape the world and the nature of international relations for decades to come. Instead, Iraq contributed to the emergence of a world in which power is more widely distributed than ever before and U.S. ability to shape this world much diminished.

To be fair, it is too soon to calculate additional benefits should Iraq stabilize and come to resemble the model society that many of the war's advocates suggested it would be. But such "success" is highly unlikely, and even if it were to come about, it would do nothing to erase the considerable costs of the policy. More likely is a future in which the costs of U.S. policy continue to mount (albeit at a reduced pace) and Iraq remains divided and falls far short of constituting a normal much less model country.

Still others would say that the principal problem with the second Iraq war was with its implementation, that it was a necessary and even desirable undertaking but that it was carried out poorly so that its costs were increased and benefits decreased. Wherever one comes out on the advisability of the war, it is hard to dispute the criticisms over the conduct of the war and the aftermath. Indeed, such decisions as to go to war with a relatively small number of troops, to demobilize (or not work to remobilize) the Iraqi army, to extend de-Ba'athification beyond the most senior levels—these and other criticisms are frequently made and widely accepted for good reason. The one question that needs to be raised in this context is whether, given the nature of Iraqi society and its political culture, a "neat" and successful outcome would have materialized if the United States had gone about the war and its aftermath with far more troops and with far better decisions about how to manage Iraqi reconstruction. It is not at all obvious this would have been the case, although it is highly likely that things could and would have turned out better had policies been better.

From this last point one can derive an important insight, one that informed much of what was taught at the Kennedy School of Government during my years there. Implementation is not a second-order concern. Execution is every bit as important as policy design. A good idea that is not or cannot be successfully implemented (with success defined as an acceptable ratio between benefits and costs) is either not a good idea or an idea that ought not be pursued. Just as much attention if not more ought to be given to implementing the policy as to developing it in the first place.

This conclusion relates in turn to the matter of process—in Washington as opposed to the field. Both the development and the execution of foreign policy require rigorous attention. To be sure, formal decision-making processes can be time-consuming, can increase the chance of leaks, can stifle innovation, and are no guarantee against groupthink and error. But it is also true that rigorous and inclusive policy development mechanisms can improve the quality of policy, protect leaders from themselves and the shortcomings of those around them, and increase the odds that implementation faithfully reflects what is sought. It is no coincidence that the administration of George H. W. Bush fared relatively well in Iraq. There was and is a close correlation between the quality of policy and the quality of the process that produces it. By contrast, George W. Bush paid a price for the informality of national security decision making during much of his administration. There was little systematic consideration of the pros and cons of going to war versus alternative policies. Policies that would shape the aftermath of the conflict received scant interagency oversight. It is worth noting that the most successful phase of policy on the ground that included the so-called surge in early 2007 resulted from a far more careful and rigorous policy review back in Washington.

One thing those involved in a policy process need to be aware of is assumptions. This applies equally to intelligence analysts and policy makers. In the first Iraq conflict, most people assumed that Saddam would not invade Kuwait and that he would be unlikely to survive its liberation. Both assumptions proved wrong. In the second conflict, just about everyone assumed that Iraq possessed weapons of mass destruction and that everything Saddam Hussein was doing could be explained by his determination to hide and protect these weapons from the international inspectors. Many involved in decision making also assumed that coalition forces would be well received by the population and that Iraq would quickly evolve into a model society that would stimulate democratic reform throughout the region. It is difficult to exaggerate just how inaccurate these assumptions turned out to be. It is essential that a culture and procedures be created within the government in which even basic and widely shared assumptions are challenged and tested and alternative explanations are put forward and subjected to scrutiny.

There is much more to be said about intelligence and policy and the relationship between the two. Intelligence analysts must interact closely with policy makers in order to know what questions and issues are relevant. And they must be willing to say what they think to policy makers even if it is not what the latter want to hear. There is always the danger that in doing so, intelligence analysts will forfeit access and influence. It is a risk worth taking, because telling policy makers what they want to hear and not what they need to hear is a recipe for ruin. Just as dangerous is an environment in which policy makers pressure analysts to produce judgments that support preferred policies. And policy makers can further undermine themselves by choosing to heed only those bits of intelligence that bolster their preferences. The best protection against all of the above is the presence of men and women of integrity on both sides of the relationship. Added insurance comes from instituting a robust national security policy process, competitive analysis, and multiple layers of oversight.

There is also the matter of the general and the particular. A principal lesson of Vietnam, an earlier war of choice, was the danger in allowing global designs—in that case, the global effort against communism—to blind decision makers to local realities, which in Vietnam often translated into the appeal of nationalism in the North and the scourge of corruption in the South. It is not a good idea to choose to go to war against a country when its society is so little understood.

Much the same holds for Iraq. Widely held notions of the potential for democratic transformation ran up against the hard reality of Iraq's history and political culture, Saddam's legacy, and the country's religious, ethnic, tribal, and geographic divisions. As was the case in Vietnam, local realities trumped global abstractions. And again like Vietnam, the resulting war of choice proved to be far more difficult and costly than anticipated.

Sanctions turn out to be an extraordinarily complex foreign policy instrument. As a rule of thumb, their effectiveness increases to the degree they enjoy considerable international backing, are buttressed by military force, and allow for humanitarian exceptions to lessen their impact on innocents. International backing in turn can be increased if essential parties and states are subsidized to offset the costs of compliance. But even in ideal circumstances, sanctions tend to be limited in what they can accomplish. They can influence behavior and selected capabilities, but they cannot be expected to produce fundamental changes in actions, capacities, or nature in a limited amount of time. Sanctions could not force Saddam Hussein to leave Kuwait. What is more, not all that sanctions accomplish is positive, in the sense that they can work against certain policy ends. In the case of Iraq, sanctions actually made it less difficult for Saddam Hussein to maintain control at home while they created sympathy for him and his country abroad. Still, sanctions coupled with inspections and select applications of military force did help to contain Saddam to a considerable degree—and arguably could have accomplished even more if everything that could have been done had been done to strengthen them.

Both Iraq wars support the argument that more force is better, both in the battlefield and post-battlefield aftermath phases of a conflict. It is less difficult to reduce force levels than to raise them. Also, an intervening country only has so much time before it begins to wear out its welcome and produce resentment and resistance. This too argues for concentrating effort so more can be accomplished before nationalism reasserts itself, which it inevitably will. Alas, this rule, that it is easier to build down than up, was violated in both Iraq and Afghanistan.

The issue of democracy promotion merits broader discussion. Iraq was and is part of a much larger debate about the priorities of American foreign policy and how much those priorities ought to be tied to promoting democracy around the world. This issue of the purpose of U.S. foreign policy constitutes one of the principal fault lines of the American political debate. It also reflects one of the principal differences between the administrations of the forty-first and forty-third presidents.

There is one school of thought that focuses mostly on what a state does beyond its borders. According to this school, the nature of a state is secondary, in part because external behavior is judged to count for more, in part because it is judged that modifying the nature of a society is simply too ambitious and difficult a task to be undertaken except when there is no choice. This was the preferred approach of President George H. W. Bush and most of his senior aides.

A second school of thought holds that the nature of another society matters most, partly because of what is moral, but also because of the belief that democratic states are likely to treat not just their citizens but also their neighbors better. This is the so-called democratic peace theory, one embraced by George W. Bush and many around him and articulated by this president in his second inaugural: "The best hope for peace in our world is the expansion of freedom in all the world." It is true that mature democracies tend to act more peacefully in their dealings with other mature democracies. But partial or immature democracies can be quite aggressive and easily captured by populism and nationalism. And building a mature democracy will at best prove a long-term enterprise, and even then is likely to prove difficult if not impossible. It can take years of effort that will prove expensive in practice, uncertain in results, and often resented by locals who question American motives and Americans who question the costs. It is important to keep in mind that American notions of democracy are neither universal nor inevitable. To proclaim, as President Bush did in that same inaugural address, that "America's vital interests and our deepest beliefs are now one" does not bear scrutiny. The United States has a vital interest in China helping to limit North Korea's nuclear program and in cooperating to slow climate change, just as we have a vital interest in Russia's helping to limit Iran's nuclear program and safeguarding its own nuclear weapons and materials. We may believe that both countries should be full democracies, but a belief is markedly less than a vital interest. All of this should have cautioned against making the creation of an Iraqi democracy so central to the case for the second Iraq war; all of this should reinforce the notion that the principal business of American foreign policy ought to be the foreign policy and not the domestic nature of other countries.

This argument is easy to caricature. It is not an all-or-nothing proposition. It is important to give people in Muslim countries a choice beyond authoritarian regimes and the mosque lest opposition to repressive and corrupt elites pave the way for illiberal religious extremists to come to power. The remedy here, though, is improving education, promoting the rule of law, and protecting civil society. Elections have a role, but closer to the end of the process of democracy building than to the start. Using military force to oust regimes and build democracies is simply too costly and too uncertain in results to constitute a sustainable approach to U.S. foreign policy.

It is important to reflect on the use of military force more broadly. There can be no serious debate about the need and legitimacy to act in self-defense, which was the rationale of the first Iraq war and the response against Afghanistan after 9/11. Preemptive strikes—attacks on capabilities that are about to be used—are also widely accepted, which is logical, given that they are a form of self-defense. The problem tends not to be political so much as being sure of the intelligence and possessing the ability to act on it. Preventive strikes—attacks on capabilities that are either developing or mature but where there is no suggestion of imminent use—are something else. The Israeli attack on Iraq's Osirak reactor in 1981 was a preventive action, as was the second Iraq war. (The much-discussed possibility of attacking Iranian nuclear installations would also qualify.) Preventive strikes should not be ruled out as a matter of principle, but neither should they be depended on. Beyond questions of feasibility and retaliation, preventive strikes run the risk of making the world less stable, both because they might actually encourage proliferation (governments could see developing or acquiring their nuclear weapons as a deterrent) and because they would weaken the long-standing norm against uses of force other than in situations of self-defense.

Both Iraq wars began with battlefield successes, but both ran into trouble in the aftermath. The costs of the trouble were far greater the second time because U.S. goals were so much more ambitious. The United States needs a military that can cope as well with nontraditional conflicts as it can with battlefields. Fighting unconventional wars ought to be an equal if not greater priority than preparing to fight wars with great or medium powers. This will entail building and maintaining a larger military, one with greater capacity to deal with the sort of threat environments being encountered in Iraq and Afghanistan. It calls, too, for greater involvement by all agencies of the U.S. government and for the building of a civilian counterpart to the military reserves that would provide a pool of human talent to assist with basic nation-building tasks. It also validates the continuing need for economic and military assistance to develop the capacities of states so that with time they are in a better position to meet their responsibilities to their citizens and their neighbors.

The last lesson is that it is important not to overlearn lessons. The conclusion here is that the first Iraq war was a war of necessity that was well advised, whereas the second Iraq war was a war of choice that was ill-advised. But the point is not to rule out all wars of choice. Rather it is to emphasize that the decision to undertake them should only be taken after the most rigorous assessment of the likely costs and benefits of acting—as well as the likely costs and benefits of pursuing other policies, including not acting. The standards for wars of choice must be high if the human, military, and economic costs are to be justified. There are unlimited opportunities to use military force—but limited ability to do so. The words of John Quincy Adams, the only other son of a U.S. president to assume that office, are worth recalling here: while noting that the United States is the "well-wisher to the freedom and independence of all," Adams also advises that this country "goes not abroad in search of monsters to destroy." Yes, Saddam Hussein was a monster, but that did not justify the decision to go to war to oust him. Even a great power needs to husband its resources. American democracy is ill-suited to an imperial foreign policy where wars are undertaken for some "larger good" but where the immediate costs appear greater than any benefits. Wars of choice are thus largely to be avoided—if only to make sure there will be adequate will and ability to pursue wars of necessity when they materialize.

APPENDIX

United States Department of State

Washington, D.C. 20520

RELEASED IN FULL $R5$

INFORMATION MEMORANDUM   September 26, 2002
        S/ES

<u>SECRET/NOFORN/NODIS</u> DECAPTIONED
DECL: 09/26/12

TO: The Secretary

FROM: S/P - Richard N. Haass

SUBJECT: Reconstruction in Iraq - Lessons of the Past

     If we end up going to war with Iraq, we need to be prepared to win the ensuing peace. Although no single historical analogy provides a roadmap for how to proceed in "the days after," the history of post-conflict reconstruction helps to identify and prioritize the challenges we would face in a post-war Iraq. This memorandum draws upon insights derived from the study of over 20 experiences with post-conflict reconstruction.

     The memorandum highlights four themes:

- The starting point for any reconstruction effort is an assessment of the nature of the problem we propose to tackle. This is primarily a function of a country's existing level of political, economic, and social development. In making this assessment, relevant factors include the country's experience with democracy, good governance, and market economics, state apparatus and bureaucracy, economic resources, level of education, middle class, and shared national identity.

- We must decide the scale of our ambitions. These can range from merely the restoration of a basic level of internal order and selective disarmament to the establishment of a fully democratic country. The larger the gap between our ambitions and the situation we inherit, the larger must be our commitment in time and resources.

- We must apply resources to the right priorities in the right way. Successful reconstruction encompasses five core elements: physical security; humanitarian relief and repatriation; physical and economic reconstruction; establishment of legitimate and effective governance; and stabilization of the regional environment. The decision of

SECRET/NOFORN/NODIS
Classified by S/P Director Richard N. Haass
Reason: E.O. 12958 1.5 (b) and (d)

UNCLASSIFIED

who will lead and administer – or "own" – the overall effort
as well as its individual components is critical.

- History has specific lessons for post-conflict Iraq, seven of
  which are identified in part IV below. They stress that we
  should prevent a security vacuum after Saddam's ouster,
  transform the existing oil-for-food program into a mechanism
  that supports humanitarian relief as well as the other
  elements of the reconstruction effort, promote an Iraqi-based
  political process to move the country toward self-government,
  and prevent neighbors from meddling in Iraq.

The cases of post-conflict reconstruction analyzed for this
study are Afghanistan; Bosnia; Cambodia; the Caribbean, 1900–
1930s (Cuba, Dominican Republic, and Haiti); Central America,
1980s-1990s (El Salvador, Nicaragua, and Panama); East Timor;
Germany, Post-World War I; Germany, Post-World War II; Greece;
Haiti, 1990s; Italy; Japan; Kosovo; Mozambique; Philippines,
1902-1946; Somalia; South Korea; South Vietnam; and Western
Europe, Post-World War II.

I. The Starting Point for Reconstruction: What is Inherited?

A successful post-conflict reconstruction effort must be
based on a firm understanding of the magnitude of the challenge.
History shows that a country's level of political, economic, and
social development fundamentally affects the nature and
difficulty of post-conflict reconstruction. The level of
development encompasses both a country's "hardware," such as its
state apparatus, economic infrastructure, and communications and
transportation networks, and its "software," such as a shared
sense of national identity, familiarity with democracy, human
capital, experience with a market economy, and professional
bureaucrats.

The cases of post-conflict reconstruction fall across a
range. At one end are cases with countries that possess well-
developed nation-state "hardware" and "software." These efforts
involve primarily fixing what has been broken, by earlier misrule
and/or conflict. The reconstruction of Western Europe following
World War II is one such effort. Countries like France and
Holland endured over four years of German occupation and then
suffered physical damage during their liberation. After
liberation, however, their citizens resumed the familiar ways of
democracy and commerce and could rely upon most of their basic
political, economic, and social institutions without fundamental
transformation. They also decided how to handle on their own
terms such issues as punishing collaborators. Reconstruction
focused on alleviating the immediate humanitarian crisis,
creating a hospitable security environment, priming the pump of

the European economies with the infusion of Marshall Plan aid, and encouraging regional economic integration.

Although necessarily much more intrusive, the post-World War II effort to reconstruct West Germany falls near Western Europe on the spectrum. Germany suffered widespread destruction during the war and over a decade of Nazi rule. Still, even amid the rubble of 1945, West Germany possessed the basis for a strong, successful nation-state because of its educated population, pre-war capitalist economy, institutions of governance with some degree of popular acceptance and people experienced running them, some history of democratic politics, and a common national identity. After removal of top Nazi officials and the demobilization of Germany's military, Western occupation authorities supervised the establishment of a strong democracy and economy within a matter of years.

At the other end of the range are cases that involve attempts to build from scratch effective and legitimate government structures, a viable economy, and the human capital to make them work. The successes are fewer and the failures greater because of the magnitude of the task. In Somalia in 1992, for instance, no effective state existed, the country was impoverished in every respect, and warlords and bandits ruled by brute force. When the United States and the international community intervened, they entered a country in name only and had to do everything for themselves. When the international community scaled back its efforts, Somalia was little changed.

Iraq's level of development places it in the middle of this range. Iraq possesses some of the capacity for a viable state, including rich economic resources, familiarity with elements of a market economy, a strong state apparatus, a largely secular, educated middle class, a talented diaspora community, and experienced managers, entrepreneurs, and bureaucrats. At the same time, Iraq lacks experience with democracy, has endured economic sanctions and international isolation, and is riven by fractious ethnic, tribal, and clan relations. The devastation of war would add to the challenges. The authoritarian rule by Saddam's Sunni faction and the fact that the Kurdish region in northern Iraq has been effectively autonomous for over a decade also present legacies to overcome.

II. The Scale of Our Ambitions

In post-conflict reconstruction, you usually get what you pay for. The next step, therefore, is to determine how ambitious we want the reconstruction effort to be. Our commitment in time and resources must be calibrated to both the scale of our ambitions and the situation we inherit.

The historical cases underscore that the ambitions for post-conflict reconstruction vary considerably. At one end of the range are efforts with minimal ambitions like restoring a basic level of order and security and/or alleviating an immediate humanitarian crisis; they do not aim at transforming a political culture or creating economic prosperity. Equally important, these efforts tend to focus on addressing immediate imperatives. The level of commitment in resources and time is relatively low. This is "nation building lite."

American interventions in the Caribbean in the early part of the twentieth century fit this mold. Although many Americans may have wished Cuba, the Dominican Republic, and Haiti would become stable, prosperous, and democratic countries, U.S. objectives ultimately stressed the maintenance of political stability and commercial development tied to American interests. When democratic government faltered, rule by a "strong man" was accepted and the underlying sources of future instability left unaddressed. Similarly, in the case of Haiti in 1994, our six-month military engagement eliminated massive human rights violations and floods of boat people, but left an impoverished country with little democratic governance. In Somalia in 1992-94, the mission faltered when the international community shifted its ambitions from addressing the humanitarian disaster to trying to rebuild the nation's fractured polity without increasing its level of commitment accordingly.

By contrast, there are cases where the ambitions for reconstruction have been the building or re-building of a stable democracy, a robust capitalist economy, and liberal political culture. Such efforts can also address broader issues of regional security, including the sources of previous international conflict or instability. These ambitious reconstruction efforts tend to be guided by longer term concerns. They are demanding enterprises, requiring significant commitment of money, material, and manpower for years and even decades. They constitute full-scale nation building.

The reconstruction of Europe and Japan following World War II are the examples par excellence of such nation building. While much smaller in absolute terms than those following World War II, the reconstruction efforts in East Timor, Kosovo, and Bosnia are likewise ambitious. In all three, the international community aims to establish reasonably stable, peaceful, prosperous, and democratic countries. In Kosovo, for example, NATO provides overall security, the UN oversees civil administration including the creation of a police force and judiciary, the OSCE helps build civil society and democratic institutions, and the EU focuses upon economic reconstruction.

UNCLASSIFIED

And in all three, the international community is committed to ensuring basic security to prevent any backsliding toward instability and thereby permitting the other elements of the reconstruction effort - from micro-credit lending to training police forces - to take root and come to fruition.

Turning to Iraq, we have not yet decided on how ambitious our reconstruction effort might be and the level of commitment we will make. These decisions will be shaped by the situation on the ground when Saddam falls. If Saddam is overthrown by a coup before we invade Iraq and the successor regime takes steps to meet our primary concerns, i.e., WMD disarmament and denying safe haven and support to terrorists, then we are unlikely to confront a situation calling for full-scale nation building. As we monitor the new regime's progress on other fronts of concern to us - such as the treatment of etnnic minorities - our efforts can then focus on alleviating any humanitarian crisis and helping revitalize Iraq's economy. Our limited commitment to nation building would reduce our leverage to shape the new Iraq, but also would reduce our costs and risks.

However, once we cross the Rubicon by entering Iraq and ousting Saddam ourselves, we will have much greater responsibility for Iraq's future. Our stated commitment to rebuild a better Iraq will then be put to the test. The likelihood of a more ambitious post-conflict reconstruction of Iraq will increase correspondingly.

The following figure (p. 6) summarizes the findings of the case studies, plotting them against ambition of the effort and the magnitude of the task. The "successes" clump together where high ambition, and thus commitment, is applied to the task of reconstructing relatively well-developed states.

The enlarged oval shows that, based on Iraq's level of development and on historical precedent, the successful full-scale nation building reconstruction of Iraq is possible, but will most likely require an ambitious effort - one commensurate with those in South Korea, Greece, Italy, and Japan.

UNCLASSIFIED

UNCLASSIFIED

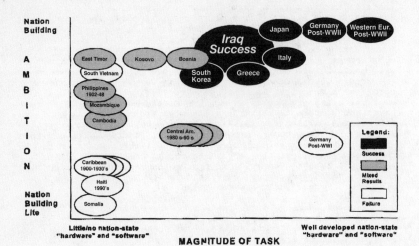

III. Specific Levers for Successful Reconstruction

History shows that success requires five core elements: (a) physical security; (b) humanitarian relief and repatriation; (c) physical and economic reconstruction; (d) establishment of legitimate and effective governance; and (e) stabilization of the regional environment. To make all these elements succeed individually and as a coherent whole, international coordination and burden sharing are necessary. This demands, in turn, clear demarcation of who should lead each component of the effort.

Physical Security - First and Foremost

Every past reconstruction success was built upon a bedrock of basic security. Without order and security at the local level, all else is jeopardized: the patterns of everyday life and commerce will not resume, refugees will not return home, private investment will remain scarce, and NGOs and international organizations will not operate.

Thus, the effective and rapid demobilization or co-opting of indigenous armed forces, militias, and internal security

UNCLASSIFIED

UNCLASSIFIED
SECRET/NOFORN/NODIS
7

apparatus is critical. In cases like Italy, Germany, and Japan,
Allied military forces accomplished this rapidly and then worked
with local indigenous police forces and civil authorities to
maintain order at the local level. In Mozambique, an effective
international peacekeeping force reined in the Government and
RENAMO forces and rapidly organized a disarmament,
demobilization, and reintegration effort that sent over 80,000
troops to demobilization camps. These forces were disarmed,
offered vocational training programs, transported to their place
of origin, and given two years of stipends provided on a monthly
basis at their places of origin. The UN and OAS oversaw similar
demobilization efforts in El Salvador and Nicaragua respectively.
In Kosovo in 1999, the entry of international forces and the
promise of security led over a million Kosovar refugees to flood
back into the country in a matter of weeks. In Mozambique,
Central America, and the Balkans, demining operations facilitated
the return of civilians and ex-combatants to their homes.

By contrast, as recent experiences in Afghanistan, Bosnia,
Haiti, Kosovo, and Somalia highlight, delay in bringing order to
everyday life during the initial phases of reconstruction can be
costly. Warlords and organized crime syndicates swiftly fill any
vacuum created by the absence of security, police, and judicial
authority. Once in place, these forces prove difficult to
dislodge and constitute "spoilers" that challenge the entire
reconstruction effort. In the Balkans, for example, the delay in
establishing effective police and courts allowed criminals to
burrow into the society and economy with corrupting implications
we still confront. Similarly, in Afghanistan today we are paying
the price for the delay in expanding ISAF and/or shifting our OEF
operations toward internal security. More dramatically, basic
order was never restored in Somalia, thus making the costs of
doing business prohibitive for international organizations and
NGOs and thereby leading to the termination of most external
assistance after the departure of international forces in 1994.

The security situation in Iraq promises to be complicated by
considerable settling of scores and jockeying for position.
Unchecked, such struggles - fed perhaps by external "meddlers"
like Iran - could undermine prospects for successful
reconstruction. Moreover, a chaotic post-conflict environment is
more likely to permit the dispersal of Iraq's current arsenal of
weapons of mass destruction and erode national unity in the face
of divisions among the Sunnis, Shiites, and Kurds.

Humanitarian Relief; Physical and Economic Reconstruction

In every success, immediate humanitarian relief and steady
improvement in economic conditions helped secure popular support.
Rapid and tangible signs of the reconstruction of physical and

UNCLASSIFIED

economic infrastructure are essential to creating a sense of
return to normal, the better for both the population's material
well-being and its morale. The honeymoon for new authorities may
be short-lived, however: if high expectations are confronted with
delays or backsliding, frustration and discontent may provide
openings for internal spoilers and external meddlers.

After both world wars, the provision of humanitarian
assistance and economic aid helped shore up fragile governments.
The Marshall Plan, for example, infused 2.5 percent of the GNP of
the recipient countries between 1948 and 1951, restored
confidence in the economic future, and bolstered the democratic
governments throughout the region in the face of internal and
external Communist pressure. The way the plan was administered
involving intra-European consultations on how to best allocate
the assistance - simultaneously increased Europeans' sense of
"ownership" as well as broader cooperation.

Today, conversely, we are beginning to see signs of the
corrosive effects on the Afghan Transitional Administration's
authority of its inability to mobilize widespread reconstruction
efforts, its limited resources relative to some regional
warlords, and the growing perception of unfulfilled promises.
Our efforts to generate international resources for highly
visible projects - including road construction, schools, and
health facilities - will be essential to maintaining popular
support for the Karzai regime. Similarly, the failure of the
governments of Presidents Aristide and Preval in Haiti to
demonstrate significant improvements in health, education, and
housing following the restoration of the democratically elected
government in 1994 contributed to popular and business cynicism
that has resulted in debilitating political stalemate.

In the immediate aftermath of a war, Iraq is likely to face
a serious humanitarian crisis. More than half the Iraqi
population depends upon rations and war will exacerbate this
humanitarian situation, spawning refugee flows and disrupting the
oil-for-food program. It is promising that both UNHCR and IOM
are well advanced in their planning; we will need to ensure that
there are adequate resources available to support such efforts.

Looking further into the future, Iraq enters a post-conflict
economic situation with certain advantages. Iraq has significant
oil resources that should provide a ready supply of cash.
Working out an effective mechanism to tap these resources is
essential. Indeed, reconstruction in Iraq could break the
historical mold and become self-supporting. It will also be
important to make sure that claims by creditors - including
Russia, France, Germany, and Japan - and those seeking

reparations for past wrongs - such as Kuwait - do not undermine the rebirth of the economy.

Establishing Effective and Legitimate Governance

Long-term success hinges on establishment of effective and legitimate governance. Ultimately, the citizens themselves need to take responsibility for their own affairs, deciding who stays in power, who is welcomed from exile, and who is punished. The practical dilemmas arise in defining how this transition to local rule should be accomplished, how fast, and by whom. The role of the international community in this process - which can lead to picking winners and losers - is among the most sensitive and vexing questions that face us in Iraq.

For starters, there is no such thing as a clean slate. Although distasteful, success often requires compromise with individuals associated with the previous regime. The case studies highlight the importance of not throwing out potentially stabilizing elements of the former regime. These elements can - unless they are thoroughly discredited - be harnessed to support reconstruction, maintain order, offer important local knowledge, and act as a source of continuity between past and future. Following World War II ambitious plans in both Germany and Japan to eliminate members of the old regime from future government and break up economic cartels were in practice radically scaled back. At times former enemies must work together. After signing peace accords and taking concrete, irreversible actions to demonstrate their commitment to peace, rebel leaders in Mozambique, El Salvador, and Nicaragua were accepted as legitimate politicians and even afforded significant government roles.

A divide often emerges between those who remained inside the country during the conflict and the opposition in exile, with its different experience and foreign support. There are also often profound divisions within these two groups, along regional, ethnic, tribal, or class lines, as we have seen in Afghanistan.

Backing one faction prematurely can have significant costs and unforeseen consequences down the road, as we learned in Vietnam when we tacitly supported the military coup against President Diem in 1963. Once you back a faction, it becomes difficult to back off when things go badly. Yet, allowing free rein to such factional struggles for power risks fragmentation and even the outbreak of full-scale civil war.

The Allies' approach to the liberation of French territory during World War II is instructive. The Allies worked with both the Free French abroad and collaborators from the Vichy regime to achieve military victory (as in North Africa), and assisted

resistance forces in France of all ideological stripes. De
Gaulle emerged as leader of the Free French in spite of the
preferences of other Allied leaders. Following the war, the
French were allowed to chose their leadership democratically,
with De Gaulle going into the political wilderness. The United
States covertly assisted existing non-Communist parties to help
preserve internal stability. In the harder cases of Germany,
Italy, and Japan, the Allies supervised the phased expansion of
native governance over a period of years from the local to the
national levels.

     In Afghanistan, the international community – under strong
U.S. and UN leadership – drew together all acceptable pretenders
to power in Bonn and insisted that they reach an accord on future
governance within given parameters. This "shot-gun wedding"
approach was able to draw on long-established internal structures
– especially the loya jirga – and enjoyed the symbolic blessing
of a unifying national figure, King Zahir Shah.

     Together these cases suggest that one proven approach
between the extremes of picking winners and losers and letting
the factions fight it out is to work to establish the boundaries
for a reasonably transparent and democratic process and let the
citizens decide. Similarly, while it is in our interest and our
power to insist on full accountability for past abuses and to
disqualify the senior-most ranks of the current regime from
participating in the post-Saddam government, the particular
mechanism for transitional justice – such as a tribunal or a
truth and reconciliation commission – should be left to the
successor government.

     Ethnic divisions and history of divided rule under Saddam
Hussein make the risk of Iraq's fragmentation a serious concern.
Iraq lacks recognized national figures – like Emperor Hirohito in
Japan, King Sihanouk in Cambodia, and King Zahir Shah in
Afghanistan – that could provide a unifying symbol for the entire
country during post-conflict reconstruction. Furthermore, Iraq
will face considerable tensions between local power brokers
associated with the previous regime and outside opposition groups
with uncertain support within Iraq, all exacerbated in turn by
ethnic tensions.

The Regional Dimension

     In bad regions with a history of neighbors threatening one
another, reconstruction may require neighborhood renewal to
succeed. The role of neighbors in either mediating or fueling
disputes is fundamental. Countries in bad neighborhoods risk
spill-over from armed combatants, refugees, arms flows, and
direct meddling.

For example, it took the transformation of the regimes in
Rhodesia/Zimbabwe and South Africa to majority rule to cut off
the main external support for the RENAMO rebel movement in
Mozambique and help drive it to the bargaining table. It also
paved the way for regional organizations – especially the
Southern African Development Community – to play an active role
in mediating among the parties. Similarly, progress in resolving
civil conflicts in Central America during the 1980's and 1990's
was mutually supportive, opened the door for OAS engagement, and
helped eliminate sources of safe haven, illicit arms transfer,
financial resources, and other support for hold-outs.

Neighbors also need to be reassured that a rejuvenated past-
offender will not return to old ways. This is best illustrated
by the different outcomes of efforts to reconstruct Germany after
the two world wars. After World War I, the western powers did
not sustain a unified front to redefine Germany and its role in
Europe, with catastrophic consequences. The reconstruction of
Germany was approached in a fundamentally different manner
following World War II. Success came by nurturing a robust
democracy, placing limits on German sovereignty vis-a-vis its
regional role (e.g., limits on its military, prohibitions against
having nuclear weapons), and anchoring Germany to the rest of
Western Europe as part of a broad and sustained project of
regional strategic, political, and economic integration. A
complex web of institutions, starting with the European Coal and
Steel Community and extending to the EU, NATO, OSCE and other
networks of today, was spun to bind Germany's future to its
neighbors and thereby reassure them.

Iraq is situated in a troubled neighborhood, due in large
part to its own making. Many of its neighbors can be expected to
try to shape – overtly or covertly – the future Iraq before any
reconstruction effort begins. Turkey could move to occupy
northern Iraq to ensure that Kurdish nationalism there does not
spill over and fuel irredentist tendencies amongst its own large
Kurdish minority. Iran, attacked by Baghdad in the past, will
likely seek to expand its influence in Iraq through contacts with
Iraqi Shiite Muslims and through longstanding relationships with
Kurdish parties in the north. Iran could also unilaterally seek
to rectify some of its outstanding territorial disputes with
Iraq, particularly if Turkey moved into northern Iraq. Should
the Baath party remain in power in Baghdad, Syria too could seek
to exert influence through its contacts with the party.

We should begin bilateral consultations now to lay down
clear redlines to prevent such meddling. We should also try to
establish a regional mechanism – akin to the 6+2 in Afghanistan
to help manage policies among Iraq's neighbors in the near term.

If successful, we should then look to build upon this foundation new regional organizations to manage security concerns and promote economic ties in the region over the long term.

Organizing the International Effort

Broad international involvement in reconstruction spreads the burdens, brings special expertise to bear, and lends added international legitimacy. Without leadership and effective coordination, however, such diverse international participation can increase friction, create huge coordination problems, and undermine the reconstruction effort. When considering a relatively ambitious undertaking, past reconstruction efforts reveal three basic approaches: (a) the "MacArthur model," (b) a coalition with separate zones of control, and (c) a "national" coalition effort where the country's reconstruction is administered through centralized and unified command.

The MacArthur model comes from the American occupation of Japan following World War II. Although acting nominally under Allied auspices, the United States effectively ran the reconstruction of Japan unilaterally with General Douglas MacArthur exercising nearly unchecked authority. The single supreme American proconsul proved effective in Japan and greatly simplified the formulation of policy by minimizing debate among the Allies. The United States in 1945 was willing and able to pay for such unilateral control by accepting the full burdens of occupation and reconstruction.

Such an unilateral approach in Iraq, however, would have significant downsides: it would increase the price of reconstruction for us and decrease our ability to draw others in as stakeholders. It could also be perceived as a crude imperial grab for oil and power in the Middle East, and would likely encounter internal and regional resistance over the long term.

A second approach shares the burdens of occupation and reconstruction among an international coalition by dividing the country into administrative zones under the control of different foreign powers. This was done in part of Germany after World War I, and then again after World War II. Korea was also famously divided at the 38th parallel to separate American and Soviet zones of occupation in 1945. In these cases, however, the lack of an effective unified command resulted in the occupying powers pursuing different policies in their zones, leading in turn to significant confrontations that undermined the overall reconstruction effort. In the 1920s, for instance, the French fomented separatist movements in the Rhineland against the wishes of the other powers, while in the cases of post-World War II

UNCLASSIFIED
13

Germany and Korea, supposedly temporary administrative lines soon marked the permanent division of the countries.

By contrast, the division of Kosovo into security zones administered by individual NATO members has proven relatively effective because of a high degree of coordination, a combined command structure, a commonality of interests among external actors, and the comprehensive reconstruction efforts of international organizations such as the UN, OSCE, and EU that cross zone boundaries.

Dividing Iraq into separate occupation zones, however, would be very risky, given the high degree of ethnic fragmentation, the potential re-emergence of regional warlords, and the divergent interests of potential participants in an international force.

In recent decades, the "national" coalition approach has been most common and effective. It involves a mix of international actors - countries, international organizations, and NGOs - operating typically under an UN mandate. It tends to be a logical extension of the structure that helped secure the end to conflict, such as a UN peacekeeping operation or a "coalition of the willing." The effort is usually led by a single country or international authority - such as Australia initially in East Timor, the United States in Haiti in 1994, or a UN Special Representative in Mozambique. Such a structure draws on the comparative advantage of each coalition partner. In Afghanistan, under the umbrella of over-all U.S. leadership, the UN is supporting political reconstruction, the Turks are leading ISAF, the Germans are helping restore the police and judicial systems, the British are working on drug eradication, the Japanese and Saudis are providing key financial resources, etc. Typically, a coalition effort will draw on existing international coordination mechanisms - such as economic recovery programs of the IMF and World Bank - and may be accompanied by a donor's conference to ensure international support.

The "national" coalition approach with firm U.S. leadership in practice, if not formally, is the most promising for any major reconstruction effort in Iraq. On principle, since the benefits of the ouster of Saddam will be shared, so should the burdens of rebuilding Iraq. Out of practical need, the United States does not possess the resources, expertise, or public support to sustain alone an ambitious reconstruction effort in Iraq. Operating under UN auspices will furnish international legitimacy, which will in turn encourage and provide political cover for other nations as well as international organizations and NGOs to contribute to the effort. Ideally, like in Afghanistan, an experienced and reliable non-American - and preferably non-Westerner - Brahimi figure with a UN title would

UNCLASSIFIED

be given authority over the coordination of the civilian elements
of the reconstruction. This would help reinforce both inside and
outside Iraq that this is not a neo-colonial venture. We should
begin dialogue now with the likely partners in such an operation.

The composition of the post-conflict security force will
depend upon the details of how Saddam falls and the international
forces committed to action in Iraq. However, given our
significant interests in Iraq, such as ensuring the complete
disarmament of Iraq's WMD arsenal and the stability of the
region, the United States should retain leadership of the
military component of the reconstruction effort.

Finally, pursing the "national" coalition approach has the
added advantage of providing chips in the pre-conflict bargaining
for support for and participation in action to oust Saddam.

IV. Seven Lessons for Iraq

- We must decide on the scale of our ambitions in Iraq,
  recognizing that goals that go beyond disarmament and regional
  stability and seek to build democracy, prosperity, and good
  governance will require a heavy commitment in resources,
  military involvement, and diplomatic engagement. The
  strategic importance of Iraq points toward ambitious long-term
  goals. In the near term, we need to maintain tactical
  flexibility in the tools we use so as to tailor our policies
  to events on the ground - such as whether a coup occurs before
  U.S. troops are in Iraq.

- We must prevent a security vacuum from emerging in Iraq that
  could be exploited by internal spoilers, encourage external
  meddlers, and preclude reconstruction and humanitarian
  efforts. This may require the rapid deployment of external
  military and policing forces, demobilization of Iraqi
  combatants, actions to control emerging warlords, and rapid
  rebuilding of internal security and judicial structures.

- We should help formulate specific plans to transform the UN
  oil-for-food program into a mechanism that will simultaneously
  support the humanitarian needs of the Iraqi people, fund the
  broader reconstruction effort, and address outside claimants'
  justified interests. The sooner consultations with others
  begin the better since agreement on these mechanisms might
  persuade countries, such as Russia, that their interests would
  be protected after the toppling of Saddam's regime. At the
  same time, the United States should avoid taking "ownership"
  of the Iraqi oil industry.

- We should preclude only a small number of members of the old regime — the upper echelons of the Baath Party, the military, and the security services, as well as any indicted war criminals — from participating in the post-Saddam political order. We will most likely need the assistance of many associated in some way with the old regime to maintain order and establish a new viable state. Careful screening of potential leaders, however, is essential to maintain the credibility of any successor government, as are transitional justice arrangements to ensure accountability for past actions.

- We should avoid imposing a particular ruler or party on Iraq, but cannot allow Iraq to degenerate into chaos, civil war, and warlordism that would threaten the stability of the entire region. We should work with our partners to launch a political process that will enable the Iraqi people to move toward self-government in a timely and responsible manner. The international community should dictate the parameters of such a process and insist on a minimum degree of transparency and respect for good governance, but we should avoid pressing for a specific outcome.

- We need to contain potential meddling by Iraq's neighbors, as well as by other international actors, that can undermine the effort to achieve even our most minimal goals in Iraq. We need to maintain broad and active bilateral dialogues with these countries, forge a 6+2-like forum for coordination among Iraq's neighbors and the most interested outside powers, and, looking to the future, strive to develop new mechanisms to manage security concerns in the region as well as promote economic linkages. In trying to renew this troubled neighborhood, we should reinforce the principle that a united Iraq at peace with its neighbors is in the interest of all, and that there will be costs for interference in this outcome.

- We should begin now to identify the international structures that will assist not only the security arrangements in a post-Saddam Iraq, but also our efforts at humanitarian relief, economic and physical reconstruction, state-building, and regional harmony. While our preference should be for the "national" coalition approach, which highlights joint responsibility and contribution from all interested parties, strong U.S. leadership is essential given the stakes in Iraq. We should assert forceful, public leadership of the security operations, and then guide the other components of the reconstruction effort from behind the scenes as we are now doing in Afghanistan.

ACKNOWLEDGMENTS

ALL BOOKS ARE collective efforts, and this is no exception. Many people agreed to be interviewed, provided detailed comments on one or more drafts, or both. I want to thank Drew Erdmann, Marc Grossman, Martin Indyk, Ken Juster, John McLoughlin, Susan Mercandetti, Jami Miscik, Peggy Noonan, Meghan O'Sullivan, Richard Plepler, Colin Powell, Bruce Riedel, Gideon Rose, Brent Scowcroft, Don Steinberg, and Larry Wilkerson for sharing their time and insights. The resulting book is better informed and just plain better for all their help.

It was John Chipman who first mentioned that I might find some reference to wars of necessity and choice in traditional Jewish literature, and Noah Feldman who provided the specifics. My thanks to both.

The crew at Simon & Schuster was professional and supportive at every step. Here I want to single out Lisa Healy, Irene Kheradi, Roger Labrie, Victoria Meyer, Tom Pitoniak, Karen Thompson, Brian Ulicky, and, above all, Alice Mayhew. Alice was excited about this project from the get-go, and her enthusiasm and belief in it and me never wavered.

Esther Newberg has been my agent for more than fifteen years despite enduring differences over politics and, more important, baseball. She has been and remains a true friend.

I had significant help from people here at the Council on Foreign

Relations. Evan Langenhahn did the first assembly of relevant documents. Eva Tatarczyk, Jeff Reinke, Jessica Legnos, and Chris Moree assisted me in countless ways that freed up the necessary time for this project. Lisa Shields and her staff worked hard to get the result noticed. Above all, though, I want to express my debt to Charley Landow for his day-in, day-out assistance. Charley has been a smart, patient, and tireless resource in dealing with citations, research needs, and much more.

Speaking of documents, I want to note my appreciation to Mark Ramee, Margaret Grafeld, Jane Diedrich, and Whitley Wolman of the State Department, all of whom assisted in facilitating U.S. government review of this manuscript and both access to and declassification of once classified materials and documents. Nevertheless, the opinions and characterizations in this book are mine and do not necessarily represent official opinions of the United States government.

And while we are on the subject of disclaimers, let me add one more. I am fortunate to be the president of the Council on Foreign Relations, but in no way do I speak for the organization, which takes no institutional positions, or for its members, who prize their independence. Again, this book reflects my own views and judgments, no more and, I'd like to think, no less

Anyone who has written a book knows how hard it is, not just for the individual doing the writing but for those living with the author. My family—my wife Susan, my son Sam, and my daughter Francesca—thus deserves special mention and extensive thanks. Susan, a world-class editor, provided invaluable advice and wise guidance from start to finish. But I also want to make a more personal point. No one can hold down a full-time job, write a book, and at the same time be the ideal husband and father, at least not if you need several hours of sleep per night. I am fortunate and then some in having a family that allows me to do what I want and need to do even if it comes at some cost.

NOTES

A NOTE ON SOURCES

I served on the National Security Council staff for all four years of the administration of George H. W. Bush and at the Department of State for the first two and a half years of the presidency of George W. Bush. A surprising amount of material has been declassified and made public by the first Bush administration. Understandably, much less has been made public from the just-concluded administration of the forty-third president, but here I drew on some of the memoranda I wrote that were subsequently declassified. In both cases, I benefited greatly from interviews with former colleagues and the detailed comments by quite a few former colleagues to a draft of this book. I also took advantage of the memoirs of others as well as some excellent books written by journalists and historians. And of course I made good use of other public sources.

As noted above, I benefited greatly from the writings of others. There are several valuable memoirs touching on the presidency of George H. W. Bush. In addition to *A World Transformed* (New York: Knopf, 1998), the book the forty-first president coauthored with Brent Scowcroft (in the interest of full disclosure, I should add that I assisted with it), there are the memoirs of James A. Baker III with Thomas M. DeFrank, *The Politics of Diplomacy: Revolution, War & Peace, 1989–1992* (New York: G. P. Putnam's Sons, 1995); Colin Powell with Joseph E. Persico, *My American Journey* (New York: Random House, 1995); and H. Norman Schwarzkopf with Peter Petre, *It Doesn't Take a Hero: The Autobiography* (New York: Bantam, 1992). The most useful books on the backdrop to the first Iraq war as well as the war itself are Christian Alfonsi, *Circle in the Sand: Why We Went Back to Iraq*

(New York: Doubleday, 2006); Rick Atkinson, *Crusade: The Untold Story of the Persian Gulf War* (Boston: Houghton Mifflin, 1993); Michael R. Gordon and Bernard E. Trainor, *The Generals' War: The Inside Story of the Conflict in the Gulf* (Boston: Little, Brown, 1995); Bob Woodward, *The Commanders* (New York: Simon & Schuster, 1991); Steven A. Yetiv, *Explaining Foreign Policy: U.S. Decision-Making & the Persian Gulf War* (Baltimore: Johns Hopkins University Press, 2004); and *Triumph Without Victory: The Unreported History of the Persian Gulf War*, authored by the staff of *U.S. News & World Report* (New York: Times Books, 1992).

The literature surrounding the presidency of George W. Bush is considerably larger despite the fact it is more recent. There already are a number of published memoirs by individuals who served in the administration, including George Tenet with Bill Harlow, *At the Center of the Storm: My Years at the CIA* (New York: HarperCollins, 2007); Douglas J. Feith, *War and Decision: Inside the Pentagon at the Dawn of the War on Terrorism* (New York: Harper, 2008); L. Paul Bremer with Malcolm McConnell, *My Year in Iraq: The Struggle to Build a Future of Hope* (New York: Simon & Schuster, 2006); Tommy R. Franks with Malcolm McConnell, *American Soldier* (New York: ReganBooks, 2004); and Scott McClellan, *What Happened: Inside the Bush White House and Washington's Culture of Deception* (New York: Public Affairs, 2008). Somewhat tangential to Iraq but thoughtful and relevant is Jack L. Goldsmith, *The Terror Presidency: Law and Judgment Inside the Bush Administration* (New York: Norton, 2007). Many, many more are sure to come.

It is impossible to write about this presidency and not make use of four books authored by Bob Woodward and published by Simon & Schuster: *Bush at War* (2002), *Plan of Atttack* (2004), *State of Denial* (2006), and *The War Within* (2008). These books, while technically secondary sources, come close to being primary sources given Woodward's unique access and reporting. Two books on George W. Bush that I found to be useful were Jacob Weisberg, *The Bush Tragedy* (New York: Random House, 2008) and Robert Draper, *Dead Certain: The Presidency of George W. Bush* (New York: Free Press, 2007). On President Bush's first secretary of state, I would cite Karen DeYoung, *Soldier: The Life of Colin Powell* (New York: Knopf, 2006).

There is a large and growing literature devoted to the second Iraq war and in particular to its aftermath. Here I would highlight George Packer, *The Assassins' Gate: America in Iraq* (New York: Farrar, Straus & Giroux, 2005);

Rajiv Chandrasekaran, *Imperial Life in the Emerald City: Inside Iraq's Green Zone* (New York: Knopf, 2006); Michael R. Gordon and Bernard E. Trainor, *Cobra II: The Inside Story of the Invasion and Occupation of Iraq* (New York: Pantheon, 2006); Thomas E. Ricks, *Fiasco: The American Military Adventure in Iraq* (New York: Penguin, 2006); Todd S. Purdum and the *New York Times* staff, *A Time of Our Choosing: America's War in Iraq* (New York: Times Books, 2003); and Larry Diamond, *Squandered Victory: The American Occupation and the Bungled Effort to Bring Democracy to Iraq* (New York: Owl, 2005). A useful Iraqi perspective is Ali A. Allawi, *The Occupation of Iraq: Winning the War, Losing the Peace* (New Haven: Yale University Press, 2007). For the U.N. dimension, see David M. Malone, *The International Struggle Over Iraq: Politics in the UN Security Council 1980–2005* (New York: Oxford University Press, 2006).

CHAPTER 1: A TALE OF TWO WARS

PAGE

9   *The first Iraq war cost:* See U.S. Department of Defense, *Conduct of the Persian Gulf War,* Final Report to Congress, April 1992, p. 725. The full text is available at www.ndu.edu/library/epubs/cpgw.pdf.

9   *The second war has cost:* For a worst possible, that is, most expensive, case analysis, see Joseph E. Stiglitz and Linda J. Blimes, *The Three Trillion Dollar War: The True Cost of the Iraq Conflict* (New York: Norton, 2008). See also U.S. Congress Joint Economic Committee, *War at Any Price? The Total Economic Costs of the War Beyond the Federal Budget,* 110th Cong., 1st sess., November 2007.

10   *Speaking in 1982 during Israel's war in Lebanon:* Menachem Begin, Address by Prime Minister Begin at the National Defense College (speech, National Defense College, Jerusalem, August 8, 1982), www .mfa.gov.il/MFA/Foreign%20Relations/Israels%20Foreign%20Rela tions%20since%201947/1982-1984/55%20Address%20by%20 Prime%20Minister%20Begin%20at%20the%20National.

11   *I introduced the phrases:* Richard N. Haass, "Wars of Choice," *Washington Post,* November 23, 2003, p. B7.

11   *Asked by Tim Russert:* George W. Bush, interview by Tim Russert, *Meet the Press,* NBC, February 8, 2004.

11   *Maimonides, one of the great scholars in the annals of Judaism:* See

Maimonides, *The Code of Maimonides,* Book 14, *The Book of Judges,* trans. Abraham M. Hershman, Yale Judaica Series, ed. Julian Obermann, Louis Ginzberg, and Harry A. Wolfson, three (New Haven: Yale University Press, 1949); and Noah Feldman, "War and Reason in Maimonides and Averroës," in *The Ethics of War: Shared Problems in Different Traditions,* ed. Richard Sorabji and David Rodin (Hants, U.K.: Ashgate Publishing Limited, 2006).

15 *I was increasingly unhappy with the policy:* Richard N. Haass, *The Opportunity: America's Moment to Alter History's Course* (New York: PublicAffairs, 2005).

15 *Called "Wars of Choice:"* Haass, "Wars of Choice."

16 *My late dear friend:* David Halberstam, *The Coldest Winter: America and the Korean War* (New York: Hyperion, 2007), p. 660.

CHAPTER 2: THE WINDING ROAD TO WAR

PAGE

17 *C. L. Sulzberger, one of the leading columnists of his day:* C. L. Sulzberger, "Foreign Affairs: East and West of Suez," *New York Times,* July 21, 1967, p. 23.

18 *The State Department, after noting "regret":* Fred Farris, "U.S. Won't Rush In to Fill Gap," *International Herald Tribune,* January 17, 1968, p. 1.

18 *Senate majority leader Mike Mansfield: Washington Star,* "Plugging the Gap as Britain Pulls Out," editorial, January 21, 1968, p. E-1.

18 *Kissinger recounts in his memoirs:* Henry Kissinger, *White House Years* (Boston: Little, Brown, 1979), p. 51.

19 *In the end, the centerpiece:* See "U.S. Policy in the Persian Gulf— Response to NSSM 66," declassified memo from the NSC Interdepartmental Group for Near East and South Asia to the National Security Adviser, March 10, 1970.

19 *The comments were later codified:* See Kissinger, *White House Years,* pp. 224–25.

20 *Months later, on a visit to Iran:* See Jimmy Carter, *Keeping Faith: Memoirs of a President* (New York: Bantam, 1982), p. 437.

21 *By 1978, when it became clear:* Zbigniew Brzezinski, *Power and Principle: Memoirs of the National Security Adviser 1977–1981* (New York: Farrar, Straus & Giroux, 1983), pp. 355–56.

21 *Brzezinski was not exaggerating:* Brzezinski, *Power and Principle,* pp. 354, 398.

21 *"Let our position be absolutely clear":* See U.S. Department of State, *American Foreign Policy Basic Documents 1977–1980* (Washington, D.C., 1983), p. 55.

22 *This tendency to view events:* Alexander M. Haig, Jr., *Caveat: Realism, Reagan, and Foreign Policy* (New York: Macmillan, 1984), p. 30.

24 *Haig was onto something:* Haig, *Caveat,* p. 79.

26 *This development triggered alarm:* George P. Shultz, *Turmoil and Triumph: My Years as Secretary of State* (New York: Charles Scribner's Sons, 1993), p. 235.

26 *The war itself, which lasted some eight years:* For information on the Iran-Iraq War, see, for example, Efraim Karsh, *The Iran-Iraq War: A Military Analysis,* Adelphi Papers 220 (London: International Institute for Strategic Studies, 1987); Efraim Karsh, *The Iran-Iraq War 1980–1988,* Essential Histories (Oxford: Osprey, 2002); and Ralph King, *The Iran-Iraq War: The Political Implications,* Adelphi Papers 219 (London: International Institute for Strategic Studies, 1987). For the lives lost in the war, see Micheal Clodfelter, *Warfare and Armed Conflicts: A Statistical Encyclopedia of Casualty and Other Figures, 1494–2007,* 3rd ed. (Jefferson, N.C.: McFarland & Company, Inc., 2008), pp. 627–29. For the economic costs, see Hooshang Amirahmadi, "Economic Reconstruction of Iran: Costing the War Damage," *Third World Quarterly* 12, no. 1 (1990): 26–47, and Kamran Mofid, "Economic Reconstruction of Iraq: Financing the Peace," *Third World Quarterly* 12, no. 1 (1990): 48–61.

26 *Diplomacy would not bear fruit:* United Nations Security Council, Resolution 598, July 20, 1987, www.un.org/Docs/scres/1987/scres87.htm. All U.N. Security Council resolutions can be found at www.un.org/documents/scres.htm.

27 *"While the United States basically adhered to the policy":* Shultz, *Turmoil and Triumph,* p. 237.

27 *It is interesting to note:* Brzezinski, *Power and Principle,* p. 506.

27 *Iraq turned it down:* Shultz, *Turmoil and Triumph,* pp. 237–38.

28 *The Reagan administration went along:* For information on Operation Earnest Will, see Senate Committee on Armed Services, *U.S. Military Forces to Protect "Re-Flagged" Kuwaiti Oil Tankers,* 100th Cong., 1st sess., June 5, 1987–June 11, 1987, S. Hrg. 100–269.

28 *"I did not want to let the United States"*: Shultz, *Turmoil and Triumph*, p. 926.

29 *These actions, coupled with setbacks:* "Words of Khomeini: On Islam, the Revolution and a Cease-Fire," *New York Times,* July 23, 1988, sec. 1, p. 5.

30 *Even assuming the worst:* A good deal of this analysis is derived from the work of Kenneth Juster. See, for example, Kenneth I. Juster, "The Myth of Iraqgate," *Foreign Policy,* no. 94 (1994): 105–19.

32 *For a while it looked like it would be:* See Alfonso Chardy, "Bush Adviser Suggested Shift in Nicaragua Policy," *Miami Herald,* December 2, 1988, p. 23D.

36 *What made him particularly unhappy:* Richard N. Haass, "Paying Less Attention to the Middle East," *Commentary* 82, no. 2 (1986): 22–26; and Richard N. Haass, "Ripeness and the settlement of international disputes," *Survival* 30, no. 3 (1988): 232–51.

36 *This must have been enough:* See Rowland Evans and Robert Novak, "House Foreign Affairs Chief Shifts, Favors PLO Negotiations," *Elyria (Ohio) Chronicle-Telegram,* February 7, 1989, p. A-4.

37 *Iran also garnered some notice:* George Bush, Inaugural Address (Washington, D.C., January 20, 1989), bushlibrary.tamu.edu/research/public_papers.php?id=1&year=1989&month=01.

38 *It was clear even before the visits:* For a discussion of the concept of ripeness, see Richard N. Haass, *Conflicts Unending: The United States and Regional Disputes* (New Haven: Yale University Press, 1990).

41 *Baker called upon the Arab world:* James Baker, "Principles and pragmatism: American policy toward the Arab-Israeli conflict" (speech, American Israel Public Affairs Committee, Washington, D.C., May 22, 1989), accessed via www.findarticles.com.

44 *It is important to make this clear:* One book that does this well is Richard Reeves, *President Kennedy: Profile of Power* (New York: Simon & Schuster, 1994).

46 *National Security Directive 26:* The White House, *National Security Directive 26,* October 2, 1989, bushlibrary.tamu.edu/research/pdfs/nsd/nsd26.pdf.

48 *There was also the realization:* This policy of constructive engagement did not meet with universal favor. See, for example, Paul A. Gigot, "A Great American Screw-Up: The U.S. and Iraq, 1980–1990," *National Interest* 22 (1990–91): 3–10; Zachary Karabell, "Backfire: US Policy

Toward Iraq, 1998–2 August 1990," *Middle East Journal* 49, no. 1 (1995): 28–47; and Dan Oberdorfer, "Missed Signals In the Middle East," *Washington Post Magazine*, March 17, 1991, pp. 19–23, 36–41.

49 *Years later, allegations regarding:* For background on Iraqgate, see, for example, Elaine Sciolino, "Iraq Policy Still Bedevils Bush as Congress Asks: Were Crimes Committed?" *New York Times*, August 9, 1992, p. A18; and David Shaw, "Iraqgate—A Case Study of a Big Story With Little Impact," *Los Angeles Times*, October 28, 1992, p. A1. For examples of the charges, see Brian Duffy, Stephen J. Hedges, and Elizabeth Pezzullo, "Cover-up," *U.S. News & World Report*, October 26, 1992, pp. 51–58; and Mortimer B. Zuckerman, "The Arrogance of Power," editorial, *U.S. News & World Report*, October 26, 1992, p. 112. For the wrap-up of the story, see Neil A. Lewis, "Inquiry Finds No U.S. Involvement in the Iraqi Arms Buildup," *New York Times*, January 24, 1995, p. A15. For criticism of the press's role in the story, see, for example, Stuart Taylor, Jr., "Mediagate: Anatomy of a Feeding Frenzy," *American Lawyer*, November 1994, pp. 85–92; David Mastio, "Take Your POP," *Forbes Media Critic*, Summer 1995, pp. 86–91; and C. Robert Zelnick, letter to the editor, *Foreign Policy*, no. 100 (1995): 177–79. For administration policy, see, for example, Lawrence S. Eagleburger, *US Policy Toward Iraq and the Role of the CCC Program, 1989–90*, prepared testimony before the House Committee on Banking, Finance, and Urban Affairs, 101st Cong., 2nd sess., May 21, 1992.

49 *Yet Gore, too, seemed unable or unwilling to understand:* For an account of Gore's speech, see Elaine Sciolino, "Gore Says Bush's Efforts to Befriend Iraqi Leader Led to Gulf War," *New York Times*, September 30, 1992, p. A21. The full text and video excerpts of the speech are available at www.reasons-for-war-with-iraq.info/gore_speech_9-29-92.html.

50 *Saddam made matters worse:* See, for example, Strobe Talbott, "America Abroad," *Time*, April 30, 1990, p. 50.

51 *Around the same time, a bipartisan group:* See Jackson Diehl, "U.S. Maligns Him, Iraqi Tells Senators," *Washington Post*, April 13, 1990, p. A26.

52 *We succeeded, although as is almost always the case:* For an overview of the 1990 Indo-Pakistani crisis, see P. R. Chari, Pervaiz Iqbal Cheema,

and Stephen P. Cohen, "The Compound Crisis of 1990," in *Four Crises and a Peace Process: American Engagement in South Asia* (Washington, D.C.: Brookings Institution, 2007); and Sumit Ganguly and Devin T. Hagerty, "The 1990 Kashmir Crisis," in *Fearful Symmetry: India-Pakistan Crises in the Shadow of Nuclear Weapons* (Seattle: University of Washington Press, 2006).

55 *I signed the necessary documentation:* See Michael Wines, "White House Blocks Furnace Export to Iraq," *New York Times*, July 20, 1990, p. A3.

55 *For the first and only time in my career:* Jesse Helms, speaking on September 13, 1990, 101st Cong., 2nd sess., *Congressional Record*, p. S13025.

56 *The State Department declared on July 18:* Richard Boucher, State Department Regular Briefing, Washington, D.C., July 18, 1990, Federal News Service transcript, accessed via Nexis. See also "US Reaction to Iraqi Threats in the Gulf," declassified cable from U.S. Department of State to U.S. embassies in the Middle East, July 24, 1990.

56 *Kuwait turned down the U.S. offer:* See Joseph Fitchett, "Kuwait Reportedly Rejected U.S. Military Aid Before Iraqi Invasion," *International Herald Tribune*, October 3, 1990, p. 6.

56 *She was widely criticized for her performance:* For a record of Glaspie's meeting with Saddam, see *New York Times*, "Excerpts from Iraqi Document on Meeting with U.S. Envoy," September 23, 1990, sec. 1, p. 19. For information on the criticism of Glaspie, see Elaine Sciolino, "Envoy's Testimony on Iraq Is Assailed," *New York Times*, July 13, 1991, sec. 1, p. 1. For more on these issues, see Jillian Dickert, "Twisting in the Wind? Ambassador Glaspie and the Persian Gulf Crisis (A)," Kennedy School of Government, Harvard University, Case Program, Case no. C16-91-1056.0 (Cambridge, Mass.: Harvard University, 1991); Jillian Dickert, "Twisting in the Wind? Ambassador Glaspie and the Persian Gulf Crisis (B)," Kennedy School of Government, Harvard University, Case Program, Case no. C16-91-1057.0 (Cambridge, Mass.: Harvard University, 1991); and Jillian Dickert, "Twisting in the Wind? Ambassador Glaspie and the Persian Gulf Crisis (Update)," Kennedy School of Government, Harvard University, Case Program, Case no. C16-92-1057.1 (Cambridge, Mass.: Harvard University, 1992).

57 *This last point was the bottom line:* April Glaspie, "Saddam's Mes-

sage of Friendship to President Bush," declassified cable from U.S. Embassy Baghdad to U.S. Department of State, July 25, 1990. For excerpts from Glaspie's cable to Washington as well as the State Department's response, see *New York Times*, "U.S. Messages on July 1990 Meeting of Hussein and American Ambassador," July 13, 1991, sec. 1, p. 4. See also James A. Baker, III, with Thomas M. DeFrank, *The Politics of Diplomacy: Revolution, War & Peace, 1989–1992* (New York: G. P. Putnam's Sons, 1995), p. 272.

57 *The message we did send:* For the full text of the message to Saddam, see Michael R. Gordon, "Pentagon Objected to Bush's Message to Iraq," *The New York Times,* October 25, 1992, sec. 1, p. 14.

59 *The intelligence community sounded the alarm:* See Zachary Karabell and Philip Zelikow, eds., "Prelude to War: U.S. Policy Toward Iraq 1988–1990," Kennedy School of Government, Harvard University, Case Program, Case no. C16-94-1245.0 (Cambridge, Mass.: Harvard University, 1994), p. 29.

CHAPTER 3: DESERT SHIELD

PAGE

60 *Resolution 660, which demanded:* United Nations Security Council, Resolution 660, August 2, 1990, www.un.org/Docs/scres/1990/scres90 .htm.

61 *The Soviets then went a step further:* James Baker and Eduard Shevardnadze, Text of Joint Statement and Press Conference by Secretary of State James A. Baker III, and Foreign Minister Eduard Shevardnadze at Vukunovo II Airport Moscow, August 3, 1990, Federal News Service transcript, accessed via Nexis.

61 *Indeed, it is worth noting:* Baker, *The Politics of Diplomacy,* pp. 1–16.

61 *The president caused problems for himself:* George Bush, Remarks and an Exchange With Reporters on the Iraqi Invasion of Kuwait, Washington, D.C., August 2, 1990, bushlibrary.tamu.edu/research/public_ papers.php?id=2123&year=1990&month=8.

62 *"I am aware as you are":* George Bush and Brent Scowcroft, *A World Transformed* (New York: Knopf, 1998), p. 322.

62 *The second NSC meeting on the crisis:* Declassified notes, Meeting of the National Security Council, the White House, Washington, D.C., August 3, 1990.

62 *"My personal judgment is that the stakes"*: Bush and Scowcroft, *A World Transformed,* p. 323.

67 *We had scheduled a fourth NSC meeting:* Declassified notes, Meeting of the National Security Council, the White House, Washington, D.C., August 5, 1990.

69 *Asked by the waiting journalists:* George Bush, Remarks and an Exchange With Reporters on the Iraqi Invasion of Kuwait, Washington, D.C., August 5, 1990, bushlibrary.tamu.edu/research/public_papers .php?id=2138&year=1990&month=8.

69 *Baker later described it:* Baker, *The Politics of Diplomacy,* p. 276.

69 *"Each international crisis also puts the spotlight"*: Maureen Dowd, "The Guns of August Make a Dervish Bush Whirl Even Faster," Reporter's Notebook, *New York Times,* August 7, 1990, p. A8.

69 *That in turn led William Safire:* William Safire, "Face Time," On Language, *The New York Times,* September 9, 1990, sec. 6, p. 26.

70 *August 6 was also the day:* Declassified notes, Meeting of the National Security Council, the White House, Washington, D.C., August 6, 1990.

71 *"I will tell you how you will be defeated"*: Declassified cable from U.S. Embassy Baghdad to U.S. Department of State, August 6, 1990.

73 *The address underscored the four principles:* George Bush, Address to the Nation Announcing the Deployment of United States Armed Forces to Saudi Arabia (speech, Washington, D.C., August 8, 1990), bush library.tamu.edu/research/public_papers.php?id=2147&year=1990& month=8.

74 *As you might expect:* For a speechwriter's perspective, see Peggy Noonan's wonderful memoir, *What I Saw at the Revolution: A Political Life in the Reagan Era* (New York: Random House, 1990).

74 *"Up to now, the most pellucid prose"*: William Safire, "Mr. Bush Hires a Writer," Essay, *New York Times,* February 11, 1991, p. A19.

74 *A few days later, the Arab League condemned:* Kim Murphy, "Arab Leaders Call for Troops to Halt Iraqis," *Los Angeles Times,* August 11, 1990, p. A1.

75 *In 1973, the United States consumed:* See U.S. Department of Energy, Energy Information Administration, "World Petroleum Consumption, 1960–2006," accessed via www.eia.doe.gov/emeu/international/oil consumption.html, and "Petroleum Imports by Country of Origin, 1960–2007," accessed via www.eia.doe.gov/emeu/aer/petro.html.

76 *Alan Greenspan wrote in his memoir:* Alan Greenspan, *The Age of Turbulence: Adventures in a New World* (New York: Penguin, 2007), p. 463.

77 *A week after the Oval Office speech:* George Bush, Remarks to Department of Defense Employees (speech, Washington, D.C., August 15, 1990), bushlibrary.tamu.edu/research/public_papers.php?id=2165& year=1990&month=8.

85 *So on August 20:* George Bush, Remarks at the Annual Conference of the Veterans of Foreign Wars (speech, Baltimore, August 20, 1990), bush library.tamu.edu/research/public_papers.php?id=2171&year=1990& month=8.

85 *On the left, Jesse Jackson:* See, for example, Alexander Cockburn, "Beat the Devil," *Nation,* September 24, 1990, pp. 298–99.

85 *Nevertheless, by the end of August:* The White House, *National Security Directive 45,* August 20, 1990, bushlibrary.tamu.edu/research/ pdfs/nsd/nsd45.pdf.

87 *The president wanted the meeting:* Bush and Scowcroft, *A World Transformed,* pp. 361–62.

88 *The two countries declared:* Joint Statement of the United States and the Soviet Union, Helsinki, Finland, September 9, 1990, Federal News Service transcript, accessed via Nexis.

89 *"A hundred generations have searched":* George Bush, Address Before a Joint Session of the Congress on the Persian Gulf Crisis and the Federal Budget Deficit (speech, United States Capitol, Washington, D.C., September 11, 1990), bushlibrary.tamu.edu/research/public_papers .php?id=2217&year=1990&month=9.

91 *As a result, the United States introduced a resolution:* United Nations Security Council, Resolution 672, October 12, 1990, www.un.org/ Docs/scres/1990/scres90.htm.

96 *The plan was unimaginative:* See Bush and Scowcroft, *A World Transformed,* pp. 380–81.

96 *This is where Brent's being national security advisor:* For a discussion of the relations between civilian and military leaders in wartime, including this episode, see Eliot A. Cohen, *Supreme Command: Soldiers, Statesmen, and Leadership in Wartime* (New York: Free Press, 2002).

97 *This was consistent with one of the basic tenets:* Colin L. Powell, "U.S. Forces: Challenges Ahead," *Foreign Affairs* 72, no. 5 (1992): 32–45.

98   *He exploded—at me:* For Baker's version of events, see Baker, *The Politics of Diplomacy,* pp. 329–30.

102 *A front-page story in the* New York Times: R. W. Apple, Jr., "The Collapse of a Coalition," *New York Times,* December 6, 1990, p. A1.

102 *Former president Jimmy Carter:* See John Whiteclay Chambers II, "Jimmy Carter's Public Policy Ex-Presidency," *Political Science Quarterly* 113, no. 3 (1999): 405–25, especially pp. 414–15; and Maureen Dowd, "Despite Role as Negotiator, Carter Feels Unappreciated," *New York Times,* September 21, 1994, p. A1.

102 *Senator Sam Nunn, normally something of a hawk:* See Senate Committee on Armed Services, *Crisis in the Persian Gulf Region: U.S. Policy Options and Implications,* 101st Cong., 2nd sess., September 11, 1990–December 3, 1990, S. Hrg. 101–1071.

102 *I found it noteworthy:* See David Pace, "Nunn Says Opposing Gulf War Ruined Chances at Presidency," *Chicago Sun-Times,* December 26, 1996, p. 20.

103 *The president was moved to write:* George Bush, "Why We Are in the Gulf," *Newsweek,* November 26, 1990, p. 28.

103 *The former was the passage:* United Nations Security Council, Resolution 678, November 29, 1990, www.un.org/Docs/scres/1990/scres90 .htm.

104 *That said, the president pressed him hard:* Declassified notes, One-on-One Meeting with Prime Minister Shamir of Israel, the White House, Washington, D.C., December 11, 1990.

104 *One of my favorite moments:* George Bush, Exchange With Reporters Prior to a Meeting With Hostages Released by Iraq, Washington, D.C., December 13, 1990, bushlibrary.tamu.edu/research/public_papers .php?id=2556&year=1990&month=12.

108 *I also drafted a letter:* The White House, Statement by Press Secretary Fitzwater on President Bush's Letter to President Saddam Hussein of Iraq, January 12, 1991, bushlibrary.tamu.edu/research/public_papers .php?id=2617&year=1991&month=1.

111 *The history of sanctions suggested some modesty:* For analysis of sanctions, see, for example, Richard N. Haass, ed., *Economic Sanctions and American Diplomacy* (New York: Council on Foreign Relations, 1998); Richard N. Haass and Meghan L. O'Sullivan, eds., *Honey and Vinegar: Incentives, Sanctions, and Foreign Policy* (Washington, D.C.: Brookings Institution, 2000); and Gary Clyde Hufbauer et al., eds., *Economic*

Sanctions Reconsidered, 3rd ed. (Washington, D.C.: Peterson Institute for International Economics, 2008).

113 *This is the classic debate:* For background on the war powers debate, see, for example, National War Powers Commission, *National War Powers Commission Report* (Charlottesville, Va.: Miller Center of Public Affairs, 2008); and Charles A. Stevenson, *Congress at War: The Politics of Conflict since 1789* (Washington, D.C.: National Defense University Press/Potomac Books, 2007).

113 *He says as much in the book:* Bush and Scowcroft, *A World Transformed,* p. 446.

115 *National Security Directive 54:* The White House, *National Security Directive 54,* January 15, 1991, bushlibrary.tamu.edu/research/pdfs/nsd/nsd54.pdf.

CHAPTER 4: WAR OF NECESSITY

PAGE

116 *We also included language:* George Bush, Address to the Nation Announcing Allied Military Action in the Persian Gulf (speech, Washington, D.C., January 16, 1991), bushlibrary.tamu.edu/research/public_papers.php?id=2625&year=1991&month=01.

116 *"Korea is a small country":* Harry Truman, Radio Address Delivered by the President on July 19, 1950, on the Korean Situation and Its Implications (speech, Washington, D.C., July 19, 1950), www.trumanlibrary.org/whistlestop/study_collections/korea/large/week2/kw_112_1.htm.

118 *Everyone in the room had a good laugh:* For a review of Baker's testimony, see Thomas L. Friedman, "Baker Rebukes Israel on Peace Terms," *New York Times,* June 14, 1990, p. A3.

122 *The focus was for obvious reasons:* George Bush, Address Before a Joint Session of the Congress on the State of the Union (speech, Washington, D.C., January 29, 1991), bushlibrary.tamu.edu/research/public_papers.php?id=2656&year=1991&month=01.

122 *The statement suggested "a cessation of hostilities would be possible":* U.S. Department of State, Joint Statement by Secretary of State James A. Baker III, and Soviet Foreign Minister Alexander Bessmertnykh, Washington, D.C., January 29, 1991, Federal News Service transcript, accessed via Nexis.

122 *Clearly Baker and Dennis Ross had not anticipated the reaction:* For
     President Bush's and Scowcroft's version of events, see Bush and Scow-
     croft, *A World Transformed,* pp. 460–61; for Baker's, see Baker, *The
     Politics of Diplomacy,* pp. 391–95.

123 *I spent a few hours in the bowels of the Pentagon:* See John A. Warden,
     III, *The Air Campaign: Planning for Combat* (Washington, D.C.:
     Pergamon-Brassey's International Defense Publishers, 1989). See also
     Richard T. Reynolds, *Heart of the Storm: The Genesis of the Air Cam-
     paign against Iraq* (Maxwell Air Force Base, Ala.: Air University Press,
     1995).

127 *On February 22 we released:* George Bush, Remarks on the Persian
     Gulf Conflict (speech, Washington, D.C., February 22, 1991), bush
     library.tamu.edu/research/public_papers.php?id=2729&year=1991&
     month=2.

127 *I drafted the short remarks:* George Bush, Address to the Nation An-
     nouncing Allied Military Ground Action in the Persian Gulf (speech,
     Washington, D.C., February 23, 1991), bushlibrary.tamu.edu/research/
     public_papers.php?id=2734&year=1991&month=2.

129 *The president told Norm:* For Schwarzkopf's account, see H. Norman
     Schwarzkopf, with Peter Petre, *It Doesn't Take a Hero: The Autobiog-
     raphy* (New York: Bantam Books, 1992), pp. 469–70.

129 *Schwarzkopf accurately recounted all this:* See H. Norman Schwarz-
     kopf, interview by David Frost, . . . *Talking with David Frost,* PBS,
     March 27, 1991. See also Ann Devroy and R. Jeffrey Smith, "Bush,
     Cheney Dispute General on End of Fighting," *Washington Post,* March
     28, 1991, p. A1; Patrick E. Tyler, "General's Account of Gulf War's End
     Disputed by Bush," *New York Times,* March 28, 1991, p. A1; and R.
     Jeffrey Smith, "Bush Phones Schwarzkopf in Bid To End Controversy
     Over Cease-Fire," *Washington Post,* March 29, 1991, p. A14.

131 *The president spoke to the American people:* George Bush, Address to
     the Nation on the Suspension of Allied Offensive Combat Operations
     in the Persian Gulf (Washington, D.C., February 27, 1991), bush
     library.tamu.edu/research/public_papers.php?id=2746&year=1991&
     month=2.

132 *A week later, he spoke:* George Bush, Address Before a Joint Session of
     the Congress on the Cessation of the Persian Gulf Conflict (Washing-
     ton, D.C., March 6, 1991), bushlibrary.tamu.edu/research/public_
     papers.php?id=2767&year=1991&month=3.

134 *Schwarzkopf was determined to avoid:* Schwarzkopf, *It Doesn't Take a Hero,* p. 481.

135 *The Safwan meeting was seen:* For an account of the meeting, see Schwarzkopf, *It Doesn't Take a Hero,* pp. 484–90.

135 *Schwarzkopf makes just this point:* Schwarzkopf, *It Doesn't Take a Hero,* p. 489.

137 *Before the rebellions took some of the glow:* George Bush, Address Before a Joint Session of the Congress on the Cessation of the Persian Gulf Conflict (speech, Washington, D.C., March 6, 1991), bush library.tamu.edu/research/public_papers.php?id=2767&year=1991& month=3.

139 *We were getting hammered in the press:* For examples, see William Safire, "Follow the Kurds to Save Iraq," Essay, *New York Times,* March 28, 1991, p. A25; William Safire, "Bush's Moral Crisis," Essay, *New York Times,* April 1, 1991, p. A17; William Safire, "Bush's Bay of Pigs," Essay, *New York Times,* April 4, 1991, p. A23; and William Safire, "The Decline of the East," Essay, *New York Times,* April 29, 1991, p. A17.

140 *Three years and thirty thousand:* Clodfelter, *Warfare and Armed Conflicts,* pp. 697–712.

140 *I had taught (with Professor Ernest May):* Richard E. Neustadt and Ernest R. May, *Thinking in Time: The Uses of History for Decision Makers* (New York: Free Press, 1986).

142 *On the security side:* United Nations Security Council, Resolution 687, April 3, 1991, www.un.org/Docs/scres/1991/scres91.htm.

144 *Progress in the theater:* See Bob Woodward, *The Commanders* (New York: Simon & Schuster, 1991).

146 *The points I'd prepared:* George Bush, The President's News Conference, Washington, D.C., September 12, 1991, bushlibrary.tamu. edu/research/public_papers.php?id=3372&year=1991&month=9.

147 *The final version sought to set a tone:* George Bush, Remarks at the Opening Session of the Middle East Peace Conference in Madrid, Spain (speech, Madrid, Spain, October 30, 1991), bushlibrary.tamu .edu/research/public_papers.php?id=3566&year=1991&month=10.

149 *A National Intelligence Estimate was actually published:* Central Intelligence Agency, "Saddam Husayn: Likely to Hang On," National Intelligence Estimate, June 1992, accessed via www.foia.cia.gov.

151 *Raines refused, saying Tyler had it:* See Patrick E. Tyler, "U.S. Said to

Plan Raids on Baghdad If Access Is Denied," *New York Times*, August 16, 1992, sec. 1, p. 1. For the administration's response to Tyler's story, see Thomas L. Friedman, "Bush Says Politics Is Not Motivation in Plans for Iraq," *New York Times*, August 17, 1992, p. A1.

CHAPTER 5: THE CLINTON INTERREGNUM

PAGE

154 *It was also an awkward issue:* Michael Kelly, "Clinton Defends Position on Iraqi War," *New York Times,* July 31, 1992, p. A13.

155 *The one time Iraq gained prominence:* Thomas L. Friedman, "Clinton Backs Raid but Muses About a New Start," *New York Times,* January 14, 1993, p. A1. See also Thomas L. Friedman, "Clinton Affirms U.S. Policy on Iraq," *New York Times*, January 15, 1993, p. A1.

156 *Iraq never quite disappeared, though:* Madeleine Albright, with Bill Woodward, *Madam Secretary: A Memoir* (New York: Miramax, 2003), p. 272.

156 *The address was delivered:* Martin Indyk, "The Clinton Administration's Approach to the Middle East" (speech, Washington Institute for Near East Policy, Washington, D.C., May 18, 1993), www.washington institute.org/templateC07.php?CID=61. For the background to this speech, see Martin Indyk, "Dual Containment," in *Innocent Abroad: An Intimate History of American Peace Diplomacy in the Middle East* (New York: Simon & Schuster, 2009), pp. 30–43.

157 *There was no talk of regime change:* Anthony Lake, "Confronting Backlash States," *Foreign Affairs* 73, no. 2 (1994): 45–55.

157 *Not surprisingly, the new policy:* Again, see Indyk, "Dual Containment," in *Innocent Abroad.* See also, for example, F. Gregory Gause, "The Illogic of Dual Containment," *Foreign Affairs* 73, no. 2 (1994): 56–66.

158 *Containment, the foreign policy doctrine:* Kennan's "Long Telegram" outlining containment was published as the famous "X article" in 1947 by *Foreign Affairs.* See X [George F. Kennan], "The Sources of Soviet Conduct," *Foreign Affairs* 25, no. 4 (1947): 566–82.

159 *My involvement in Iraq:* For a sampling of work during this period, see Richard N. Haass, "The U.S. Military Can't Create a New Iraq," *Washington Post,* October 12, 1994, p. A23; Richard N. Haass, "He's back," *The Boston Globe,* April 2, 1995, p. 67; Richard N. Haass, prepared

testimony before the House Committee on National Security, 104th Cong., 2nd sess., September 26, 1996; Richard N. Haass, "Why we won't invade," *Washington Times,* November 20, 1997, p. A21; Richard N. Haass, "Stay Strong on Iraq," *Washington Post,* January 29, 1998, p. A19; and Richard N. Haass, "Containing Saddam," *Washington Times,* November 10, 1998, p. A21.

160 *The administration thus favored:* United Nations Security Council, Resolution 986, April 14, 1995, www.un.org/Docs/scres/1995/scres95 .htm.

161 *Months later, in October 1997:* United Nations Security Council, Resolution 986, October 23, 1997, www.un.org/Docs/scres/1997/scres97 .htm.

162 *What influenced it:* "Iraq Weapons of Mass Destruction Programs," U.S. Government White Paper, February 13, 1998, www.globalsecurity .org/wmd/library/news/iraq/1998/whitepap.htm.

162 *Madeleine Albright made this clear:* Albright, *Madam Secretary,* pp. 276–77.

163 *There was: coercive force:* For a discussion of this concept, see Richard N. Haass, *Intervention: The Use of American Military Force in the Post–Cold War World* (Washington, D.C.: Carnegie Endowment for International Peace, 1994), especially pp. 53–55.

164 *Secretary of State Albright explicitly acknowledged just this:* Albright, *Madam Secretary,* pp. 286–87.

164 *"Through constant confrontation":* Samuel R. Berger, Advance Text of Remarks To Be Delivered by Samuel R. Berger, Assistant to the President for National Security Affairs (speech, Stanford University, Palo Alto, Calif., December 8, 1998), Federal News Service, accessed via Nexis.

164 *This pressure took several forms:* See, for example, *Weekly Standard,* "Saddam Must Go," editorial, December 1, 1997, p. 11.

164 *Paramount among these:* Project for the New American Century, "Letter to President Clinton on Iraq," January 26, 1998, www.newameri cancentury.org/iraqclintonletter.htm.

165 *My description of U.S. policy:* Richard N. Haass, "The United States and Iraq: A Strategy for the Long Haul," Brookings Policy Brief Series 7, Brookings Institution, October 1996, www.brookings.edu/papers/ 1996/10iraq_haass.aspx?p=1.

165 *I also worried about the consequences:* Richard N. Haass, "U.S. Op-

tions in Confronting Iraq," prepared testimony before the House Committee on International Relations, 105th Cong., 2nd sess., February 25, 1998, Federal News Service transcript, accessed via Nexis; and Richard N. Haass, "Iraq: Can Saddam Be Overthrown?" prepared testimony before the Senate Committee on Foreign Relations Subcommittee on Near Eastern and South Asian Affairs, 105th Cong., 2nd sess., March 2, 1998, Federal News Service transcript, accessed via Nexis.

166 *In October 1998, it passed: Iraq Liberation Act of 1998,* Public Law 105–338, 105th Cong., 2nd sess., October 31, 1998.

166 *Tony Zinni, the marine general:* See Vernon Loeb, "General Wary of Plan To Arm Groups in Iraq; Commander in Gulf Fearful of 'Rogue State,'" *Washington Post,* January 29, 1999, p. A19. See also Daniel Byman, Kenneth Pollack, and Gideon Rose, "The Rollback Fantasy," *Foreign Affairs* 78, no. 1 (1999): 24–41.

166 *And speaking at the National Press Club:* Samuel R. Berger, Remarks by Samuel R. Berger (speech, National Press Club, Washington, D.C., December 23, 1998), clinton3.nara.gov/WH/EOP/NSC/html/speeches/19981223.html.

166 *The international inspections effort had effectively ended:* See United Nations Security Council, Resolution 1284, December 17, 1999, www.un.org/Docs/scres/1999/sc99.htm.

167 *He named in order of priority:* See Bill Clinton, *My Life* (New York: Knopf, 2004), p. 935.

CHAPTER 6: THE 9/11 PRESIDENCY

PAGE

169 *I left behind a copy:* Richard N. Haass, *The Reluctant Sheriff: The United States after the Cold War* (New York: Council on Foreign Relations, 1997).

170 *Later on they would come to call themselves:* James Mann, *Rise of the Vulcans: The History of Bush's War Cabinet* (New York: Viking, 2004).

171 *Even Kennan harbored grave doubts:* George F. Kennan, *Memoirs: 1925–1950* (New York: Pantheon, 1967), p. 467.

172 *The hearing before the Senate Foreign Relations Committee:* Senate

Committee on Foreign Relations, 107th Cong., 1st sess., April 25, 2001, FDCH Political Transcripts, accessed via Nexis.

173 *In the end, I spent more than an hour:* See, for example, Toby Harnden, "N. Ireland No Longer Priority; Bush Turns Issue over to State Dept.," *Chicago Sun-Times,* March 12, 2001, p. 21; Al Kamen, "U.S. Loses Its Seat; Powell Loses His Cool," *Washington Post,* May 7, 2001, p. A17; Niall O'Dowd, "Bush 'Peace Envoy' Favored British: Nominee Critical of Clinton Role," *New York Irish Voice,* March 20, 2001, p. 3; and Robin Wright, "Richard Haass Gets Four Key Jobs as Powell Seeks to Reduce the Number of Special Envoys," *Los Angeles Times,* March 15, 2001, p. A6.

174 *The policy "answer" to this:* See Meghan L. O'Sullivan, *Shrewd Sanctions: Statecraft and State Sponsors of Terrorism* (Washington, D.C.: Brookings Institution, 2003).

175 *This initiative would not reach fruition:* United Nations Security Council, Resolution 1409, May 14, 2002, www.un.org/Docs/scres/2002/sc2002.htm.

175 *It did, as Ron Suskind details:* See Ron Suskind, *The Price of Loyalty: George W. Bush, the White House, and the Education of Paul O'Neill* (New York: Simon & Schuster, 2004), pp.70–75.

176 *In both instances, the countries' nuclear programs:* On Iran, see William J. Broad and David E. Sanger, "Iran Said to Have Nuclear Fuel for One Weapon," *The New York Times,* November 20, 2008, p. A12; and, for a more detailed picture, International Atomic Energy Agency, "Implementation of the NPT Safeguards Agreement and relevant provisions of Security Council resolutions 1737 (2006), 1747 (2007), 1803 (2008), and 1835 (2008) in the Islamic Republic of Iran," Report by the Director General, November 19, 2008, www.iaea.org/Publications/Documents/Board/2008/gov2008-59.pdf. On North Korea, see Helene Cooper, "In Disclosure, North Korea Contradicts U.S. Intelligence on Its Plutonium Program," *The New York Times,* May 31, 2008, p. A12.

177 *Meanwhile, I got busy with policy planning:* For an analysis of issues related to policy planning, see Daniel Drezner, ed., *Avoiding Trivia: The Role of Strategic Planning in American Foreign Policy* (Washington, D.C.: Brookings Institution, 2009).

177 *I ended up giving:* My speeches from my tenure as director of the Policy Planning Staff can be found at 2001-2009.state.gov/s/p/rem.

180 *We know now that 84 percent of the hard currency:* See Charles Du-
elfer, *Comprehensive Report of the Special Advisor to the Director of
Central Intelligence on Iraq's Weapons of Mass Destruction,* Central
Intelligence Agency, September 30, 2004, https://www.cia.gov/library/
reports/general-reports-1/iraq_wmd_2004/index.html. The most complete study of the "oil-for-food" program and corruption surrounding
it is contained in two reports: Independent Inquiry Committee into the
United Nations Oil-for-Food Programme, *Report on the Management
of the Oil-for-Food Programme,* September 7, 2005; and Independent
Inquiry Committee into the United Nations Oil-for-Food Programme,
Report on the Manipulation of the Oil-for-Food Programme, October
27, 2005. Both are available at www.iic-offp.org/documents.htm.

180 *I thought former CentCom commander:* Steven Lee Myers, "Iraqis
Ask U.S. to Do More to Oust Saddam," *New York Times,* July 3, 2000,
p. A7.

182 *I did not intend it:* Thom Shanker, "White House Says the U.S. Is Not
a Loner, Just Choosy," *New York Times,* July 31, 2001, p. A1.

183 *This all accorded Dick Cheney:* Mark Blanchard, "Cheney: Look Hard
at Energy Needs," United Press International, April 30, 2001, accessed
via Nexis.

186 *A good deal of the investigation:* See *The 9/11 Commission Report:
Final Report of the National Commission on Terrorist Attacks upon
the United States* (New York: Norton, 2004).

187 *(It turns out he did):* See, for example, Saud Abu Ramadan, "Arafat
Condemns Terrorist Attacks in U.S.," United Press International, Sep-
tember 11, 2001, accessed via Nexis; and "Arafat Condemns Terror
Attacks," CNN, October 10, 2001, accessed via www.cnn.com.

192 *But it is worth noting that the first instinct:* Richard A. Clarke, *Against
All Enemies: Inside America's War on Terror* (New York: Free Press,
2004), p. 32.

192 *And a number of influential voices:* See, for example, Robert Kagan
and William Kristol, "What to Do About Iraq; For The War on Terrorism to Succeed, Saddam Hussein Must Be Removed," *Weekly Standard,* January 21, 2002, p. 23; and Project for the New American
Century, "Letter to President Bush on the War on Terrorism," September 20, 2001, www.newamericancentury.org/Bushletter.htm.

195 *A perfect example was his October 16, 2003, memo:* Among Rumsfeld's most interesting snowflakes is one in which he asks, "Are we

winning or losing the Global war on Terror?" For the text, see www
.usatoday.com/news/washington/executive/rumsfeld-memo.htm.

198 *In the end, though:* See James F. Dobbins, *After the Taliban: Nation-Building in Afghanistan* (Washington, D.C.: Potomac, 2008), especially pp. 77–97.

198 *Gary Schroen, in the CIA at the time:* Gary C. Schroen, *First In: An Insider's Account of How the CIA Spearheaded the War on Terror in Afghanistan* (New York: Presidio, 2005), pp. 379–81.

200 *We also discussed what it might say:* See Condoleezza Rice, "Campaign 2000: Promoting the National Interest," *Foreign Affairs* 79, no. 1 (2000): 45–62.

CHAPTER 7: PRELUDE TO WAR

PAGE

203 *I was so confident of this outcome:* Todd S. Purdum and David E. Sanger, "2 Top Officials Offer Stern Talk on U.S. Policy," *New York Times,* February 2, 2002, p. A1.

204 *We never saw a draft:* George W. Bush, Address Before a Joint Session of the Congress on the State of the Union (speech, U.S. Capitol, Washington, D.C., January 29, 2002). For the text, see *Public Papers of the Presidents,* George W. Bush—2002, Vol. 1, pp. 129–36, accessed via www.gpoaccess.gov/pubpapers/gwbush.html.

205 *Months later (in December 2002):* Richard N. Haass, "Towards Greater Democracy in the Muslim World" (speech, Council on Foreign Relations, Washington, D.C., December 4, 2002), 2001-2009.state.gov/s/p/rem/15686.htm.

207 *It was thus with more than a little bemusement:* John J. Mearsheimer and Stephen M. Walt, *The Israel Lobby and U.S. Foreign Policy* (New York: Farrar, Straus & Giroux, 2007).

208 *The president's description of Ariel Sharon:* George W. Bush, Remarks Prior to a Meeting with Secretary of State Colin Powell and an Exchange with Reporters, Washington, D.C., April 18, 2002. For the text, see *Public Papers of the Presidents,* George W. Bush—2002, Vol. 1, p. 633, accessed via www.gpoaccess.gov/pubpapers/gwbush.html.

209 *In the end, the president did break some useful ground:* George W. Bush, Remarks on the Middle East (speech, the White House, Washington, D.C., June 24, 2002). For the text, see *Public Papers of the Presi-*

dents, George W. Bush—2002, Vol. 1, pp. 1059–62, accessed via www .gpoaccess.gov/pubpapers/gwbush.html.

210 *Demanding that others are either with us or against us:* George W. Bush, Satellite Remarks to the Central European Counterterrorism Conference (speech, the White House, Washington, D.C., November 6, 2001). For the text, see *Public Papers of the Presidents,* George W. Bush—2001, Vol. 2, pp. 1348–50, accessed via www.gpoaccess.gov/ pubpapers/gwbush.html.

210 *I tried to advance some of this thinking:* Richard N. Haass, "Defining U.S. Foreign Policy in a Post-Post-Cold War World" (lecture, Foreign Policy Association, New York, April 22, 2002), 2001-2009.state.gov/ s/p/rem/9632.htm.

211 *William Safire built his column around it:* William Safire, "The Inside Skinny," *New York Times,* April 25, 2002, p. A31.

212 *It was around this time:* For an account of the interagency group's activities, see Douglas J. Feith, *War and Decision: Inside the Pentagon at the Dawn of the War on Terrorism* (New York: Harper, 2008).

213 *The first strong public indication:* George W. Bush, Commencement Address at the United States Military Academy in West Point, New York (speech, United States Military Academy, West Point, N.Y., June 1, 2002). For the text, see *Public Papers of the Presidents,* George W. Bush—2002, Vol. 1, pp. 917–22, accessed via www.gpoaccess.gov/ pubpapers/gwbush.html.

214 *On August 5, Powell was invited:* For one account of the dinner, see Bob Woodward, *Plan of Attack* (New York: Simon & Schuster, 2004), pp. 149–51.

215 *We now know from the so-called Downing Street Memo:* See Michael Smith, "Blair Planned Iraq War from Start," *Times* (London), May 1, 2005, p. 7; and "The Secret Downing Street Memo," *Times* (London), May 1, 2005, p. 7.

216 *The opening salvo was launched:* Brent Scowcroft, interview by Bob Schieffer, *Face the Nation,* CBS, August 4, 2002; and Brent Scowcroft, "Don't Attack Saddam," *Wall Street Journal,* August 15, 2002, p. A12.

217 *They had some reason to be worried:* See, for example, Bill Keller, "The Loyal Opposition," *New York Times,* August 24, 2002, p. A13; and Michael Quinlan, "War on Iraq: A Blunder and a Crime," *Financial Times* (London), August 7, 2002, p. 15.

218 *The administration's response came:* Dick Cheney, Remarks by Vice
President Cheney at the Opening Session of the 103rd National Convention of the Veterans of Foreign Wars (speech, Gaylord Opryland
Hotel, Nashville, Tenn., August 26, 2002), Federal News Service transcript, accessed via Nexis.

218 *Much has been written:* See, for example, Ron Suskind, *The One Percent Doctrine: Deep Inside America's Pursuit of Its Enemies Since 9/11*
(New York: Simon & Schuster, 2006).

220 *I should add that Dick Cheney:* See Barton Gellman, *Angler* (New
York: Penguin, 2008), pp. 242–44.

220 *Brent Scowcroft is quoted:* See Jeffrey Goldberg, "Breaking Ranks;
What Turned Brent Scowcroft against the Bush Administration?" *New
Yorker,* October 31, 2005, pp. 54–65.

221 *That helped explain why he could oppose:* See www.youtube.com/
watch?v=YENbElb5-xY.

221 *Yet another signal of where policy was heading:* The White House,
"The National Security Strategy of the United States of America," September 2002, p. 15. The text is available at www.globalsecurity.org/
military/library/policy/national/nss-020920.pdf.

222 *A second camp housed the skeptics:* See Gellman, *Angler,* pp. 215–22.

228 *The president ad-libbed:* George W. Bush, Address to the United Nations General Assembly in New York City (speech, United Nations,
New York, September 12, 2002). For the text, see *Public Papers of the
Presidents,* George W. Bush—2002, Vol. 2, p. 1576, accessed via www
.gpoaccess.gov/pubpapers/gwbush.html.

229 *He and other senior officials regularly referred:* See Senate Select
Committee on Intelligence, *Report on Whether Public Statements Regarding Iraq by U.S. Government Officials Were Substantiated by Intelligence Information,* 110th Cong., 2nd sess., June 5, 2008.

229 *The votes were one-sided:* U.S. House of Representatives, H.J.Res. 114,
Roll Call 455, 107th Cong., 2nd sess., October 10, 2002; and U.S. Senate, H.J.Res. 114, Vote Number 237, 107th Cong., 2nd sess., October
11, 2002.

230 *The publication in October 2002:* See National Intelligence Council,
"Iraq's Continuing Program for Weapons of Mass Destruction," Key
Judgments from October 2002 National Intelligence Estimate, www
.dni.gov/nic/special_keyjudgements.html.

231 *All this helped to create an environment:* See Bob Drogin, *Curveball:*

Spies, Lies, and the Con Man Who Caused a War (New York: Random House, 2007).

231 *I know of no attempt to falsify intelligence:* For a different view of this, see Ron Suskind, *The Way of the World: A Story of Truth and Hope in an Age of Extremism* (New York: HarperCollins, 2008).

231 *On November 8, the U.N. Security Council:* United Nations Security Council, Resolution 1441, November 8, 2002, www.un.org/Docs/scres/2002/sc2002.htm.

CHAPTER 8: WAR OF CHOICE

PAGE

235 *The arguments put forward:* See, for example, Bryan Borrough et al., "The Rush to Invade Iraq; The Ultimate Inside Account," *Vanity Fair,* May 2004, pp. 228–45, 281–94.

235 *The fact that Secretary of Defense Donald Rumsfeld:* See Tommy Franks, with Malcolm McConnell, *American Soldier* (New York: ReganBooks, 2004).

236 *Such big actions appealed:* See Jacob Weisberg, *The Bush Tragedy* (New York: Random House, 2008)

237 *In January 2003, the State of the Union:* George W. Bush, Address Before a Joint Session of the Congress on the State of the Union (speech, U.S. Capitol, Washington, D.C., January 28, 2003). For the text, see *Public Papers of the Presidents,* George W. Bush—2003, Vol. 1, pp. 82–90, accessed via www.gpoaccess.gov/pubpapers/gwbush.html.

239 *My experience in Davos:* For an idea of the scene at the World Economic Forum, see, for example, Andrew Borowiec, "Forum troubled by Iraq, economy; Mood extremely anti-American," *Washington Times,* January 28, 2003, p. A15.

240 *So I sketched out some ideas:* Colin L. Powell, Remarks at the World Economic Forum (speech, World Economic Forum, Davos, Switzerland, January 26, 2003), 2001-2009.state.gov/secretary/former/powell/remarks/2003/16869.htm.

242 *He left out any reference to yellowcake:* Colin L. Powell, Remarks to the United Nations Security Council (presentation, United Nations, New York, February 5, 2003). For the text and accompanying materials, see 2001-2009.state.gov/p/nea/disarm/index.htm. For the origi-

nal reference from the State of the Union, see *Public Papers of the Presidents,* George W. Bush—2003, Vol. 1, p. 88, accessed via www .gpoaccess.gov/pubpapers/gwbush.html.

244 *This is consistent with the February 14 report:* Hans Blix, Briefing of the Security Council (speech, United Nations, New York, February 14, 2003), www.unmovic.org.

247 *I have thought a good deal about this:* See Richard N. Haass, *The Bureaucratic Entrepreneur: How to Be Effective in Any Unruly Organization* (Washington, D.C.: Brookings Institution, 1999), especially pp. 75–78.

247 *Asked precisely this by ABC's Charles Gibson:* George W. Bush, interview by Charles Gibson, *World News with Charles Gibson,* ABC, December 1, 2008.

248 *Powell would cite the anecdote:* Peter Slevin, "Serving Notice at the State Dept.; For Powell, Marshall Became an Example of Duty and Discipline," *Washington Post,* November 12, 2003, p. A21.

249 *Cordell Hull, FDR's secretary of state:* See Fred L. Israel, ed., *The War Diary of Breckinridge Long: Selections from the Years 1939–1944* (Lincoln: University of Nebraska Press, 1966), p. 388.

253 *Donald Rumsfeld infamously stated:* See U.S. Department of Defense, "Secretary Rumsfeld Town Hall Meeting in Kuwait," December 8, 2004, www.defenselink.mil/transcripts/transcript.aspx?transcriptid= 1980.

254 *No one can legitimately argue:* See, for example, James Dobbins et al., *After the War: Nation-Building from FDR to George W. Bush* (Santa Monica, Calif.: RAND Corporation, 2008).

254 *Two National Intelligence Council reports emerged:* See Senate Select Committee on Intelligence, *Report on Prewar Intelligence Assessments about Postwar Iraq,* 110th Cong., 1st sess., May 31, 2007, S. Rep. 110–76, pp. 13–91.

255 *Army chief of staff Eric Shinseki:* See Ken Guggenheim, "Army Chief: Huge Force Would Occupy Iraq," Associated Press, February 25, 2003, accessed via Nexis; and Eric Schmitt, "Pentagon Contradicts General on Iraq Occupation Force's Size," *New York Times,* February 28, 2003, p. A1. For the full transcript of Shinseki's testimony, see Senate Committee on Armed Services, 108th Cong., 1st sess., February 25, 2003, Federal News Service transcript, accessed via Nexis.

255 *Indeed, much of this option:* See Aram Roston, *The Man Who Pushed*

America to War: The Extraordinary Life, Adventures, and Obsessions of Ahmad Chalabi (New York: Nation Books, 2008).

256 *Garner estimates that as many as seventeen:* See Council on Foreign Relations, HBO History Makers Series with Jay Garner (meeting transcript, Council on Foreign Relations, New York, October 1, 2008), www.cfr.org/publication/17718.

257 *This story of a botched aftermath:* In addition to the sources listed at the beginning of this Notes section on the war's aftermath, two shorter pieces of note are James Fallows, "Blind Into Baghdad," *Atlantic,* January/February 2004, pp. 53–74; and David Rieff, "Blueprint for a Mess," *New York Times Magazine,* November 2, 2003, pp. 28–33, 44, 58, 72, 77–78.

257 *Much has been written about the Future of Iraq project:* The full text of the project's thirteen-volume report, as well as background information, is available at www.gwu.edu/~nsarchiv/NSAEBB/NSAEBB198/index.htm.

259 *(What little support there was:* See Samantha Power, *Chasing the Flame: Sergio Vieira de Mello and the Fight to Save the World* (New York: Penguin, 2008).

261 *The army was along with the Baath Party:* See L. Paul Bremer, III, with Malcolm McConnell, *My Year in Iraq: The Struggle to Build a Future of Hope* (New York: Simon & Schuster, 2006); and L. Paul Bremer, James Dobbins, and David Gompert, "Early Days in Iraq: Decisions of the CPA," *Survival* 50, no. 4 (2008): 21–56.

262 *It didn't help itself with the publication:* National Security Council, "National Strategy for Victory in Iraq," November 2005. The text is available at www.washingtonpost.com/wp-dyn/content/article/2005/11/30/AR2005113000376.html.

262 *The creation of the bipartisan Iraq Study Group:* See James A. Baker, III, and Lee H. Hamilton, cochairs, "The Iraq Study Group Report," December 6, 2006. The report text and other information is available through the United States Institute of Peace at www.usip.org/isg/iraq_study_group_report/report/1206/index.html.

263 *Iraq's Shia militias, most likely with the prodding of Iran:* For the debate over the surge, see, for example, Linda Robinson, *Tell Me How This Ends: General David Petraeus and the Search for a Way out of Iraq* (New York: PublicAffairs, 2008); Bing West, *The Strongest Tribe: War, Politics, and the Endgame in Iraq* (New York: Random House,

2008); and Bob Woodward, *The War Within: A Secret White House History 2006–2008* (New York: Simon & Schuster, 2008).

CHAPTER 9: TAKEAWAYS FROM TWO WARS

PAGE

268 *It is also worth noting that the first Iraq war:* For more on just-war theory applied to the Gulf War, see Peter Steinfels, "The Persian Gulf conflict and how it tested the theory of waging a just war," Beliefs, *New York Times,* February 15, 1992, sec. 1, p. 10.

270 *It is quite possible history will judge:* For a discussion of this opportunity, see Richard N. Haass, *The Opportunity: America's Moment to Alter History's Course* (New York: PublicAffairs, 2005).

270 *Instead, Iraq contributed:* See Richard N. Haass, "The Age of Nonpolarity: What Will Follow U.S. Dominance," *Foreign Affairs* 87, no. 3 (2008): 44–56.

271 *The one question that needs to be raised:* For a radical critique, see Jonathan Steele, *Defeat: Why America and Britain Lost Iraq* (Berkeley, Calif.: Counterpoint, 2008).

273 *A principal lesson of Vietnam:* See Frances FitzGerald, *Fire in the Lake: The Vietnamese and the Americans in Vietnam* (New York: Little, Brown, 1972).

275 *This is the so-called democratic peace theory:* See George W. Bush, Inaugural Address by President George W. Bush (speech, U.S. Capitol, Washington, D.C., January 20, 2005), Federal News Service transcript, accessed via Nexis.

278 *The words of John Quincy Adams:* For the full text of the quotation, see Suzy Platt, ed., *Respectfully Quoted: A Dictionary of Quotations Requested from the Congressional Research Service* (Washington, D.C.: Library of Congress, 1989), p. 120.

INDEX

Baker, James (*cont.*)
Lebanon trip of, 81–82
personality of, 98–99
Shamir's conversation with, 118–19
Banca Nazionale del Lavoro (BNL), 51, 54
Bandar bin Sultan bin Abdul Aziz al-Saud, Prince of Saudi Arabia, 65–67, 77, 79, 103
Bay of Pigs, 148, 180–81
Bazoft, Farzad, 50
Begin, Menachem, 9–10
Bell, Gertrude, 52
Berger, Sandy, 156, 164, 166
Berlin Wall, 44, 45, 53, 61
Bessmertnykh, Aleksandr, 122
Best and the Brightest, The (Halberstam), 105
Biden, Joe, 173
bin Laden, Osama, 133, 167, 190
Blackwill, Bob, 170
Blair, Tony, 215, 228, 242–43, 246, 248, 249
Blix, Hans, 244
Boschwitz, Rudy, 89
Bosnia, 9, 153, 155, 247
Brady, Nicholas, 87
Brahimi, Lakhdar, 194, 198
Bremer, L. Paul, 253, 260
Brookings Institution, 159, 165, 170, 174
Brown, Harold, 22
Brownback, Sam, 172–73
Brzezinski, Zbigniew, 21, 27, 98
Burns, Bill, 35
Bush, George H. W., 2, 3, 12, 14, 22, 32, 33, 34, 59, 63, 81, 84, 100, 148, 151, 153, 154, 155, 163, 171, 217
assassination attempt against, 156
and Baker's meeting with Aziz, 103
budget of, 88–89, 92
on going to war without congressional approval, 113–14
Gulf War ended by, 129–31
Gulf War speech of, 69
at Helsinki summit, 87–88
inaugural address of, 37–38
on Jewish lobby, 145–46
joint sessions of Congress addressed by, 88–89, 137
messages to Saddam from, 57–58, 108–9
military visits by, 123

in 1992 election, 154
Oval Office speech of, 73–74
Persian Gulf troop levels doubled by, 97–98
on post–Gulf War plans, 132
and post–Gulf War rebellions, 139
and Saddam's behavior, 245–46
Saudi trip of, 101
Shamir and, 40, 43, 104, 118, 119
speech at beginning of Gulf War, 116
State of the Union speech of (1991), 121–22
and ultimatum approach, 94
"Why We Are in the Gulf" written by, 103
Bush, George W., 3, 14, 25, 165, 167, 168–70, 247, 270, 272
Abdullah's visit to, 208
Abraham Lincoln speech of, 253
Arab-Israeli conflict speech of, 209–10
"axis of evil" speech of, 204–5
capabilities of, 236
and idea of Iraqi exile brigade, 255
Iraq containment rejected by, 158
on Iraq War, 11
Israel trip of, 170
preventive attacks favored by, 221
State of the Union speech of (2003), 237, 242
State of the Union speech of (2004), 256
U.N. address of, 228–29
"with us or against us" remark of, 210
Bush, Laura, 256
Bush (G. W.) administration:
desire to topple Saddam in, 180–82, 192, 216, 234, 237, 272
Powell's differences with, 179, 185–86

Card, Andy, 185, 195
Carter, Jimmy, 13, 20, 23, 78, 83, 102, 157, 247
Carter Doctrine, 22
Castro, Fidel, 139, 181
Central Command, 23, 96, 97, 166, 180, 235, 254
Central Intelligence Agency (CIA), 1, 34, 120, 149, 181, 186, 195, 198, 220
Chalabi, Ahmad, 251, 255–56, 260
Charles, Sandra, 34, 45, 108

ABOUT THE AUTHOR

Richard N. Haass is president of the Council on Foreign Relations, a position he has held since July 2003. He has worked for four U.S. presidents—Jimmy Carter, Ronald Reagan, George H. W. Bush, and George W. Bush—in various posts at the Departments of Defense and State and the White House. He received the Presidential Citizens Medal in 1991 for his contributions to U.S. policy during Operations Desert Shield and Desert Storm and the State Department's Distinguished Honor Award in 2003 for his role in advancing peace in Northern Ireland and reconstruction in Afghanistan. He is the author or editor of eleven books on American foreign policy and one on management. A Rhodes Scholar, he holds a B.A. from Oberlin College and the Master and Doctor of Philosophy degrees from Oxford University. He lives in New York City with his wife and two children.